A Part of History

A *Part of*
History

Aspects of the
British Experience of the
First World War

INTRODUCED BY
MICHAEL HOWARD

continuum

Published by Continuum

The Tower Building
11 York Road
London
SE1 7NX

80 Maiden Lane
Suite 704
New York
NY 10038

www.continuumbooks.com

First published 2008

British Library Cataloguing-in-Publication Data
A catalogue record for this book is available from the British Library.

ISBN 9780826498137

Typeset by YHT Ltd, London
Printed and bound by MPG Books Ltd, Bodmin, Cornwall

Contents

Notes on Contributors

Sir Michael Howard served with the British Army in Italy during the Second World War and was awarded a Military Cross. Thereafter he established the Department of War Studies at King's College London, which he left to become first Chilchele Professor of the History of War, and then Regius Professor of Modern History at Oxford, ending his professional career as Robert A. Lovett Professor of Military and Naval History at Yale. He has been awarded The Order of Merit and is a Companion of Honour. In addition to his own *History of the First World War*, his works include *The Franco-Prussian War*, *War in European History*, and most recently *Liberation or Catastrophe: Reflections on the Twentieth Century*.

Gary Sheffield is professor of War Studies at the University of Birmingham. He has published widely on military history, especially the First World War. His forthcoming book *Douglas Haig, the British Army, and The First World War* will be appearing in 2009.

Malcolm Brown contributed five volumes on the 1914–1918 war to the series of Imperial War Museum books about the two world wars, published by Sidgwick & Jackson of the Pan Macmillan group, which was awarded a Duke of Westminster Medal for Military Literature in 2005. Other books on the First World War include *Tommy Goes to War*, *Christmas Truce* (co-written with Shirley Seaton) and *Verdun 1916* (published in French in 2006 by Editions Perrin of Paris). He was the contributing British author to the book *Frères de Tranchées* by four historians, two French, one German, one British, published by Editions Perrin in 2005, republished in English in 2007 by Constable as *Meetings in No Man's Land: Christmas 1914 and Fraternization in the Great War*.

Julian Putkowski is an independent scholar with an established interest in discipline and dissent in the British Army during the First World War.

Stephen Badsey is reader in Conflict Studies at the University of Wolverhampton. Further information may be found on his website www.stephenbadsey.com.

Peter Hart is the author of several books on the Great War including *The Somme 1916*. He is the Oral Historian at the Imperial War Museum.

Nick Hewitt was born in Hull but was brought up in Surrey and attended Kingston Grammar School. He studied history at Lancaster University and War Studies at King's College, University of London, where he specialized in naval history. Nick joined the Imperial War Museum in 1995, running the National Inventory of War Memorials project for several years before becoming permanent historian on board HMS *Belfast*, a branch of the IWM, in September 2003. His research interests include most aspects of naval conflict during the two world wars, and to date he has curated six exhibitions for the ship including Ghosts of Jutland, The Commonwealth Navies 1939–1945 and Eyewitness Falklands. He is currently writing a book on the coastal convoys of the Second World War, *The Indestructible Highway*, which will be published by Pen and Sword in 2008.

Trevor Gordon Wilson was born in Auckland, New Zealand, and educated at Mt Albert Grammar School and Auckland University. He continued his studies at Oxford University, where he completed his DPhil in 1959. He has taught at the University of Adelaide since 1960, becoming professor in 1968, and is now professor-emeritus and visiting research fellow. His publications include *The Downfall of the Liberal Party 1914–1935*, *The Political Diaries of C. P. Scott*, *The Myriad Faces of War: Great Britain and the War of 1914–1918* (winner of the Adelaide Festival of Arts Literature Prize) and, with Robin Prior, *Command on the Western Front*, *Passchendaele*, *The First World War* and *The Somme*. He is now carrying out research on Britain and Europe in 1940.

Santanu Das is a lecturer in English at Queen Mary, University of London, and has held research fellowships at St John's

College, Cambridge, and at the British Academy, London. He is the author of *Touch and Intimacy in First World War Literature* and is currently working on India, empire and First World War writing.

Michael Burleigh's ten books include *The Third Reich: A New History*, *Earthly Powers: Religion and Politics from the French Revolution to the Great War*, *Sacred Causes: Politics and Religion from the European Dictators to Al Qaeda* and most recently, *Blood and Rage: A Cultural History of Terrorism*.

For nearly 30 years, **Nicholas Reeves** taught history to undergraduate and postgraduate students in west London; he still lives in Ealing. He is the author of *Official British Film Propaganda during the First World War*, *The Power of Film Propaganda – Myth or Reality?*, and a number of articles on the history of film propaganda.

Jane Potter is senior lecturer at the Oxford International Centre for Publishing Studies, Oxford Brookes University. Her book *Boys in Khaki, Girls in Print: Women's Literary Responses to the Great War 1914–1918* is published by Oxford University Press and was joint winner of the 2006 Women's History Network Book Prize. Her other publications include contributions to *The Routledge History of Women in Europe since 1700*, *Publishing in the First World War: Essays in Book History*, *The History of the Book in Scotland* (volume 4) and *The Blackwell's Companion to the Bible in Literature*. She is book reviews editor of *Women's History Network* and editor of the Wilfred Owen Association *Journal*.

Terry Charman is senior historian at the Imperial War Museum and has worked on most of the Museum's projects including the 2005 Churchill Museum Project. He has also been involved in many publications including *The First World War in Photographs*, and has been IWM advisor on films and TV series including *Foyle's War* and *My Boy Jack*. He is a frequent lecturer, broadcaster and contributor to books and journals.

Dominic Hibberd's publications include two highly praised biographies – *Wilfred Owen: A New Biography* and *Harold Monro: Poet of the New Age* – as well as selections from their poems, the critical study *Owen the Poet*, several editions and anthologies, and many articles and reviews. His most recent book, edited with John Onions, is the anthology *The Winter of the World: Poems of the First World War*. He is a Fellow of the Royal Society of Literature.

Brian Bond is one of Britain's most distinguished military historians. Emeritus professor of King's College London, he has also been a visiting fellow of Brasenose and All Souls colleges in Oxford. In 2000 he gave the Lees Knowles lectures at the University of Cambridge. His six books include *The Pursuit of Victory: from Napoleon to Saddam Hussein* and *The Unquiet Western Front: Britain's Role in Literature and History*.

Max Saunders is professor of English at King's College London, where he teaches modern English, European and American literature. He studied at the universities of Cambridge and Harvard, and was a research fellow and then college lecturer at Selwyn College, Cambridge. He is the author of *Ford Madox Ford: A Dual Life*, 2 vols (Oxford University Press, 1996), the editor of Ford's *Selected Poems, War Prose*, and (with Richard Stang) *Critical Essays* (Carcanet, 1997, 1999, 2002) and has published essays on life-writing, on Impressionism and on Conrad, James, Forster, Eliot, Joyce, Rosamond Lehmann, Richard Aldington, May Sinclair, Lawrence, Freud, Pound, Ruskin, Anthony Burgess and others.

Lyn Macdonald has established a popular reputation as an author and historian of the First World War. Her books are *They Called It Passchendaele*; *The Roses of No Man's Land*; *Somme*; *1914*, which won the 1987 Yorkshire Post Book of the Year Award; *1914–1918: Voices and Images of the Great War*; *1915: The Death of Innocence*; and her most recent, *To the Last Man: Spring 1918*, has been published by Viking. All are based on the accounts of eyewitnesses and survivors, told in their own words, and cast a unique light on the First World War.

Gavin Stamp is an architectural historian and writer and was, until recently, chairman of the Twentieth Century Society. He organized the 'Silent Cities' exhibition about the cemetery and memorial architecture of the Great War at the RIBA Heinz Gallery in 1977 and in 2006 published *The Memorial to the Missing of the Somme* (Profile Books, London).

Ian Bostridge is an acclaimed tenor, well known for his performances as an opera singer and as a song recitalist. He studied at the universities of Oxford and Cambridge, where he read history and philosophy. He received his doctorate from Oxford, on the significance of witchcraft in English public life from 1650 to 1750, in 1990, and was a post-doctoral fellow at Corpus Christi College, Oxford, before embarking on a career as a singer, having won the 1991 National Federation of Music Societies Award and support from the Young Concert Artists' Trust. In 2004, Ian Bostridge was awarded the CBE for his services to music.

Terry Castle has taught at Stanford since 1983. She specializes in the history of the novel, especially the works of Defoe, Richardson and Fielding, and in the study of eighteenth-century popular culture. She has taught courses on Gothic fiction, women in eighteenth-century literature, psychoanalytic theory, opera, the literature of the First World War, and lesbian writing. She has written seven books: *Clarissa's Ciphers: Meaning and Disruption in Richardson's 'Clarissa'* (1982); *Masquerade and Civilization: The Carnivalesque in Eighteenth-Century English Culture and Fiction* (1986); *The Apparitional Lesbian: Female Homosexuality and Modern Culture* (1993); *The Female Thermometer: Eighteenth-Century Culture and the Invention of the Uncanny* (1995); *Noel Coward and Radclyffe Hall: Kindred Spirits* (1996); *Boss Ladies, Watch Out! Essays on Women, Sex, and Writing* (2002); and *Courage, Mon Amie* (2002). She writes regularly for the *London Review of Books*, the *New Republic* and other magazines and journals.

Esther MacCallum-Stewart is a postgraduate researcher at SMARTlab, the University of East London. Her work investigates the representation of war in popular culture, in particular through digital narratives and games. She is currently writing on the ways warfare is represented in video games and online worlds, and has recently contributed work to *Digital Culture, Play,* and *Identity, A World of Warcraft*® *Reader*.

Tony Pollard is one of Britain's leading battlefield archaeologists. He has worked with the Field Archaeology Unit of University College, London, and is currently a senior project manager at the University of Glasgow. He has carried out pioneering work on battlefields in Zululand and North Africa, and as a forensic archaeologist he has worked with police forces throughout Britain.

Dan Todman is senior lecturer in Modern History at Queen Mary, University of London. He specializes in the military, social and cultural history of Britain's twentieth-century wars. His 2005 book, *The Great War: Myth and Memory*, also published by Continuum, won the Times Higher Education Supplement Young Academic Author of the Year award. Dr Todman is currently working on a new history of Britain in the Second World War.

Introduction

The term 'The First World War' was coined by a sardonic journalist soon after the conflict, and only became official once the Second had begun. Until then it had been 'The Great War' for all the leading participants with the interesting exception of the Germans, who, having no doubt about its scope and the issues at stake, termed it *Das Weltkrieg* from the very beginning. But the melancholy spondee 'The Great War' still has profound resonance – and not just for the rapidly disappearing generation who endured the conflict. On war memorials throughout the country the casualties of the Second World War usually come as a mercifully brief appendix to the horrifying list of the young men, all too often from the same village families, who were killed in the First. The losses suffered by the British people in 1939–45 were tragic enough, but it is those endless lists of the dead and missing, inscribed on the walls of the Menin Gate at Ypres, on the Thiepval memorial and on the Passchendaele cemetery at Tyne Cot, that haunt the collective memory and dominate all subsequent narratives of the First World War.

Although Britain and her allies *won* the First World War – a fact that is often overlooked in subsequent controversy – victory celebrations were brief and quickly overshadowed by collective mourning for the dead. There is no national memorial of triumph in London; only a cenotaph – an empty tomb – and an 'unknown soldier' buried in Westminster Abbey to remind us of the scores of thousands who have no known grave. Once a year we observe two minutes' silence in memory of that 'sacrifice'. It is not surprising that the question poses itself: sacrifice for what? On the altar of what bloodthirsty god?

To understand this emphasis on loss rather than victory, we have to recall not only the events of the war itself but what happened, or rather what did not happen, in the succeeding years. If victory had resulted in increased prosperity and more stable peace, the price might have been more acceptable. Indeed

for a decade after 1918 British public opinion suspended judgement, coming to terms with the terrible memories of the Western Front but not as yet condemning them. After all, the
German menace (and no one doubted that there *had* been a
German menace) had been defeated. The British Empire had
been not only preserved but extended. The domestic standard of
living was being gradually improved. The intractable problems of
European conflict seemed to be yielding to patient diplomacy.
Then at the end of the decade it all collapsed. Economic ruin,
sweeping eastward from the United States, shattered both
domestic security and international peace. A new generation
published unvarnished memoirs of front-line horrors that
unleashed accumulated bitterness against the statesmen whose
deliberations round their green tables had precipitated the war,
and the claret-swigging generals, safe in their chateaux, who had
conducted it; stereotypes that became firmly lodged in the public
mind and have remained there ever since. For much of British
public opinion – and even more of French – the lesson seemed
clear: no more war. For the Germans, embittered both by the loss
of the war and the hardships of the peace, it was more
ambivalent. The war had been terrible, but that made it all the
worse that they should, so they believed, have been cheated of
victory. If another war had to be fought to redress the balance, it
must be conducted with a skill and decisiveness so evidently
lacking in the first.

For most of the twentieth century the historiography of the
First World War was largely a quest for blame. Who was
responsible for starting it? Who was responsible for its sanguinary
conduct? And, for the Germans, who was responsible for their
defeat? Only recently have historians begun to escape from this
obsession, to see the conflict, as the title of this book suggests, as
'a part of history': a terrible and tragic event certainly, but one
that must be understood in its context, and explained rather
than condemned.

For British historians, the task is to explain not only why the
war came about but why Britain became involved in it at all;
then, once involved, why she concentrated on the Western
Front rather than using her sea power to pursue the more flexible
and limited strategy indicated by her traditional 'way of war'; and
finally, once committed to the Western Front, whether it was
necessary to conduct operations in a manner that involved such
appalling losses. In answering these questions the historian has to

consider not so much possible alternatives as how these alternatives presented themselves at the time – if indeed they presented themselves at all; and what were the cultural parameters, the 'unspoken assumptions'; not just of the decision-makers but of the societies on whose behalf they made those decisions. The world of 1914 was not that of 2008. It was not even that of 1918. To revisit it requires a degree of imaginative understanding that precludes easy acts of judgement and condemnation.

In 1914 only a small number of specialists understood what a major war would involve. It was generally assumed that a prolonged conflict would be unsustainable if only for purely economic reasons, and so could not possibly happen. Expectations of future war were therefore based on the experiences of the European conflicts fought half a century earlier between 1859 and 1871, which had been both brief and decisive; so it was for this kind of war that military planners had prepared and that public opinion expected in August 1914. By the end of the year the belligerent armies had run out of ideas and ammunition without reaching a decision, but nonetheless the war went on. Public opinion in France, Germany and not least Britain had by this time made it impossible to stop. The Germans seemed within an ace of winning; the French could not make peace so long as the Germans occupied a fifth of their territory; while the British had barely begun to fight.

In August 1914 British public opinion had been divided over the wisdom of taking part in the war at all. The rising power of Germany was certainly seen as a menace, but the French and Russians were far from popular. The first were considered volatile and unreliable, the second autocratic and oppressive, while both were Britain's historic enemies. Then Germany's invasion of Belgium, followed by her ruthless treatment of Belgian civilians, rapidly united both Conservatives who feared German power, and Liberals who believed in the rights of small nations; while the success of German armies during the following weeks made it clear not only that Germany might very well win the war but that if she did she would establish a power-base in Europe that would make the Napoleonic threat appear trivial. The British Empire was at the height of its power, and public opinion, as expressed not only in the poetry of Rupert Brooke but in every press editorial throughout the country, responded almost gladly to the challenge. If the German armies in the west had fulfilled von Schlieffen's expectations and defeated France in a *Schlacht ohne*

Morgen, a battle without a tomorrow, the war would have probably gone on much as the Napoleonic Wars had gone on and the Second World War would go on, as a struggle between German land power and British sea power. But they did not. The British Expeditionary Force was not swept into the sea as its successor was to be at Dunkirk 25 years later, but remained on the continent. Its destinies were now inextricably linked with those of its French allies, whether they liked it or not.

At the end of 1914, however, there still seemed to be a strategic alternative. Britain was already raising a huge army in Kitchener's atypical expectation – shared by few of his countrymen and none of his contemporaries in Europe – that the war would last for years. But need all those armies be committed to the Western Front? Neither Winston Churchill at the Admiralty nor Kitchener himself at the War Office thought so. British maritime power surely offered a strategic alternative. So the Dardanelles expedition was launched, in the hope of outflanking the enemy and exploiting the power of the Russian ally. But whatever the validity of this strategy on paper, operational failure put an end to it.

Even so, there still remained strong pressure in London to avoid total commitment to a 'continental strategy' and to rely instead on sea power and economic pressure to support Britain's allies and undermine the enemy, as had been done so effectively in the days of Napoleon. But the French argued, and the British High Command in France argued with them, that if the Allies did not continue to attack in France the Russians would collapse and Germany could then deploy her full strength irresistibly to the west. In retrospect we cannot say whether that would necessarily have been the case, but at the time the argument appeared irresistible. Kitchener remarked philosophically, 'We cannot make war as we would like to, but as we must.' So the British acquiesced in Joffre's great autumn offensive, in which their share was the Battle of Loos. The bloody repulse they there suffered they attributed to bad staff work, poor training and lack of firepower. Next time they would do better.

Next time was the Battle of the Somme, some six months later. They did not do better, and Trevor Wilson explains in his chapter why they did not. German defences were not to be overcome simply by large numbers of men backed by enormous quantities of artillery, especially when the men were only partially trained, their officers inexperienced and the artillery shells hastily manufactured and often ineffective. The Germans themselves, better-trained professionals though they were, had done no better when they had attacked the French at Verdun three months earlier. In consequence the High Command on both sides was coming to the conclusion that the war could not be won by traditional techniques of manoeuvre but only by attrition: the wearing down of the forces of the other side until out of sheer weakness they had to surrender. That meant not only the total mobilization of available manpower into the army but the mobilization of industry to provide them with war material and of the population to support both and to endure all the deprivations entailed. The Germans, who had suffered almost as much on the Somme from British artillery as had the British from German machine guns, termed it a *Materielschlacht*, a war of materiel rather than men.

It is not surprising that by the end of 1916 voices were being raised in all the belligerent countries insistently calling for peace. In Russia they were strong enough to promote revolution, and would probably have done so in Austria-Hungary if that ramshackle empire had not been propped up by their German ally. In France they provoked a political crisis. In Britain they were less influential: in spite of the losses on the Somme, British casualties were still significantly less than those of both her enemies and her allies. But dissatisfaction with the conduct of the war brought about a change of government and the advent to power of a radical prime minister, David Lloyd George, who did not conceal his dissatisfaction with the military conduct of the war. The option of peace, now being energetically canvassed by President Woodrow Wilson, was still not seriously considered in London: the attitude of the German government still hardly made it a plausible option. By the end of 1916 the military authorities in Germany had virtually usurped control of the government, and their war aims were uncompromising: in the west, Belgium was to be virtually annexed and the French coast to be controlled down to the mouth of the Somme; in the east, German frontiers were to be extended deep into Russian territory and along the Baltic coast. What they aimed to create was the *Grossdeutschland* that Hitler would establish in 1940. The German government did not dare make these claims explicit, but they were well enough known to render any serious talk of peace out of the question. So again, the war went on; and when the Germans tried to break the deadlock with the introduction of unrestricted submarine warfare in February 1917, it went on with the assistance of the United States.

By mid-1917 the situation of the Allies seemed increasingly desperate. Russia was disintegrating. The French armies were in a state of mutiny. The submarine blockade of the British Isles seemed to be working very effectively. The United States was now a co-belligerent, but would be incapable of providing effective help for another year, by which time Germany seemed likely to have won the war. It was against that background that Haig took the decision to renew his offensive on the Western Front that has gone down in history under the name of Passchendaele.

There were certainly, or appeared to be, alternatives. Those offered by Lloyd George, that the allies should shift their offensive to Italy or the Middle East, hardly stand up to strategic analysis. At best these were minor theatres where no serious decision could be expected. More plausible was that proposed by the French themselves and some voices in England, not least that of Winston Churchill: the Allies should remain on the defensive in the west and build up their resources, including their new weapons of aircraft and tanks, until American help made it possible to attack with a crushing superiority. But such a proposal met with a visceral resistance from the military authorities, who could deploy some convincing arguments in favour of continuing the offensive. If they remained on the defensive, argued Haig, the Germans would discover the full extent of French weakness and finish them off. Russia would collapse and the full force of German power could then be switched to the west. But if the British armies continued to attack, they would continue to grind down German manpower and increase the pressure on the German home front where the cry for peace was becoming increasingly insistent. Further, a victory in 1917 would be a victory for the British Empire, with all the consequences that would flow from it for the subsequent peace, whereas a victory postponed until 1918 would be one for the United States, a power far from friendly to British imperial status and interests.

In any case the military could argue that lessons had been learned from the Somme. They had now abandoned hope of deep breakthroughs and decisive manoeuvres. Instead they were learning how to use infantry and artillery in intimate cooperation to seize limited objectives, consolidate them and move on only when their base was secure, leaving the enemy with the alternatives either to abandon his positions or himself to take heavy losses in counter-attack. Operations conducted along these lines, they believed, could now ensure success at acceptable cost.

Unfortunately the Germans had also learned their lessons on the Somme. Their heavy casualties on that charnel battlefield, they believed, had been due partly to holding their forward positions in such strength that British artillery had been able to inflict punishing losses on them, and partly because of a determination that not an inch of ground should be yielded and that any lost must be retrieved by immediate counter-attack. Now they reorganized their defences in great depth, their forward positions held by widely separated machine-gun posts and their main forces kept well back beyond enemy artillery range. British shells would now fall not on German troops but on open ground, making it impossible to traverse. When Haig eventually launched his offensive in July 1917, unseasonable downpours helped churn the low-lying fields over which British troops had to attack into impassable mud. Nonetheless the offensive ground on: 240,000 dead, wounded and missing were added to the 600,000 already suffered on the Somme, and to the names on the village war memorials.

As for the effect on the Germans, Haig was certainly misled by over-optimistic assessments of their losses. Nonetheless, the German experiences of Passchendaele were little less dreadful than those of the British, and the strain on civilian morale and military manpower was becoming almost intolerable. True, by the end of the year Russia had collapsed, but the Austrian Empire was not far behind, and there were mutterings of revolution in Germany itself. We cannot say how different the situation would have been had the British Army not been battering the Germans throughout the autumn at such frightful cost to themselves, but the news coming out of Germany certainly gave Haig every incentive for carrying on. Indeed the internal situation in Germany at the beginning of 1918 was so precarious that the High Command knew that if they did not win the war within the next few months they would have lost it.

The subsequent events were dramatic. In March, Ludendorff launched his offensive in the west that very nearly broke through the Allied lines. The Allies just survived the crisis and counter-attacked, this time with American help. By now the British military had thoroughly learned their trade. Their operational objectives were realistic; cooperation between infantry and artillery had been perfected, and not only tanks but low-flying aircraft had been integrated into the team. Losses were still heavy, but there was now something to show for them. It is surely a matter for regret that in the mourning of the losses incurred in the First World War the ultimate triumph of this 'Battle of the Hundred Days' has been almost forgotten.

Nonetheless the question remains: was it all worth it? If the cost of victory was so heavy, would it not have been better if Imperial Germany had been allowed to win the war, whether by acknowledging defeat in 1914 or accepting her peace terms two years later? Some historians have pointed out that the plans put forward by German economists in 1916 for a *Mitteleuropa,* an integrated European economy monitored from Berlin, were little different from the European Union that eventually came into being, monitored from Brussels. If only European statesmen had been more flexible and their generals less stubborn, might not this solution have come about half a century sooner and Europe, instead of destroying itself and slaughtering a generation of its young men, have emerged as a Great Power in its own right, even if one under German leadership?

Perhaps. But if the Germany of 1916 was not that of Adolf Hitler, neither was she that of Konrad Adenauer. Power was contested between an authoritarian, militaristic and increasingly proto-fascist right wing and a liberal-socialistic left, and every military success strengthened the hand of the former. Victory in war would have established their dominance, not only in Germany, but over Europe as a whole, and with it their determination to destroy Britain's naval supremacy and to reduce her to the status of a second-rate power as they had done to France in 1871. That at least was the perception in Britain itself, which was why, for better or worse, neither elite nor popular opinion in Britain across the political spectrum for a moment considered defeat to be an option. Reserves of national pride, built up over generations, were not yet exhausted. Politicians and generals were reviled for the way in which they conducted the war, but not for fighting it at all. Had the war dragged on for another year the situation might have been different, but by then American public opinion rather than British would have been the decisive factor. As it was, Britain won the war of attrition, at huge and tragic cost. But she would never be the same again.

MICHAEL HOWARD

Chapter 1

Military Revisionism: The Case of the British Army on the Western Front

Gary Sheffield

Comparing the literature available in 2007 with that in print 40 years earlier, it is clear that scholarly perceptions of the British Army of the First World War have been transformed. In the mid-1960s, John Terraine was ploughing a fairly lonely furrow in his defence of the generalship of Douglas Haig. Revision of the wider reputation of the army that fought on the Western Front (the British Expeditionary Force, or BEF) had scarcely begun. With some notable exceptions the riches that had become available with the opening of the military archives in the Public Record Office were little exploited by military writers. Much was made of partisan memoirs of participants such as Churchill and Lloyd George; secondary works; and a handful of published primary sources – Robert Blake's highly selective 1952 edition of Haig's papers was a particular favourite. Terraine's judgment of the 'instant history' books produced in this period as 'rubbish' is as sound as ever four decades on.

Today the situation is very different. The British Army of the First World War is a dynamic area of scholarly research. There is an emerging consensus that the First World War saw a transformation in the conduct of warfare, and the British Army played a leading part in it. In four years it evolved from a small professional force into a large citizen army of volunteers and conscripts, learning literally how to fight 'on the job', while conducting operations under unpropitious circumstances against an extremely effective enemy at a time when battle itself was undergoing changes that were revolutionary in nature. It was a mighty act of improvisation. Historians have highlighted the BEF's 'learning curve' (more accurately described as a 'learning

1

process'), in which new technology and techniques emerged by a process of trial and error and were incorporated into a way of fighting that reached a peak of effectiveness in 1918. These included improvements and innovations in artillery, staff work, logistics, cavalry, communications, aircraft and armour; the development of infantry tactics based on the light machine gun; and the emergence of operational techniques. This list is by no means exclusive. Tactically, in the latter part of the Somme (1916), Messines and the initial stages of Arras (1917) and in much of Third Ypres (or Passchendaele, 1917) the BEF proved highly effective. Crucially, in the victorious battles of the Hundred Days operational effectiveness was joined to tactical effectiveness and this helped produce victory.

Such arguments are not new. Many of the points being made by revisionists today can be found in the interwar books (such as divisional and regimental histories) and articles, in for example the *Army Quarterly*. The relatively obscure nature of these sources was such that high-profile works critical of the high command, such as Lloyd George's *War Memoirs* and the books of Liddell Hart (which chimed in with the *Zeitgeist* of the chattering classes of the late 1920s and early '30s), proved far more influential. This helps answer the question sceptics sometimes pose – why has it taken until now for this version of history to emerge?

The conduct of the war on the Western Front by the BEF inspires passion on both sides of the argument. Ultimately, it comes down to casualties. To risk parody, traditionalists are encumbered by a large amount of cultural baggage. Often viewing the war though the prism of 'disillusionment', influenced by the poetry of Wilfred Owen and *Oh! What a Lovely War*, traditionalists see the huge number of dead, wounded and missing, allied to the absence of decisive victories, as evidence of the criminal stupidity of the generals, who failed to learn from their experiences and persisted with outdated methods. Revisionists are apt to be viewed as apologists for mass murder. For their part, revisionists are inclined to scorn ignorance of the most basic facts of military history, to argue that the losses need to be placed in context (overall the British Empire had fewer losses than France and Germany, and statistically some Second World War battles were more lethal than those of 1914–18) and stress the importance of the difficult, but ultimately successful, learning curve which did result in decisive victories in 1918.

Counting from the pioneering efforts of Terraine and Correlli

Barnett in the 1960s, the revisionist school of historians is now in its third generation. Two features of the current cohort are noteworthy. First, a sizeable number do not have a conventional academic background or post, instead pursuing research as a hobby in addition to their day job or in retirement. Members of the Western Front Association (founded 1980) have been responsible for the production of a large body of research. This is inevitably patchy in quality, but the best is excellent. Many individuals have added scholarly rigour to their enthusiasm and interest by undertaking part-time postgraduate research. King's College London has a distinguished record in this regard, and non-traditional students at other universities such as Sunderland are producing interesting work. Arguably the most significant group are the students on the University of Birmingham's MA in British First World War Studies, which began in 2002. These mostly mature students have produced some excellent dissertations, and some have moved on to working on PhDs. This 'professionalization' of military history as a hobby is a very significant development. It has broadened and democratized the field of scholars working on the British Army of the First World War, and has diverted into serious research a very able group of people who otherwise would have been unlikely to have taken this path.

Second, whereas in the past cultural and military historians of the First World War tended to glare at each other from opposite sides of an academic No Man's Land, in recent years there has been a profitable interchange in ideas. A major factor in this has been the emergence of a group of younger scholars who are at home in both disciplines. In theses, conferences and books they have drawn fruitfully from both traditions and have helped to break down barriers. This has resulted in a perceptible softening in attitudes from some of the old and bold in both camps. As someone who has long advocated that a total conflict like the Great War deserves total history, I can only welcome this.

Alongside these positive developments, there is plenty of evidence that the war on the Western Front offers an extreme example of the dichotomy between academic and non-scholarly views of history. An astonishingly large number of bad popular books on the First World War continue to be published, or, in the case of one or two of the Pen and Sword's 'Military Classics [sic]' series, republished. In them one can read the familiar tales of British military incompetence, as well as watch television programmes with the same theme. While some are rehashes of the instant histories of the 1960s, a few contain a sprinkling of archival references in an attempt to gain spurious academic credibility. However, they either ignore recent scholarship or show little sign of having understood it. Some scholars take the view that it does not matter that inaccurate views have such a grip on the popular imagination. I disagree. History should not be merely a debate among academics but should reach out to engage with the widest possible audience.

Television and radio producers have in recent years proved willing, occasionally, to incorporate revisionist elements into portrayals of the Great War, albeit often with caution. Such revisionism had obviously passed by one student who contacted me recently to ask whether I agreed with the thesis that there was a conspiracy by British generals to kill a generation of young British men who lacked sufficient manliness by sending them into battle to be slaughtered. This correspondent had apparently learned from GCSE history that the problem lay in the generals' obsessions with cavalry charges.

More seriously, all too often a gulf also exists between the views of academic military historians and those of scholars in other branches of the discipline. One would not be able to guess the existence of the revisionist school from Peter Clarke's *Hope and Glory: Britain 1900–1990* (1996). In this otherwise admirable work the author, Professor of Modern History at Cambridge, betrays his reliance on the works of A. J. P. Taylor, Basil Liddell Hart and Paul Fussell rather than modern military historical scholarship. Eleven years on, it seems that little has changed. In *The Decline and Fall of the British Empire 1781–1997* (2007) Piers Brendon played an interesting variation on a theme, as he disparaged the BEF by contrast with the Canadian Corps. Here he perpetuates some myths in following a line beloved of Canadian nationalist historians. This has, however, been debunked by a number of historians, including Canadians, who have pointed out, among other things, the huge input by individual British officers into the evolution of Canadian methods; that many Canadian soldiers were British born; and the symbiotic relationship between the Canadian Corps and the rest of the BEF. It is perhaps unfair to pick on one aspect of what is otherwise an excellent book but it does serve to illustrate the extent to which revisionist military history of the war has failed to impinge on historians of cognate subjects (although there are some notable exceptions to this rule). The reasons why this might be so are beyond the scope of this essay.

Our understanding of the BEF has thus been transformed – the question is now, how best can it be taken further forward? It is surprising how many significant lacunae there are in the historiography. One problem is that so much energy is being poured into a narrow topic: command at the very top of the BEF. Two biographies (albeit popular ones) of Haig, an edition of his pre-First World War papers and one of his 1914–18 diaries and letters appeared in the period 2005–07. Haig continues to polarize opinion. Robin Prior and Trevor Wilson have developed the hostility to Haig, discernible in their seminal study of Rawlinson, *Command on the Western Front* (1992), to such an extent in the *The Somme* (2005) that Brian Bond accused them of a 'butchers and bunglers' approach. Ian Beckett and Nikolas Gardner both took a markedly anti-Haig line in their recent studies of First Ypres and the relationships between senior commanders of the BEF of 1914 respectively. Along with some other historians, I believe that these scholars have been overly harsh on Haig, as my recent jointly edited edition of Haig's papers and my forthcoming study of *Douglas Haig, the British Army, and the first World War* make clear.

But there is a deeper point at issue. By concentrating so heavily on one, albeit important, individual, historians (including myself) have inadvertently highlighted the extent to which other areas have been under-studied. Even in the area of military commanders there is much to be done. Notwithstanding Keith Jeffrey's excellent biography of Henry Wilson, there is scope for a full-scale study of Wilson as CIGS in the last year of the war. Robertson's career as QMG and then Chief of Staff of the BEF in 1914–15 is a neglected area. None of Haig's army commanders has a truly satisfactory modern scholarly biography. The ideal would be a combination of the techniques used by Prior and Wilson in their *Command on the Western Front* and a conventional 'life'. Plumer's papers were destroyed on his death, but a systematic exploitation of Second Army's war diaries and other documents might produce sufficient for a military study. The careers of Allenby, Byng, Gough and Birdwood as army commanders are in need of reassessment based on up-to-date research. Further down the command hierarchy, very little has been written about individual corps, divisional or brigade commanders, although there are some important exceptions to this rule. More generally, although the corps level of command has been well covered by Andy Simpson and there are some pioneering essays in Sheffield and Todman's 2004 collection, there is some basic work still to be done in this area. The commander–chief-of-staff relationship – an area frustratingly neglected by Prior and Wilson in their work on Rawlinson – is an obvious area for study.

Logistics is fundamental to the success or otherwise of any army. Ian Malcolm Brown's pioneering 1998 study has created a starting point for future research, but so far little else has been done. There is, however, a great deal of scope for exploration of logistics, especially since Brown devoted disappointingly little attention to the critical issue of how the BEF's logistic services adapted to the demands of an offensive mobile campaign in the Hundred Days of August–November 1918. Rob Thompson's eagerly awaited University of Birmingham PhD will undoubtedly shed more light on the topic. An equally crucial area – training – is also under-explored, although Alistair Geddes's 2007 University of Birmingham MA dissertation on Solly-Flood made a significant contribution to our pool of knowledge. Jim Beach's recent University College London PhD on British intelligence on the Western Front is a truly original piece of work which highlights the extent to which historians of strategy and operations, writing without a detailed knowledge of the intelligence picture available to Haig, have been working in the dark.

Books on battles have always been popular subjects with both authors and publishers, but even here there are some surprising omissions. There has been no scholarly treatment of the Battle of Arras as a whole, and only one popular book, since the official history of 1940. For many years, there was nothing worthwhile on Loos, but even following the recent appearance of three books on the battle the last word has not been said on the subject. The BEF's other actions of 1915 are still poorly covered. The Somme and Third Ypres continue to be popular, but even here detailed studies of individual episodes such as Morval and Polygon Wood would be valuable. This is especially true of the 1918 Hundred Days campaigns, which is much better covered than was the case a few years ago but still leaves significant scope for study. In the meantime, individual titles in the hybrid history-cum-battlefield-tour guides in the *Battleground Europe* series, although variable in quality, offer some useful insights.

In 2007, then, scholarship on the British Army of the First

World War is in a healthy state. A glance back over the previous three or four decades will confirm the extent to which the agenda has moved on. However, there is still much work to be done, including on some fairly fundamental topics. More worryingly, both non-scholarly military history and 'mainstream' history appear to be resistant to revisionist work on the BEF. Unless the problems caused by the cultural baggage associated with the First World War are overcome, revisionist historians run the risk of ending up merely talking to each other.

Further Reading

Beckett, Ian F. W. (2004), *Ypres: The First Battle, 1914*. Harlow: Pearson.

Beckett, Ian F. W. and Stephen Corvi (eds) (2005), *Haig's Generals*. Barnsley: Pen and Sword.

Brown, Ian Malcolm (1998), *British Logistics on the Western Front 1914–1919*. Westport, CT: Praeger.

Griffith, Paddy (1994), *Battle Tactics of the Western Front*. New Haven, CT: Yale UP.

Lloyd, Nick (2007), *Loos 1915*. Stroud: Tempus.

Prior, Robin and Trevor Wilson (1992), *Command on the Western Front*. Oxford: Blackwell.

Sheffield, Gary (2001), *Forgotten Victory: The First World War – Myths and Realities*. London: Headline.

Sheffield, Gary and Dan Todman (eds) (2004), *Command and Control on the Western Front: The British Army's Experience 1914–18*. Staplehurst: Spellmount.

Sheffield, Gary and John Bourne (eds) (2005), *Douglas Haig: War Diaries and Letters 1914–1918*. London: Weidenfeld and Nicolson.

Simpson, Andy (2006), *Directing Operations*. Staplehurst: Spellmount.

Chapter 2

The British Tommy

Malcolm Brown

I have in my possession a small 'Official Copy' Bible, dating from the 1880s, of which I am extremely proud. It belonged to a British soldier who served in India during the late years of the Victorian age. Annotations inside make clear that it was issued to Private William George Brown who enlisted at Cardiff on Saturday, 12 September 1885 'for 7 years in the Army and 5 in the researve [sic]', and arrived in India on Saturday, 30 January 1886, being posted to Winourie Barracks, Poona.

To declare my interest, William George Brown was my grandfather. From the details given above it can be deduced that he was a genuine 'Tommy' of Rudyard Kipling vintage. What scenes he saw, what actions he was involved in during his years in India, he never divulged, though perhaps something can be assumed from his reaction when my father, also called William George Brown, decided in the second year of the Great War that, being of suitable age, it was his duty to enlist. 'All right,' said my grandfather, 'enlist if you want to, but *nothing with the bayonet, nothing with the bayonet.*' My father duly volunteered, also in Cardiff, but joined the Royal Army Medical Corps. So he too became a Tommy, but not of the fighting kind, though he was still a proud soldier. I recall that when I asked him what his rank had been, he replied with a twinkle: 'I rose to the rank of private.' I guess many of his kidney made the same cheerful claim.

In the 1930s my parents bought a book by the then popular writer Arthur Mee, which he called his *Hero Book*. It was full of the standard names with which heroism has been associated through the ages: from Socrates to Grace Darling via Francis Drake and Abraham Lincoln. But the section of the book which fascinated me was the one about the very recent Great War, then far nearer in time than we are now to the Falklands conflict.

It included a striking drawing entitled 'The Man Who Won the War'. And who was this figure so credited? Was it Lloyd George or Haig or Foch or any other political or military grandee? No, it was the honest-to-goodness, shilling-a-day, British Tommy, complete with standard issue tin-hat and .303 rifle.

Arguably the mid-1930s was a good time to honour the ordinary British Tommy, but let no one assume he was so honoured during the war itself. He had had a hard life with the constant threat of a hard death, and he was at the beck and call of the army in which he served every hour he breathed.

A classic definition of the Tommy's status and condition is to be found in that jewel of a book *The Long Trail*, subtitled *Soldiers' Songs and Slang 1914–1918*, edited by John Brophy and Eric Partridge. Originally published in 1930, its reissued edition in 1965 was prefaced by a forthright essay by Brophy entitled 'After Fifty Years'. Brophy was himself a former private in the King's Liverpool Regiment who had contrived to enlist in 1914 when under 15, so he knew his subject. This was how he described the lot of the men who responded to the nation's call to arms in 1914 and after:

> They had engaged to serve, twenty-four hours a day, seven days a week, fifty-two weeks a year, for an undetermined number of years, as private soldiers in a complex organisation incidentally designed to enforce the will of each and every superior on those in the lowest ranks of all, to make them jerk into action at the word of command, stand still at the word of command, go anywhere and do anything at the word of command. In order to carry out what they had conceived, for the most part romantically and generously, as a patriotic duty, the young civilians were compelled to a preliminary process not unlike what would now be called conditioning. It involved an almost total surrender of personal liberty and an immediate, unconsidered obedience to orders . . .

In an earlier compilation entitled *The Soldier's War*, published in 1929, John Brophy had included in a brief glossary a definition of a well known military term which was evidently considered far too extreme for inclusion in the Brophy / Partridge anthology launched in the following year; it packs implicitly a certain amount of anger:

Attention: to stand to attention it was necessary to have: eyes front, heels together, feet at an angle of forty-five degrees to each other, thumbs in line with the seams of the trousers, no expression, glazed eyes and a vacant mind, merely keeping the nerves alert, ready to galvanise at the next command.

This, Brophy was effectively saying, was the ground-base of subjection in which the ordinary Tommy was firmly fixed in the culture of the British Army. As for the consequences of any infringement of this harsh code, in his 1965 essay he listed them as follows:

The penalties for disobedience ranged from a temporary loss of leisure, if any, a temporary loss of pay and some extra duties, through pack drill – mostly marching at speed with rifle and full equipment (which weighed about sixty pounds) to specialised forms of punitive imprisonment and, on active service, Field Punishment No 1: this involved the offender subsisting on a diet of bread and water and, lashed by hands or ankles to a wheel or a gate, being exhibited to his comrades in one of the ancient postures of crucifixion. ... As soon as a private soldier realised the power of the organisation to which, body and soul, he now belonged, he realised also that, while he might learn certain ways of outwitting it, outwardly he had no choice but to submit. Any form of direct defiance was worse than useless.

In this catalogue of disadvantage the item that hits the hardest is surely that almost medieval concept of Field Punishment No. 1, a sanction which provoked so much shock among other elements in the BEF that there were known cases of, for example, Australian troops angrily taking men down. The following is the reaction of one deeply shocked British soldier, Private Archie Surfleet, 13th Battalion, East Yorkshire Regiment, who witnessed a man undergoing this grim ordeal on the Somme front in 1916:

A lot of guns were lined up very regimentally and a number of limbers, spotlessly polished, stood beside them. At first, I could not believe my eyes, but as we came quite close to the guns, I saw that one of the artillerymen was lashed with rope to the wheel of one of the limbers. He was stretched out, cruciform-fashion, his arms and legs wide apart, secured to the wheel. His head lolled forward as he shook it to drive away the flies. I don't think I have ever seen anything which so disgusted me in my life and I know the feelings amongst our boys was very near to mutiny at such inhuman punishment. The expression on the face of this half-crucified gunner got us all groggy. I have never heard such expressions of disgust from the troops before. I'd like to see the devils who devised this having an hour or two lashed up like that.

Another demeaning element in the life of the ordinary private soldier as emphasized by John Brophy was that 'the Army only rarely allowed a private soldier to be an individual; he was a name and a regimental number, and on returns of strength was likely to be shown as one of so many "rifles". If and when he were killed or wounded, another man took over the rifle. It was all very understandable but, to the private soldier of 1914–18, left alone for a few rare moments with his own thoughts, hardly reassuring.'

Pioneered far back by such as John Brophy, there has been over many years a growing counter-culture, the aim of which is to give the silent mass the chance to speak. When in 1989 I began a 15-year labour of compiling five volumes in the Imperial War Museum series about the 1914–1918 war I saw this as one of my prime aims. In the event no act of positive discrimination was required to shoehorn them into the text. They were there because of the sheer quality of their description; and, it should be stressed, my concentration was deliberately on the largely unexplored evidence produced *at the time*, as opposed to the often unreliable testimony of survivors whose impressions could often be seriously distorted by hindsight.

To give substance to this claim I offer brief profiles of three Tommies whose writings still resonate in the memory.

Private Daniel Sweeney was a regular of the Lincolnshire Regiment who had served for seven years before war came, much of his time in trouble with the authorities. He was redeemed in 1914 by being contacted by a lady Sunday school teacher seeking for a Tommy to write to; he fell in love with and eventually married her, while pouring out his heart to her in a spate of letters so vivid and outspoken they are now collected in five bound volumes in the Imperial War Museum. He never disguised anything, but just let her know how it was. This is his comment on the consequences of an attempted raid on the German trenches in May 1916:

> It is simply murder at this part of the line. There is one of our officers hanging on the German barbed wire and a lot of attempts have been made to get him and a lot of brave men have lost their lives in the attempt. The Germans know that we are sure to try and get him in so all they have to do is to put two or three fixed rifles on to him and fire every few seconds – he must be riddled with bullets by now: he was leading a bombing party one night and got fixed in the wire – the raid was a failure.

A raid by the Germans in November 1917 prompted the following confessional, almost heartbroken, account. An officer's servant at this time, he was in a dugout with two other servants when the raid began:

> They began to throw bombs down into the dugout but we were safe as long as we kept clear of the stairs. Presently I heard someone coming down the stairs – I shouted 'Who are you?' – he said something but I pulled my trigger and he said no more, he rolled down to me with two men very much alive following him up. I let go at them, one I killed, the other died later, the other two servants shot five, and one was wounded. The German that I shot who died afterwards was a fine looking man. I was there when he died, poor chap – I did feel sorry but it was my life or his, he was speaking but none of us could understand a word he said, to tell you the truth I had a tear myself – I thought to myself perhaps he has a Mother or Dad also a sweetheart and a lot of things like that. I was really sorry I did it but God knows I could not help myself.

This was Sweeney's reaction to the late stages of the Third Battle of Ypres, generally known as Passchendaele.

> Our boys are having a terrible time in the trenches, up to the Waist in Mud and Water. Just like a ditch full of water. Each side of the Menin Road there are dead horses and men, cars, motor lorries in their hundreds, it is death to go

off the road, as the mud is so deep. It is nearly death as it is as he is shelling all along the road ...

The Somme was bad enough but this is a thousand times worse.

It should be added that Sweeney was one of countless ex-servicemen who in post-war Blighty failed to find gainful employment until the next world crisis in 1939.

Another Tommy whose story seems a seminally tragic one was Private Jack Mudd, 2 / 4th Battalion, The London Regiment, Royal Fusiliers, who took part in a dawn attack in the Ypres salient on 26 October 1917. Shortly before, he wrote a long letter to his wife, now on permanent display at the IWM, of which the following extracts show something of its poignant quality (Marie was their young daughter):

We are expecting to go up again in 2 or 3 days, so dearest pray hard for me and ask Marie for God will not refuse her prayers, she doesn't know the wickedness of this world ... God bless you all. I love you more than ever. I long to take you in my arms again, what a lot we have missed but please God it will make it all the sweeter when I see you ...

Out here dear we're all pals, what one hasn't got the other has, we try to share each others troubles, get each other out of danger. You wouldn't believe the Humanity between men out here. Poor little Shorty, one of the fellows that came out with me, he used to tell me about his young lady, his Hilda. He used to make me laugh with his talk, but unfortunately he will never see her again poor fellow, he would give me half of everything he had. Still dear I don't want to make you sad, but it just shows you how we seem to stick together in trouble, It's a lovely thing is friendship out here.

Please God it won't be long before this war is over, we are pushing old Fritz back, I don't think he will stand the British boys much longer and then we will try and keep a nice home. I know the value of one now.

Private Mudd went 'missing' in the subsequent attack. His body was never found. He effectively became part of the mud of the Ypres salient. He is commemorated on one of the memorial panels of Britain's largest military cemetery in Flanders, indeed in the world, Tyne Cot.

A vigorous and opinionated Tommy whose diary, for me, superbly transcends the old view of the ordinary soldier as dull and inarticulate was Private Robert Cude of 7th Battalion, The Buffs (East Kent) Regiment, who served for much of his time in France as a battalion runner. He came through the war buoyantly, worked in a factory for many years and ended his career with a flourish as a film extra in the first of the James Bond movies, *Dr No*. His diary, like Sweeney's letters, is held in bound volumes in the IWM's archives. For a man with virtually no formal schooling he could write with remarkable precision and skill. He could also, by his own description, be 'venomous'. This is his comment on a brigadier general who had been dismissed for incompetence. He wrote of his successor:

> At first sight he suits, for he looks a thorough soldier. The other old woman has gone back to England to act as housekeeper to a Suffragette, at least, that is all he is fit for, and I think everyone in the Brigade is unanimous in that opinion.

Yet in 1916, when a brigadier general he approved of was sent home for refusing to commit his battalions to an action which he saw as futile, Cude was vehement in his support:

> He has been relieved of his command, for what? Being a human man. He will carry with him the good wishes of the whole Brigade and we can never forget the man who would wreck his career rather than be a party – however unwilling – to the annihilation of troops under his command.

Typically he had no sympathy for the staff. Thus this entry in early 1917:

> Nothing doing today 16th Feb, except Divisional HQ move up. Wonders will never cease. They will get hurt one of these days and it seems such a pity to see such brightly decked men so near the line.

Or this, also in 1917, when the 18th Division's Artillery HQ was shelled: 'We laughed until the tears ran down our faces watching the flower of England's greatness – the STAFF – running for dear life.'

His attitude stemmed from two causes. One was the assumption that officers given staff posts were not up to the demands of serving in the line. The other was the belief, widely held, that the staff, who gave the orders which others carried out, despised the ordinary fighting soldier while being spared the dangers to which that long-suffering individual was constantly prone. Searching for a definition of the 'infantryman's lot in wartime', Cude described it as being 'treated as less than nothing by big wigs in scarlet who direct operations without taking a man's share of the burden'.

He also shared the basic hostility of those engaged in the fighting to those who lived safely away from it. When members of the latter group won medals while deserving members of the first group were ignored, his 'venom' could be particularly strong:

> The officer i/c 18th Div Baths has been given the DSO for his valuable services, whereas Officers (Junior) in the Battn go through the bitterest of the War, unhonoured, except perhaps for a wooden cross! The inequality of it is simply astounding, and one marvels at the courage of the men who wear the medals that were won in Tea shops or over Mess tables, whereas they were instituted for service in the field.

Cude did not ask for or want a comfortable life. Bored when out of the line, he could express the wish to be back in it. And he could write thus of a harassing day on the Somme in which his activities as a runner – on this occasion a mounted one on a bicycle – had put him in conflict with one of the Western Front's constant hazards – mud:

> I have had to push my cycle, in company with other 'Runners', over roads three-inch deep in mud! Arrive midnight and drop into sleep straight away, awaking 7.30 a.m. feeling completely washed out, for am still soaked to the skin. It is all in a day's march however, and we are on 'Active Service', so must grumble but carry on.

'Must grumble, but carry on.' If there is one sentence out of the innumerable accounts I have studied which sums up the attitude of the British Tommy on the Western Front, 1914–1918, it is surely this one. No wonder it could be claimed that, somehow or other, against the odds, despite his lowly status, it was he who won the war.

Further Reading

Brophy, John and Eric Partridge (1965), *The Long Trail*, London: Andre Deutsch; republished (2008) as The Daily Telegraph *Dictionary of Tommie's Songs and Slang*, with a new Introduction by Malcolm Brown. Barnsley: Frontline Books.

Brophy, John (1929), *The Soldier's War*. London: J.M. Dent.

Brown, Malcolm (1978 / 1999 / 2005), *Tommy Goes to War*. London / Stroud: J. M. Dent / Tempus.

Holmes, Richard (2004), *Tommy: The British Soldier on the Western Front, 1914–1918*. London: HarperCollins.

Middlebrook, Martin (1971 / 2003), *The First Day on the Somme*. London / Barnsley: Allen Lane / Leo Cooper.

Simpson, Andy (1993), *Hot Blood & Cold Steel, Life and Death in the Trenches of the First World War*. London: Tom Donovan.

Malcolm Brown's Imperial War Museum books (see Notes on Contributors) on the First World War, on 1914, the Western Front, the Somme, and 1918, make extensive use of soldiers' first-hand accounts held in the Museum's archives.

Chapter 3

Tommyrot: The Shot at Dawn Campaign and First World War Revisionism

Julian Putkowski

No evidence was found to lead us, including the Judge Advocate General, to think that the convictions were unsound or the accused were treated unfairly at the time ... I appreciate the distress which surviving relatives of the soldiers concerned still feel ... and I greatly sympathise with them ... The authorities at the time took the view that deserters had to receive due punishment because of the effect of desertions on military capacity and morale ... shell-shock did become recognised as a medical condition during the First World War. And where medical evidence was available to the court, it was taken into account in sentencing and in the recommendations on the final sentence made to the Commander-in-Chief. Most death sentences were commuted on the basis of medical evidence.

John Major, 10 February 1993

In August 2006, the British government declared that it would grant posthumous conditional pardons to British soldiers who had been executed by the army for military offences (other than murder) committed during the First World War. Exactly why Tony Blair's administration abruptly departed from a sustained and virtually unqualified endorsement of John Major's no-pardons policy invites speculation, and a definitive account will doubtlessly emerge in due course.

In the meantime it is easier to compare the reactions of the executed men's families and their supporters with the annoyed response of a relatively small group of self-styled 'revisionist' military historians. The former did not achieve all they desired but the historians' undisguised anger about the announcement invites reflection about the revisionists' objectivity, collective agenda and political values. In considering their reaction, account also needs to be taken of the perceived challenge posed by the *Shot at Dawn* campaign to the revisionists' interpretation of the First World War.

Public reaction at home and abroad to news about the pardons was generally positive. The executed men's surviving relatives and supporters of the 'Shot at Dawn' pardons campaign were understandably delighted, and the move was welcomed by the Irish, New Zealand and Canadian governments. Yet it was also universally apparent that the British government's gesture was miserly compared with the fulsome pardon that had been enacted by the New Zealand government in 2000. Nor would the outcome have satisfied Judge Anthony Babington, the author of *For the Sake of Example* (1983) in which he surveyed and expressed informed doubts about the fairness of the wartime capital courts martial. Rather than a generic pardon, Babington always advocated the initiation of a case-by-case independent judicial review but his opinion could not be solicited because he died in 2004.

Parliament was never granted the opportunity to decide between a generic pardon and a case-by-case review, the choice embodied in the 'War Pardons' Private Members Bill, initially proposed in 1992 by Andrew Mackinlay MP. However, more than a decade had elapsed since he had declared that those who were 'shot at dawn' were already recognized as brave soldiers by 'the highest court in the land – British public opinion'. Mackinlay may have been guilty of hyperbole in what he stated but there was also overwhelming evidence of sustained popular support for posthumous pardons.

The Secretary of State for Defence, Des Browne, had done well to overcome entrenched institutional opposition by an ad hoc coalition of Conservative politicians, senior academics, retired military officers and sundry Westminster 'shadow-warriors'. Many *Shot at Dawn* campaigners felt the capital courts martial judgements should have been quashed and the executed men's campaign medals ought to have been restored but recognized Browne's achievement and refrained from open criticism.

Other interested parties, albeit of a contrary persuasion, felt less inhibited, including the BEF commander-in-chief's son, the second Earl Haig, who complained about the change in government policy. In an interview published by *The Guardian*, Earl Haig complained that it was not possible to 're-write history' and insisted:

> My father took a lot of trouble anxiously going into these cases late into the night. The majority were not shot. Courts martial were carefully done ... He did not just sign on the dotted line. It was a terribly sad situation and some of the soldiers were genuinely shell shocked. But many were rogues, persistent deserters and criminals, or they were guilty of cowardice.

If recent parliamentary reform had not divested him of a seat in the House of Lords, Earl Haig declared he would have voted against the granting of posthumous pardons, and concluded, 'I think public opinion on World War One is not always sound. It may be ill-informed basically.'

Aside from declaring his voting preferences, Earl Haig aired more than a personal apologia for his father's exercise of the death penalty during the First World War – he also reflected the views of First World War revisionist historians. In general, revisionist perspectives about the British Army during the First World War maintain that anti-militarism, 'anti-war' mythology and 'anti-First World War effusions by non-historians' have culturally subverted public opinion about the First World War.

In accounting for the bamboozlement of the British public, revisionists exercise reductionism in much the same way that doctrinaire Marxists used to do when called upon to explain the persistence of proletarian, non-revolutionary 'false consciousness'. However, instead of promoting class warfare, revisionists seek to explain the development and remedy the persistence of what they regard as misrepresentation and popular misunderstanding about Britain's involvement in the war.

Their reasoning is often prefaced by a positive affirmation of the British government's justifications for going to war in 1914. In terms of international relations, the revisionist position is essentially realist, though with a nod in the direction of 'just war' theory via accompanying denunciations of German autocracy and atrocities committed by the Kaiser's forces in Belgium and northern France. With reference to the conduct of the war, it is less easy to identify a clear revisionist consensus. However, the most influential interpretation has recently been expressed in Gary Sheffield's book, *Forgotten Victory*, in which he maintains that the allied success during the summer of 1918 was due to British military prowess: tactical developments (a 'learning curve'); intelligent and imaginative leadership; British technical improvisation; and native ingenuity – and a measure of belated assistance by the USA.

Sheffield and his fellow revisionists agree that soldiers' disenchantment and war-weariness, where it existed, has been exaggerated, that in reality the rank and file regarded themselves as victors and reckoned Field Marshal Haig to have been a great leader. Revisionist thinking also affirms that during the First World War British public opinion generally supported the war effort but that after hostilities ceased, the populace failed to recognize, sustain and celebrate the military achievement. Revisionists reason that the sheer human and material cost, post-war economic vicissitudes and negative interpretations about the conflict shaded and then shaped popular disillusionment about the human and material losses as well as the outcome of the peace settlement.

Correlli Barnett's view, reprised by Brian Bond, was that by the early 1930s, 'We won the war' sentiment had been eroded by the malign influence of best-selling anti-war poetry and prose; Lloyd George's 'self-exculpating and mendacious' war memoirs; Remarque's *All Quiet on the Western Front* (book and film); and the inadequacies of contemporary military historians. Although he continued to bemoan the negative influence of middle-class poets, and 'lachrymosely emotional' public reaction to the First World War, for his book *Audit of War* Correlli Barnett garnered an appreciative response from Margaret Thatcher's cabinet ministers.

Revision of Field Marshal Haig's much-criticized wartime leadership was energetically pursued by John Terraine and blossomed during the 1960s and 1970s. Although Terraine eschewed archival research and remained resolutely partisan, his seminal contribution to revisionism continues to be acknowledged in more scholarly texts, latterly crafted by Gary Sheffield, John Bourne and fellow members of the Douglas Haig Fellowship.

During the 1980s Correlli Barnett's and Terraine's perspectives were sythesized and amplified by members of the British Commission for Military History, leading luminaries of the Western Front Association and historians associated with the

Royal Military Academy, Sandhurst, and the War Studies Department of King's College, London University. Revisionist academics, including Brian Bond, Ian Beckett, Keith Simpson MP and, to a lesser extent, Stephen Badsey, continue to figure prominently but during the past 20 years their perspectives have been sustained and further elaborated by a second generation of revisionists.

The latter have established a significant institutional presence at Birmingham University's First World War Studies Centre, Canterbury University and Queen Mary College, University of London, and include in their ranks: John Bourne, Gordon Corrigan, Keith Grieves, William Philpott, Gary Sheffield, Peter Simkins, Michael Snape, Dan Todman, John Connolly and a dozen or two scholarly fellow-travellers. Virtually all profess to share Terraine's and Correlli Barnett's distaste for *Oh! What a Lovely War!* (play and film); 1930s 'Futility of war' sentiment; 1960s counter-culture and anti-militarism and (anti-) war poetry. During the 1990s their animus was also directed at popular television, including *The Monocled Mutineer* (BBC, 1986); the satirization of staff officers in *Blackadder Goes Forth* (BBC, 1989) and media coverage favourable to the *Shot at Dawn* campaign.

Badsey and Sheffield have repeatedly drawn attention to the harmful effect of on-screen fictional work that in their opinion replicated and reinforced stereotypes cherished by an ill-informed British public. However, the latest and most substantial formulation of the revisionists' cultural agenda is exemplified by Dan Todman's book *The Great War: Myth and Memory* (2005). Todman advances a rather simplistic interpretation of British 'popular culture', corrupted by 'myths' and emotional responses to war. His book eschews reference to any *Shot at Dawn* myths or associated controversies about coercion and military injustice but his 'Trench Fever' website directs readers to consult Colonel John Hughes-Wilson and Cathryn Corns' book *Blindfold and Alone* (2001).

Prior to publication of *Blindfold and Alone* neither Hughes-Wilson, a retired senior army intelligence officer, nor Corns, a biochemist, had figured significantly in the revisionists' ranks. However, on the basis of a magazine review written by Hughes-Wilson that had been published in the *Spectator* about the 'Unquiet Graves' Conference (Ieper, 2000), Hughes-Wilson was dubbed an 'historian' in Bond's revisionist survey *The Unquiet*

Western Front (2002). *Blindfold and Alone* was publicized as a comprehensive, reliable and 'balanced' source of knowledge about the *Shot at Dawn* executions and related issues, and in the absence of any comparable study, *Blindfold and Alone* became the revisionist vade mecum. Unfortunately, as the critical review featured on the *Shot at Dawn* website swiftly indicated, *Blindfold and Alone* addressed only a minority of capital cases and was flawed by a rash of factual errors about the executions and the *Shot at Dawn* campaign. Revisionist approval of Hughes-Wilson and Corns' work was also contested by Gerard Oram's doctoral thesis 'Military Executions during World War One' (2003) and the Irish government's *Report into the Court Martial and Execution of twenty-six Irish soldiers by the British Army during World War 1* (2004).

Notwithstanding their denunciation of both the *Shot at Dawn* book and the long-drawn-out campaign, revisionists never appear to have fully engaged with what amounted to lively and passionate public discourse about the First World War. With few exceptions, instead of deploying their skills as historians, prior to 1997 the revisionists remained content to reiterate the arguments advanced by John Major. Thereafter, they drew on John Peaty's essay in *Look to your Front* (1999), a contribution that was in substance a résumé of a 1998 Ministry of Defence review, carried out at the behest of the Armed Forces Minister, John Reid. If, after a decade of idly regurgitating ministerial statements, revisionists, individually or collectively, felt a discreet sense of embarrassment about the shortcomings of *Blindfold and Alone* then they had no one but themselves to blame. They had been afforded ample time in which to conduct original research that could have added to the sum of scholarly understanding and refined the standard of debate about the executions; that they failed to act in such a positive fashion remains for me a matter of profound regret.

A sense of a missed opportunity may also be inferred from the response of individual revisionists to the enactment of conditional pardons. Some considered the entire affair 'political' and therefore unworthy of an historian's attention. Ian Beckett, for example, dismissed the policy revision as a complete charade, declaring in his book *The Great War* (2007):

The public campaign for pardons for all save murderers, which was bizarrely upheld by the ludicrously posturing

British government in 2006, was profoundly unhistorical. It was a matter of faulty popular memory imposing contemporary values on the past, rather than an historical debate.

In Todman's Trench Fever weblog response to Browne's initial announcement about the government's change of mind, there was precious little evidence of the objectivity purportedly cherished by revisionists. Instead, Todman opted to blame a compliant media, and patronized the executed men's families:

> Well, not making old ladies cry seems like an appropriate moral stance to me, although this would seem to offer grounds for statutory pardons for pretty much any celebrated case where the criminals' families are still with us. It must be pretty difficult being a member of the Kray family nowadays – lots of comments and jokes, possibly even some discrimination. Let's pardon them so the family don't suffer. After all, they did love their dear old mum ... they've enjoyed a lot of media interest and the chance to air their grievances. They make good interviewees, and it's a nice story for the media. Relatively few historians want to be seen to be making people miserable, so they don't often get opposed when they appear on TV. As a result, it's pretty much universally accepted that their relative was innocent, or wilfully mistreated. I've yet to see a report in the press which actually engages with what shell shock might have meant in 1916, let alone the moral issue of whether, if you want to achieve big aims like winning a war for national survival, you might need to shoot a few people to encourage the rest.

In self-absolution, Todman appeared to rationalize his personal failure as an historian to engage with popular manifestation of mass culture by concluding:

> For all my bluster I don't think that you should make people miserable if you can easily avoid it, and pardoning these soldiers seems an easy way to make some people less miserable. It's bad history – in fact, this whole thing would be an excellent candidate for the Carnival of Bad History – but it might turn out to be an effective use of the past.

As for the authors of *Blindfold and Alone*, Corns said nothing in public but Hughes-Wilson was understandably miffed by the conditional pardons and possibly bewildered by the turn of events. His immediate response to an enquiry from the *Daily Telegraph* appeared rather existential: 'What we are seeing here is an attempt to reinvent the past to suit today's political correctness ... I think this leaves military law with a big question mark over it because war is not a walk in the park and different rules apply.'

Judge Babington would have given short shrift to Hughes-Wilson's reference to the application of 'different rules' but the allusion to an unidentified force attempting to 'reinvent the past' has always been very evident in revisionist writing about the First World War.

Prompted by authoritarian convictions or institutional demands, revisionists select facts with which to bolster their own emotional response to the First World War, and by extension war in general. Their own emotionalism is never explicitly acknowledged in books like *The Unquiet Western Front* or the essays in Bond's *The First World War and British Military History* (2002); instead, such failings are projected onto what are frequently imaginary opponents. In a fashion akin to the pacifists and war resisters of the 1920s, 1930s and 1960s, whose work they despise, revisionists appear to believe that some terrible corrupting force has perverted public opinion through propaganda. Instead of the merchants of death and dastardly media moguls, the revisionists, specifically Hughes-Wilson, inferred the *Shot at Dawn* campaign and the executed men's families were being duped and manipulated by a handful of individuals, whose illegitimate and irrational efforts threatened to undermine the revisionists' version of the past.

In the cold light of day, it all sounds a bit dotty and atavistic but the revisionist past exhumed by Hughes-Wilson and Corns may be glimpsed in *Blindfold and Alone*. It consists of their version of Edwardian England: 'An ordered place with the certainty that stemmed from the unshaken belief in the institutions that made up a long-established society. All classes (and most people) knew their place.' It is a land defended by a regular army whose rank and file are 'mostly recruited from the intelligent and ambitious youth of the working class', who 'volunteered to escape the tedious back-breaking or futureless manual work that was on offer in the first decade of the twentieth century'.

And the threat? Much though Hughes-Wilson may have understood otherwise, the *Shot at Dawn* threat to the past depicted in *Blindfold and Alone* was unprompted by Cold War cant or Marxist dogma. In Parliament and elsewhere, it was clear from the demands and arguments articulated by the executed men's families and their supporters that the campaign was informed by liberal perspectives and humanitarian values.

For most revisionist historians, disinterest in studying the executions and associated issues left them little alternative other than to rely on *Blindfold and Alone* and arguments that had been conjured up by civil servants in Whitehall for political purposes. Whether because of intellectual sloth or, as their socialist critics argue, the outcome of a narrow, elitist, patriarchal, white, Anglo-centric interpretation of the First World War, revisionists failed to generate for themselves a stock of reliable, well researched and analysed historical data.

Since revisionists dismissed the historical significance of contributions by 'non-historians' to public debate about the British Army's use of coercion during the First World War, there has been little imperative to alter the established tenor of their academic programmes. Their syllabi and recommended reading schedules for the study of the First World War continue to reflect a socially conservative preoccupation with hierarchy, order and rules, tactics, strategy, firepower, logistics and 'group cohesion' – which sounds less woolly than 'morale'. Students are encouraged to adopt a positivist, semi-actuarial calculation of developments on the battlefield, instead of carnage, mud, blood and weepy messiness. In Sheffield's teleological work, every battle yields 'lessons learned' to be plotted on the learning curve; Simkins exhorts historians to focus on the battlefield; Bond damns 'doom and gloom' TV Great War documentaries and 'Books with such backward-looking polemical titles as *The Donkeys* and *British Butchers and Bunglers of World War One*'. In the aftermath of the enactment of conditional pardons, there seems little sign of any change in the revisionist project. Neither is there much evidence of critical reflection by other revisionist agencies, including members of the Douglas Haig Fellowship or the British Commission for Military History, perhaps because their accommodation of barbarism and the brutality of war is rather too well entrenched. However, by way of consolation for their critics, even if the revisionists' motives have not always been easy to discern, at least their hegemonic 'Utility not Futility' message has for many years been quite open and transparent.

Further Reading

Chielens, P. and J. Putkowski (2000), *Unquiet Graves: Battlefield Guide*. London: Francis Boutle Publishers.

Dallas, G. and D. Gill (1985), *The Unknown Army*. London: Verso.

Dendooven, D. and K. Koch (eds) (forthcoming), *1915. Innocence Slaughtered? Conference Proceedings, Ieper*. London: Ashgate.

Godefroy, A. B. (1998), *For Freedon and Honour?* Nepean: CEF Books.

Jahr, C. (1998), *Gewohnliche Soldaten: Deutschen und Deserteuer im deutschen und britischer heer 1914–1918*. Gottingen: Vandenhoeck und Ruprecht.

Lister, D. (2005), *Die Hard, Aby: a boy soldier shot to encourage the others*. Barnsley: Pen and Sword Books.

Offenstadt, N. (1999), *Les Fusillees de la Grande Guerre et la memoire collective 1914–1999*. Paris: Editions Odile Jacobs.

Oram, G. (1998), *Worthless Men: Race, Eugenics and the Death Penalty in the British Army during the First World War*. London: Francis Boutle Publishers.

Oram, G. and J. Putkowski (2008), *British Army Officers Courts Martial 1914–1924*. London: Francis Boutle Publishers.

Putkowski, J. J. (1998), *British Army Mutineers 1914–1922*. London: Francis Boutle Publishers.

——(2002), *Les Fusilles de King Crater, 1 & 2*. Louviers: Editions Ysec.

Raw, D. (1997), *Bradford Pals*. Barnsley: Pen and Sword Books.

Sellers, L. (2005), *Death For Desertion: The story of the court martial and execution of Sub. Lt. Edwin Dyett*. Barnsley: Pen and Sword Books.

Walker, S. (2007), *Forgotten Soldiers: The Irishmen Shot at Dawn*. London: Gill and Macmillan.

Chapter 4

Press, Propaganda and Public Perceptions

Stephen Badsey

Almost before the First World War ended, it had begun to be re-fought in words and symbols, in a battle which would last for much longer than the war itself. Chief among the defeated nations in this second propaganda conflict, fought to establish the meaning of the war rather than to decide its outcome, was the United Kingdom. If Germany had been made to accept the 'war guilt clause' (Article 231) of the Treaty of Versailles, then within just over a decade it was the British who came to consider themselves guilty; or rather an idealistic elite, associated during the war with the Union for Democratic Control, and later with the League of Nations Union, came to believe that British propaganda lay at the heart of all that was wicked about its outbreak and conduct. There was evidence, even boasts from those responsible, that Germany had been defeated through a 'stab in the back' by the Department of Propaganda in Enemy Countries, created early in 1918 at Crewe House under Lord Northcliffe, denounced by the Germans as the 'Father of All Lies'. Isolationists in the United States were outraged that they had been tricked into the war by a British propaganda campaign against American neutrality, run by the clandestine Wellington House organisation under Charles Masterman MP.

But the greatest lies of the British propagandists seem to have been aimed at their own people, particularly over German war crimes (in the language of the time, 'outrages', 'atrocities' and 'frightfulness'), and such fictions as the story in April 1917 of the German 'corpse factory' used to convert dead bodies into glycerine, finally acknowledged as a fabrication in parliament in 1925. British lies and distortions were catalogued by Arthur Ponsonby MP in his 1928 book *Falsehood in War-time*, and ridiculed next year by Robert Graves in his *Goodbye to All That*, both books that are still in print. Such views formed one of the strongest British memories of the war.

Unfortunately, in this as in many other cases of propaganda and warfare, memory meant getting the history wrong. The campaign by Wellington House in the United States was real enough, targeting elite opinion-formers in a sophisticated manner, but like all British propaganda it was closely co-ordinated with foreign policy and grand strategy, and it did not in itself lead to American entry into the war. The supposed campaign by Crewe House was less real, starting late in 1918 and aimed more at Austria-Hungary than Germany. Although British propaganda may have played some part in the defeat of both countries, and the disintegration of the Dual Monarchy, Crewe House certainly exaggerated its achievements.

As for domestic propaganda, any claim that the British government propagandized its own people in 1914 must overcome the very considerable hurdle that there were no official British propaganda organisations in existence, and certainly no plans for a recruiting propaganda campaign. Instead, propaganda organisations went through a slow evolution in the course of the war, closely paralleling other aspects of the British war effort, as local and separate ministerial initiatives merged into a coherent national whole. Not until February 1918 was the unified Ministry of Information created, under Lord Beaverbrook. British propaganda policy was based on what Masterman called 'the propaganda of facts', an often understated approach which had much in common with British traditions in diplomacy and in espionage. This policy appeared to allow free debate and even dissent by the press and in public, as long as this debate remained within the agenda that the government had already established. If an overenthusiastic patriot produced an inflammatory poster or editorial, then this was not necessarily official policy.

Initial British opposition to the war came almost entirely from elites, and was mainly based on religious or partly religious beliefs; it became more intense and more widely based after January 1916 with the introduction of conscription and the threat to traditional labour-management power structures. But throughout the war it remained far from revolutionary, except in Ireland, and was effectively defused by a mixture of political concessions and propaganda skills. The Official Press Bureau, established on the outbreak of the war, normally went no further than to issue editors with guidance on which subjects were to be avoided or treated with caution, and the draconian powers available to the government were only rarely used. The few famous cases in the war of collisions between the press and authority, such as Repington's 'shell scandal' dispatch, Keith Murdoch's report from Gallipoli, or the 'Maurice Letter' of 1918, represent occasions on which normal practice broke down. Similarly, stories of German brutalities either had a strong basis in truth, including the war crimes committed during the invasion of Belgium, or came from sources other than the British official mind.

One of the many difficulties facing historians in understanding British mass society during the war is that, in the absence of the scientific opinion polling or sampling techniques developed some decades later, there are very few hard statistics to measure, although anecdotal and circumstantial evidence are both remarkably consistent. Popular enthusiasm for war and the widespread willingness to volunteer for active military service appear to have been largely spontaneous, not just in Great Britain but in Ireland and in the dominions of Australia, Canada and New Zealand. One plausible explanation advanced by historians for this behaviour has been that for decades British and Imperial society had not only been propagandized but militarized, and heroic efforts have been made to prove that militarism provided the mainspring for volunteerism in 1914 – but the evidence is just not there. If militarism means a loyal and disciplined subservience to the existing order, then the increasingly militant organized labour movement of 1912–14 certainly fails to fit. The efforts of the National Service League or the Navy League before the war were ineffective; the Territorial Force remained persistently understrength; and the schools' Officer Training Corps failed to produce even a fraction of the regular officers needed. Whatever motivated the volunteer movement of 1914, it was a reflection of a very deep-seated consensus within British and Imperial society; propaganda is too small a word for it.

In defining 'public opinion', most scholars now subscribe to some variant of government interaction with a wider and very informally structured 'public', led by various elites and including the press as both a participant and a mediator; and recognize the importance of these elites in responding to any political agenda. The British and dominion volunteer movement provides a unique and invaluable case-study for testing these theories. Historians rightly bemoan the fact that theirs is a discipline in which the experiment cannot be repeated. But the volunteer movement represents a rare case in which this was not so: barely more than a decade before 1914, a similar volunteer movement on a smaller scale had contributed to the Boer War of 1899–1902, including volunteers from the dominions. Although early historical research discounted the evidence from the Boer War because those who went to fight were predominantly middle class, the total who actually volunteered included a significantly higher proportion of working-class men who were rejected. The existence of these two British Imperial volunteer movements so close together in time, and so widely spread around the globe, offers the opportunity for comparative historical study, as well as a warning that any explanation based on any one country and its experience of propaganda is unlikely to yield the complete truth.

The critical role of local elites in these volunteer movements was first identified by Canadian and Australian historians, who interpreted the raising of dominion volunteers as the sinister product of collusion between the British government and local politicians of unrepresentative pro-British sympathies. This interpretation has now been overturned in favour of a recognition that the impulse to volunteer was genuine, but depended either for its origins or its maintenance on the actions of local leaders who provided a structure for the new forces and also propaganda for recruiting. The same pattern has been very clearly identified within the United Kingdom, with local leaders being particularly important in Wales, Scotland and Ireland, and in the raising of the famous 'Pals Battalions'. What has emerged from this evidence and the continuing study of volunteerism is a United Kingdom (and even an Empire) with considerable regional diversity, narrow and parochial in its horizons but in which there was still a strong enough consensus to unite the West End of London or Hampshire with Red Clydeside and Ulster, in order to fight the war.

During the first days of recruiting, propaganda initiatives and government responses ran behind the volunteer movement, leading to the creation of the Central Committee for National Patriotic Organisations in August 1914, and propaganda only became proactive when the first surge slackened in September. Even then, propaganda which later became iconic may have had only a slight impact. Alfred Leete's poster proclaiming that Kitchener 'Wants You', which appeared on 5 September, did not halt the temporary decline in recruiting following the first August rush, while the Parliamentary Recruiting Committee's total budget for posters and leaflets was less than Rowntree's of York had spent during two years before the war in promoting a single brand of cocoa.

The extent of volunteerism as an ideology has also been underestimated. When the British government introduced conscription in January 1916 it expected to find a substantial pool of 'shirkers' in the civilian workforce who had avoided military service. But the resulting supply of conscripts was barely enough to maintain the army at its existing strength against the demands made of it, and there is little reason to assume that many of these conscripts might not have volunteered anyway, as they came of age.

The loss of volunteerism in January 1916 also meant the loss for historians of a critical indicator of mass public opinion and support for the war. But the next most significant piece of evidence is the unprecedented British interest in and enthusiasm for the first of the big British propaganda documentary films, *Battle of the Somme* in August 1916, followed by similar full-length films into mid-1917, after which British official film production switched to emphasizing a twice-weekly newsreel. Film had already eclipsed music hall as the dominant working-class entertainment, with a penetration into working-class culture far greater than any newspaper. *Battle of the Somme* was seen by at least twenty million people in its first six weeks, and almost certainly by a majority of the population before the war's end, making it the essential starting point for any historical discussion of British working-class responses to the war. Although there were some protests about these films, the popular response suggests that in 1916 domestic support for the war was still strong, while anecdotal evidence and letter censorship confirms that this was also true of the fighting fronts.

Anecdotes also suggest that most British people, including serving soldiers, reacted against official propaganda chiefly when they felt that it strayed too far from the facts as they understood them, or when they believed that they were being too overtly propagandized. The majority of the British people wanted to believe in their own side's cause in the war and in eventual victory, and propaganda provided them with some of the arguments, and some of the inspiration, but only when it was closely linked to political and military events. The forms of propaganda meant to appeal to the mass of the working class drew rather superior sneers from intellectuals like Ponsonby or Graves, who failed to realize how much they were influenced by other propaganda forms. But to state the obvious, if Siegfried Sassoon had been typically representative of the British Army then it would have followed his well-publicized protest against the war in July 1917 by mutinying.

One advantage that the British enjoyed over their enemies was that from the war's start German propaganda policy was in the hands of their General Staff, which was chiefly intent on establishing to its own satisfaction why its behaviour as governed by military necessity was correct, and then announcing this in triumph to the world. One outstanding example of this was the proclamation of the punitive terms of the Treaty of Brest-Litovsk in March 1918 just days before the great offensive in the West, a blunder that did much to stiffen Allied resolve. The German Navy, also, promoted in 1917 a propaganda campaign on unrestricted submarine warfare which backfired disastrously in neutral countries. This inept German propaganda policy provided frequent gifts to Allied politicians as well as propagandists, and underlined the need for a strong institutional connection between high government policy and the low culture of film newsreels or the popular press.

In contrast, British propaganda policy was made largely by civilians. The British armed forces became involved only as part of wider policies, although there was some inevitable friction between military and civilian institutions. The chief military involvement in propaganda on the fighting fronts was through the humble propaganda leaflet, which often played an important role in helping enemy troops to surrender safely.

British military regulations were so wide-ranging that in theory for a soldier on active service to keep a diary or write a letter for publication was a punishable offence, although many examples exist in archives to show how little this was enforced. Despite bans on some fronts, private cameras were also tolerated, especially early in the war, and again many photographs survive to prove it. Private letters and photographs continued to appear in the provincial press throughout the war, making provincial newspapers a neglected source for research. Otherwise, after an unsuccessful attempt to ban the press outright from the fighting fronts, the first official war correspondents appeared in early 1915, followed by official cine-cameramen and photographers.

Most accounts have taken these men at their own valuation, as figures of importance with real powers to influence war policy. Like other members of the British propaganda machine they were allowed considerable latitude in their writings, and the belief that they either lied outright or failed to describe the horrors of the Western Front is a myth. But in practice they were highly constrained minor players, required by a variety of pressures and circumstances (including personal beliefs) to modify what they wrote. A large part of their work depended on access to senior political and military leaders, and one of their most important functions was to act as unofficial and occasional channels between elites and the mass of the media-consuming public that were not always one-way.

The greatest strains on the British war effort came in 1917, which is also the year for which the fewest reliable major sources exist for British public attitudes. From January onwards the British propaganda apparatus was being reorganized with the absorption of Wellington House into the new Department of Information; while with the entry of the United States into the war in April British propaganda policy was itself realigned, to reflect both a more domestic and a more populist agenda. It was in this context that the notorious 'corpse factory' story appeared, an isolated misjudgement reportedly made over the objections of the professional propagandists. Although such mistakes were quite exceptionally rare, like other changes in propaganda policy they may be taken as very public evidence of strains and conflicts within the British political leadership which might otherwise be less visible.

The most commonly cited measure of British home front attitudes in 1917 is the increased incidence of strikes from March onwards, usually attributed to complaints over inequalities in food distribution and profiteering. Again, the government linked its political strategy of reform closely with its propaganda initiatives, including the creation of the National War Aims Committee in August, and the despatch of King George V to Clydeside the following month for an official visit accompanied by the press and cameras. By late 1917, the government and the press lords had come to believe that while they might disagree or even despair among themselves about the war and its conduct, *pas devant les domestiques*: they must not do so in public or in print for fear of the working classes who they believed looked to them for leadership (since, according to the most pessimistic, that leadership might itself be imperilled once doubt had been created).

With the establishment of the Ministry of Information the following year, much official propaganda began to adopt an altogether more strident tone, particularly through films and cartoons, but as in 1914, British propaganda appears to have been responding to wider public opinion during the first few months of 1918, only eventually coming to direct it or revitalize it towards the war effort. The change in British grand strategy over winter 1917–18, and the persistent undervaluing of the Western Front by the government and its propaganda apparatus during the course of the year, meant that most British people had little idea in November of how they had won the war. At the same time, measured in part by anecdotal and circumstantial evidence, in the last few months of 1918 British popular enthusiasm for the war rose to a level of passion and even xenophobia that may actually have been even greater than in 1914. The exact connection between this enthusiasm (if it was not illusory), the final British military victories, and British propaganda policy remains at present one of the unsolved puzzles of the war.

Further Reading

My own writings on the press, propaganda and public perception during the First World War are listed on the 'publication' page of my personal website, www.stephenbadsey.com. Good general overviews of propaganda and the war are Philip M. Taylor, *Munitions of the Mind* (1990, Wellingborough: Stephens); Garth S. Jowett and Victoria O'Donnell, *Propaganda and Persuasion* (1986, Beverley Hills, CA: SAGE); and Nicholas Reeves, *The Power of Film Propaganda* (1999, London: Cassell). For the United Kingdom, Michael Sanders and Philip M. Taylor, *British Propaganda During the First World War 1914–1918* (1982, London: Macmillan) remains irreplaceable, joined by Gary S. Messinger, *British Propaganda and the State in the First World War* (1992, Manchester: Manchester UP); Brock Millman, *Managing Domestic Dissent in First World War Britain* (2000, London: Frank Cass); George Robb, *British Culture and the First World War* (2002, Basingstoke: Palgrave); and David Silbey, *The British Working Class and Enthusiasm for War 1914–1916* (2005, London: Frank Cass). Stephen Koss, *The Rise and Fall of the Political Press in Britain* (1981, London: Hamilton), and Martin J. Farrar, *News From the Front* (1998, Stroud:

Sutton), describe the British press and its war correspondents. For meanings attributed to the war after its end see Dan Todman, *The Great War: Myth and Memory* (2005, London: Hambledon and London), supplemented by Michael Paris, *Warrior Nation* (2000, London: Reaktion). John M. Mackenzie, *Propaganda and Empire* (1984, Manchester: Manchester UP), argues the case for imperial propaganda; for Australia, see John F. Williams, *Anzacs, The Media and the Great War* (1999, Sydney: University of New South Wales), and Jenny Macleod, *Reconsidering Gallipoli* (2004, Manchester: Manchester UP); and for Canada see Tim Cook, *Clio's Warriors* (2006, Vancouver: University of British Columbia Press). For Germany, see David Welch, *Germany, Propaganda and Total War 1914–18* (2002, London: Athlone), supplemented by John Horne and Alan Kramer, *German Atrocities 1914* (2001, New Haven, CT: Yale UP), and Isabel V. Hull, *Absolute Destruction* (2005, Ithaca, NY: Cornell UP); and for Austria-Hungary see Mark Cornwall, *The Undermining of Austria-Hungary* (2000, Basingstoke: Macmillan).

Chapter 5

Gallipoli: A Stone Unturned

Peter Hart

The study of Gallipoli has been in a straitjacket for too long. The literature of the campaign is plagued with books that are underpinned by the premise that the original concept of the Gallipoli campaign was a brilliant idea that was betrayed by a failure to divert sufficient military resources from the Western Front, incompetent local commanders and sheer bad luck. The humiliating utter failure of the campaign is hence excused by constant references to 'close run things', 'the narrowest of margins' and 'the terrible ifs'. This is a perspective that was not accepted by contemporary military experts and has been since comprehensively undermined by the return to a more rational appraisal of the military operations of the Great War.

In reality the Gallipoli campaign was a diversion of valuable military resources from the main battle against the German Army on the Western Front. All of the British external strategic imperatives were under direct threat from the Germans: if they were successful in beating France then they would achieve the domination of Europe, they could take control of the Channel ports, and their High Seas Fleet was directly challenging the supremacy of the Royal Navy implying that Britain would lose control of the seas. The German challenge had to be confronted and France could not do it alone. The bulk of the British military effort *had* to be directed onto the Western Front.

This, however, was not how the 'Easterners' saw the war. They looked back to an older maritime vision of warfare, relying on naval strength to land small expeditionary forces to make a real difference at key points across the globe. Intervention at the right time could resolve a conflict, or seize tactically significant features, before an opponent had a chance to respond. This was all very well, but signally failed to represent the nature of the threat posed by Germany – the solid muscle behind the Central Powers. In essence the Easterners were seeking an easy option; indeed, it is no coincidence that many of them were politicians. They looked to avoid the ordeal of facing the German Army and thought that they could end the war by knocking out Germany's allies or attacking her non-existent soft underbelly. And so was born the Gallipoli campaign.

It was a lunacy that never had the chance to succeed, an idiocy generated by muddled thinking. By attacking the Turks, the British merely allowed the Turks the opportunity to kill British soldiers in large numbers. Left to themselves, in the face of simple defensive measures to secure British interests in the Suez Canal and Mesopotamian oil supplies, there was nothing much the Turks could have done. But by diverting resources to Gallipoli the Allies not only exposed themselves to a greater possibility of a catastrophic defeat by the Germans but also allowed the Turks to soundly thrash them in front of the whole Muslim world. Brilliant!

The naval campaign culminating in the abortive attempt to rush the Dardanelles on 18 March 1915 was probably the best chance of any Anglo-French success. But the collected pre-dreadnoughts floundered against the Turks' integrated defence system – the bane of the amateur strategist. The heavy guns kept the battleships at a reasonable distance, the concealed artillery batteries threatened the progress of the makeshift trawler minesweepers, the mines had to be cleared before the big ships could pass, and the torpedo tubes set along the shores of the straits were a final threat. The civilian crews of the minesweepers could not carry out their task, while the Turks laid a new minefield that was not detected, and naval guns were ineffective against land targets. The end result was a disaster with three pre-dreadnoughts sinking and a badly damaged battlecruiser. Apologists insist that a renewed naval attack could have succeeded, but wiser heads at the time preferred to let the army seize the Kilid Bahr Plateau that dominates the Straits. In the later stages naval optimists pointed to the possibilities of destroyers equipped as minesweepers clearing the mines, but that overlooks the fact that when the Royal Navy had their chance, they had not made the proper preparations and they had failed. If there *had* been a chance of success then they had missed it.

When the military campaign proper finally began on 25 April it provided a veritable checklist of the defining characteristics common to British Easterner military adventures in Mesopotamia, Salonika and East Africa in 1915: a lack of realistic or well-defined goals, no coherent plan, the use of inexperienced troops, an absence of proper maps or intelligence, negligible artillery support, totally inadequate logistical and medical arrangements, a gross underestimation of the enemy, easily disrupted communications, incompetent local commanders and all overlaid with lashings of misplaced overconfidence leading to inevitable disaster.

The plans for the landings made by General Sir Ian Hamilton are often lauded but they are clearly overcomplicated and lacked any clear focus. There were two separate diversions: one at the Bulair neck of the peninsula and another launched by the French at Kum Kale on the Asiatic side of the Straits. The main landings were to be on the Helles Peninsula, at the V and W beaches, with two subsidiary flanking landings at S and X beaches, and a further landing at Y beach. Then there was a secondary major landing by the Australian and New Zealand troops at what would become known as Anzac Cove, intended to strike across the Gallipoli Peninsula to seize the Mal Tepe hill feature, before joining with the planned assault from the main British landings on the Kilid Bahr Plateau. This was the real objective: the imposing fortified massif that directly overlooked the Narrows and dominated the Peninsula. All the rest were just stepping stones to that end. Sympathy for Hamilton – an intelligent general with an attractive personality who had been placed in an impossible position – has tended to prevent any real critical analysis of his plans. But by attacking at so many different points Hamilton allowed the vastly outnumbered and thinly spread out Turks to 'just about' hold out in many different places, something that would have been impossible with just one or two really heavy blows. The well-defended V and W beaches could then have been easily outflanked, but then Hamilton and his staff never believed that the Turks would stand and fight.

The landings have been mythologized as a military achievement of the highest order by many Gallipoli authors. Much is made of Turkish machine guns, streams of lead, British heroism beyond measure and struggles against almost insuperable odds. This may well be so, but the insuperable odds were faced by the Turks, not the British. Just one battalion of Turks – some 1,000 or so men – faced 12,000 British troops, yet they and their minimal reinforcements succeeded in keeping the 29th Division penned back to the beaches for most of the first day. It may have been the first landing to be made in the face of modern weapons, but the British could hardly have done worse, or indeed the Turks much better, on 25 April. To make it plain: the British utterly bodged the Helles landings, making mistake after mistake at *every* level of command, missing any brief opportunities while ludicrously exaggerating the scale of the opposition. This is emphatically *not* a matter of doubting the courage of individual soldiers but more of accepting an endemic military incompetence that was lethally combined with troops who still had no experience of modern warfare in 1915.

Meanwhile, along the coast the landing at Anzac Cove saw a similar tale of Turkish defensive success. The grossly out-numbered Turks used all the natural advantages of the rugged terrain to stymie the Australian troops advancing to contact across broken ground through tangled undergrowth. Then when the Turks' reserves arrived the Anzacs were often isolated and overrun. By nightfall they had only carved out a minute bridgehead barely a quarter of a mile deep and everywhere overlooked by the Turks. This was a close-run thing all right, but it was not a question of near Australian success – more likely that the Turks needed only a bit more luck and they would have pitched them straight back into the sea. Yet the 'Diggers' dug in and held their ground. But they could not – and did not – make any renewed effort to attain their *real* objectives of Mal Tepe and beyond that the Kilid Bahr Plateau. For the next three months the Anzac beachhead was nothing more than a holding camp. They achieved nothing other than to defend themselves from the Turks. It was against all military odds or sense, it was heroic, it was fascinating in the extreme – but it was of negligible importance to the campaign as a whole.

The subsequent domination of the literature of Gallipoli by the Anzac story is more a reflection of the importance to the Australians of their first military campaign than a realistic assessment of their achievements. At the centre of everything was the achievement of Charles Bean in producing his massive two-volume official history of Anzac. This epic goes into incredible detail, examining the movements of groups of indi-viduals during the first day and barely widening its focus as the campaign moved on. But the growing legend of Gallipoli also led to a rash of dubious personal experience accounts riddled with incredible stories of bullet-torn beaches.

The Anzac Corps would go on to fight against the 'real enemy' on the Western Front. Here, after undergoing a painfully sharp learning curve, they more than pulled their weight to emerge as the finest Allied attacking formation in 1918. Sufficient time has now elapsed to allow a mature historical look at their performance at Gallipoli. Books from the Australian perspective have multiplied but few add much to the overall picture, as there is a general unwillingness to grasp the failure of the Anzacs, or indeed to accept the overall success of the Turks. The sheer detail in Bean means that few add much to our knowledge of the course of events, although the recent recasting of Bean's geographically dominated record of events into a chronological account by David Cameron in his book *25 April 1915* certainly highlights the sheer courage and brilliance of the Turkish defence as they faced multiple simultaneous threats across the Anzac ridges and gullies. Other sharply focused studies, such as Peter Stanley's book *Quinn's Post* or biographies such as *No Better Death: The Great War Diaries and Letters of William G Malone*, edited by John Crawford, have allowed room to explore detailed aspects of the fighting.

The campaign at Helles is never dealt with separately. Yet it was at Helles that the campaign would be decided one way or another. It was here that the main offensives were launched to try and break through the Turkish lines, to seize the Achi Baba hill that overlooks Helles with the intent of then driving on across the broken ground to Kilid Bahr. Time and time again the British, Indian and French troops heaved themselves forward in the First, Second and Third battles of Krithia, the Battle of 12 / 13 July, the Battle of Gully Ravine and the major diversionary attack in August. Here was real drama: hubristic plans, temporary successes and dreadful failures; here the bulk of the butcher's bill was paid. Throughout, they were faced by determined Turks in almost equal numbers, well dug in and determined to defend their homeland. There were violent Turkish counterattacks, when they flung themselves forward, attacking without heed down gullies that would soon be blocked by their fast-decomposing corpses. Their bones lie scattered there even now.

These were all engagements that dwarf the skirmishes at Anzac. To put it in context, the French had more troops at Gallipoli than the Australians. They fought more battles, killed more Turks and had more casualties than all the Anzac forces put together. They even had the most difficult military ground in the Kereves Dere sector where the dreaded Ravin de la Mort speaks for itself.

It is often claimed that Gallipoli was a close-run thing but this too is nonsense, as the Turks held the Allies back from their *real* objectives with relative ease. Most of the 'close shaves' of legend were incidents where the confused remnants of a company or so of Allied troops found themselves marooned in an isolated position, facing the undivided attentions of masses of fresh Turkish troops. Look at the real objectives: the passage of the Narrows. To do that they needed Kilid Bahr, but to do that they first needed Achi Baba. They couldn't get that, so they must get the village of Krithia that lay in front of it. However, that too was beyond their reach, so the Vineyard would be a stepping stone. Even that proved impossible, so the end result was men fighting and dying in their hundreds to capture Trench H12, or J13, or some other benighted irrelevance. This was mission creep at its worst. They never got anywhere near Kilid Bahr.

Worse still, that was just the *first* step to success. The Allied fleet still had to get through the Narrows, defeat the Turkish fleet, which included the dangerous German battlecruiser the *Goeben*, while avoiding any further minefields in steaming all the way across the Sea of Mamara to Constantinople; and even then they still had to secure the surrender of the Turkish government.

In August the Empire bestirred itself to send massive reinforcements for the combined British / Anzac / Indian attempt to break out from Anzac all in conjunction with the fresh landing at Suvla Bay. Here again Hamilton's plans were ludicrously overcomplicated: the right assaulting column; the right covering force; the left assaulting column; the left covering force; the attack at the Nek; the diversionary attacks at Lone Pine and German Officer's Trench; and the criminal full-scale assault with no chance of success carried out at great cost at Helles. Once again the same story: inept British commanders and plans that paid no heed to the state of the ground or qualities of the troops. The various columns blundered about, getting lost in the tangled hills and ridges. The Turks knew the ground and their superior command skills saw them baulk the British at every turn. The landing at Suvla Bay was a demonstration of incompetence that even today causes a sharp intake of breath. The senior officers at Suvla had minimal command experience and failed to 'press on'; indeed they failed to do anything much at all.

The failure of the August offensive marked the effective end of the campaign as a serious attempt to take the Straits. Simple survival became paramount everywhere on the Peninsula. Evacuation was inevitable once the dreamy Hamilton had been replaced by the far more practically minded General Sir Charles Munro. 'He came, he saw, he capitulated,' Churchill grumbled. But a far more accurate assessment was that he arrived, summed up the hopeless situation and had the courage to take the only action possible – evacuation as quickly as possible before too many German heavy guns could arrive to blast them pell-mell into the Aegean.

The Gallipoli campaign as a whole has been blessed with a marvellous literature and cursed with some bad history. The 'story' has been given a romantic glow suffused with the echoes of various Greek tragedies, in particular dwelling on the siege of Troy and filtered through the prism of officers' classical educations. This was typified by the *Hamilton Diaries*, which were not really diaries at all but an apologia designed to exculpate the men who served at Gallipoli and throw all the blame back onto the politicians in London. Even the excellent two-volume official history stylishly written by Cecil Aspinall-Oglander was hardly neutral as he had served there himself in the guise of Captain Aspinall – one of Hamilton's senior staff officers. Other writers who served there have given us wonderfully emotive accounts, as exemplified by John North's *Gallipoli: The Fading Vision* and Harold Nevinson's *The Dardanelles Campaign*. But they were biased, unwilling to accept that something that meant so much to them could have been essentially flawed.

Books covering the whole Gallipoli campaign have always been straitjacketed by the demands of publishers. What *they* require is a single-volume history covering the genesis of the campaign, the naval battle, the landings and battles at Helles, Anzac and Suvla, followed by the evacuation and authorial ponderings on who was to blame for failure. Imprisoned by this lack of space, the books fall into a similar pattern: a fairly superficial rewriting of the official histories with a dollop of an extra ingredient – often it is personal experience accounts (Robert Rhodes James, *Gallipoli*; Michael Hickey, *Galllipoli*; Nigel Steel and Peter Hart, *Defeat at Gallipoli*); sometimes authors deploy a wonderful journalistic flair to tell a rattling good tale (Alan Moorhead, *Gallipoli*; Len Carlyon, *Gallipoli*); or perhaps there is an attempt to get a new perspective as with Tim

Travers's *Gallipoli 1915*. This last makes numerous references to using Turkish sources but the publisher has not actually left him the space to deploy them in any serious manner. Specialist or academic studies – such as those of Peter Chasseaud and Peter Doyle, *Grasping Gallipoli*, and Jenny Macleod's *Reconsidering Gallipoli* and her collection *Gallipoli: Making History* – are one possible step forward.

But what we still need is a cold-eyed analysis of the fighting at Helles without having to be overly distracted by Anzac. Helles was the crux of the campaign; this was the real fight for Gallipoli. We need a detailed review of the British and Turkish plans, an investigation of the ludicrous logistical situation, the failures of command and control, an understanding of the Turkish defensive arrangements / tactics and a proper appreciation of the huge French contribution. We desperately need a collection of French personal experience accounts so that we can have a picture of their trials and tribulations. Suvla too needs a proper separate scrutiny, particularly of the Turkish movements, both locally on the Suvla Plain but also of the timetable of the arrival of the massed reserves marching down from Bulair. The Australians have begun to accelerate their work on Turkish sources, but the Turkish Official History still needs to be properly translated and made available with an expert commentary. We also need to see more translated Turkish personal experience accounts. *Gallipoli 1915: Bloody Ridge Diary* by Mehmed Fasih is a start, but contemporary literacy rates and the subsequent radical change in their written language makes future progress doubtful.

Gallipoli is a fascinating campaign and it is a beautiful place, redolent of its tragic past. But historians must beware of being sucked into thinking that it was either a justifiable operation of war or had any realistic chance of success. The Western Front was where the war would be decided and the German Army defeated. Gallipoli was a futile sideshow.

Chapter 6

Writing about Jutland: Historiography and Hysteria

Nick Hewitt

The Battle of Jutland ('Jutland') was fought between 31 May and 1 June 1916. It was the only time that the fleets of British and German big-gun 'dreadnought' battleships, which had been built at such enormous expense between 1906 and 1914, actually came to blows. The battle involved, on both sides, 250 ships and around 100,000 men. It was at times a confused and bloody action. By the morning of 1 June the fleets had separated and returned home to lick their wounds, the British having lost 14 ships and 6,094 men killed, the Germans, 11 ships and 2,551 men.

Almost immediately Jutland provided a rich seam of debate for historians, analysts and commentators to mine. In the United Kingdom, in particular, expectations of the much hyped battle fleet had been incredibly high in the years that preceded the war: the population had been conditioned to expect another Trafalgar as their right, and were bitterly disappointed when the Kaiser's ships were not sent to the bottom en masse or brought home in chains.

This chapter will investigate how British writing about this pivotal battle has changed over the years since 1916. It is not intended to provide a comprehensive reading list, although those whose interest has been stimulated will find some suggestions for further reading embedded in the text. However, the confused nature of the battle meant that much of the early literature tended to concentrate on the vexed question of who actually won the battle, and who was to blame for various perceived failures. Before beginning, therefore, it would perhaps be timid to avoid giving my own interpretation of the outcome. There are inevitably many ways to interpret such a complicated and unclear battle, but the accepted wisdom is to allow the Germans a tactical victory, on the grounds that the British lost more ships and men. My own view is that Jutland was an unequivocal British victory, both tactically and strategically.

It is unfashionable to take this line in the face of so many dead, but let us try for a moment to set them to one side and appraise the aftermath of Jutland with the cold eye of a senior commander. With the exception of the brand new battlecruiser HMS *Queen Mary*, most of the British losses were tactically insignificant. The older battlecruisers *Invincible* and *Indefatigable* were practically obsolete, and the three lost armoured cruisers certainly almost worthless. Eight destroyers were lost, out of 77 available to the Grand Fleet. Most crucially of all, only two dreadnought battleships in the main British line suffered any form of damage at all. The Grand Fleet was ready for action again the next day.

On the German side, the brand new battlecruiser *Lutzow* constituted a serious loss equivalent to the *Queen Mary*. The obsolete 'pre-dreadnought' battleship *Pommern* and the old light cruiser *Frauenlob* were insignificant, and five torpedo boats lost out of the 57 available were probably acceptable. But the loss of three modern light cruisers represented half of the total number of this valuable type of ship available to the Germans.

Furthermore, the German battleships had suffered far more than their British equivalents. Four modern dreadnoughts were damaged, three not returning to the line until the end of July. And the German battlecruisers were wrecked, two remaining out of service until the autumn. Until then the High Seas Fleet Scouting Force was reinforced by fast battleships, further reducing the size of the battle fleet.

It is my contention that perceptions of leadership at Jutland have been distorted by exploding British battlecruisers. Both Vizeadmiral Franz von Hipper (in command of the German battlecruisers) and Vice Admiral Sir David Beatty carried out their allotted roles competently and courageously, each seeking out the enemy and leading him in turn onto the guns of their main fleets, the textbook role of battlecruisers. Beatty's reputation is somewhat tarnished by signalling failures and his force's poor gunnery, although to his credit he learned from these problems.

In the fleet action the German Commander in Chief, Vizeadmiral Reinhard Scheer, led with aggression and dash. But the manoeuvre for which he is most famed is the *gefechtkehrt-wendung,* or 'battle turn away'. We should not let the fact that this was an astonishing feat of seamanship disguise that it was a well-rehearsed method of getting out of trouble. Similarly, much is made of the British inability to take advantage of the possibilities offered by a night action. But neither did the Germans, whose undoubted skills in this area were applied only to escape.

In the end, the purpose of the entire German plan, and the raison d'etre of the German fleet, was to destroy the British fleet, break the blockade and seize control of the North Sea. After only a few minutes of action with Jellicoe, Scheer realized that this was unachievable and extracted his fleet from danger. So shaken were the Germans that they never again mounted such a serious challenge to British surface hegemony, turning instead to unrestricted submarine warfare.

Jellicoe was no Nelson, and Jutland was no Trafalgar – but in 1916 Britain did not need Trafalgar. Jellicoe knew what was required and delivered it, one American newspaper writing that 'The German fleet has assaulted its jailor, but is still in jail.'

This, however, was by no means universally accepted at the time, any more than it has been since. The German fleet returned home first, tallied up the losses and announced a great victory. The British response was a disastrous Admiralty despatch, issued on 2 June, which admitted to heavy losses and strongly implied defeat. Kaiser Wilhelm II, never one to miss an opportunity for hyperbole, responded on 5 June, when he travelled to Wilhelmshaven to proclaim that: 'The English were beaten. The spell of Trafalgar has been broken. You have started a new chapter in world history.'

So began the 'Jutland Controversy', the source of prodigious expenditure of ink over the forthcoming decades. For the British, it swirled around the issues of whether they won the battle at all and, if they did, who was to blame for the perceived failure to 'Trafalgar' the Kaiser.

The latter question focused in turn on whether fault lay with Beatty, for his alleged impetuosity and glory seeking, or Jellicoe, for his supposed caution and inflexibility. Both admirals, to their credit, stayed largely aloof (at least publicly) from this poisonous internecine conflict. Jellicoe's own book, *The Grand Fleet 1914–1916* (1919, London: Cassell), rushed out almost before the guns had cooled, was diplomatic, describing Beatty as showing 'fighting qualities of the highest order'. But despite this the vitriolic public outpourings of the various friends and supporters of the two admirals dominated the historiography of Jutland for many years.

The first blow was struck by Arthur Pollen, a civilian inventor who had unsuccessfully tied to persuade the navy to adopt his design for a mechanical fire control computer and blamed Jellicoe for turning it down. On 28 November 1918 he published *The Navy in Battle* (1918, London: Chatto and Windus) in which he rather ludicrously tried to give credit for any success at Jutland to Beatty alone. Pollen was joined two years later by Beatty's chief cheerleader, the gloriously named Commander Carlyon Wilfroy Bellairs, Conservative MP for Maidstone. His *The Battle of Jutland: The Sowing and the Reaping* (1919, London: Hodder and Stoughton) was riddled with damning criticism of Jellicoe, whom he called 'a man of tearful yesterdays and fearful tomorrows'.

Jellicoe's biographer, Admiral Sir Reginald Hugh Spencer Bacon, was initially more circumspect, choosing to damn Beatty with faint praise, but when in 1933 he brought out a book specifically devoted to Jutland he seems to have felt less obliged to show restraint. In *The Jutland Scandal* (nd, London: Hutchinson) he lambasted Beatty, calling him 'inexperienced and lacking tactical experience'. He was joined by Capain J. E. T. Harper, an Admiralty navigation specialist and the officer originally charged with producing the official report on the battle. Harper finished his draft in October 1919, by which time Beatty had become First Sea Lord, and apparently he found it unacceptable. Harper refused to make the required changes and the report was suppressed. Frustrated and angry, Harper eventually published his findings himself in *The Truth about Jutland* (1927, London: John Murray), following up with an article for the *RUSI Journal* in the same year and another book, *The Riddle of Jutland: An Authentic History* (1934, London: Cassell), just a few years later. Like Bacon, he was vitriolic in his condemnation of Beatty, calling him 'tempestuous' and 'impetuous', and his supporters men who 'manifested the almost passionate belief that Beatty could do no wrong'. He did at least, however, embarrass the Admiralty into releasing his original report, albeit a truncated version.

Harper, Bacon, Bellairs and Pollen are really just the tip of the iceberg of the 'Jutland Controversy', and this brief chapter will not attempt to catalogue all of the contributions. Perhaps the most celebrated participant was Winston Churchill, who devoted several chapters of *The World Crisis* (1923–29, London: Thornton Butterworth) to the battle, generally favouring Beatty and damning Jellicoe.

Perhaps one of the most interesting books to come out at this time, *The Fighting at Jutland*, by H. W. Fawcett and G. W. Hooper, was one which pre-empted the more modern approach to history by relating the experience of the men of the Grand Fleet. Most histories of Jutland written in the interwar period were, however, tainted to a greater or lesser extent by the controversy, even the *Official History of the Great War: Naval Operations* written by Sir Julian Corbett and Sir Henry Newbolt (1920–31, London: Longmans, Green and Co.).

The debate over the 'controversy' was always fairly introverted and of little interest to the public at large. It only really began to wane once the main protagonists died, first Jellicoe in 1936 and then Beatty a year later. Finally, in September 1939, a new war brought to a close a debate which was always more about hysterical faction fighting than serious historical analysis.

Interestingly, the end of the Second World War brought about a renewed interest in the First and, in particular, attempts to understand it using the memories of those who fought at all levels, rather than just through the eyes (and egos) of long-deceased senior commanders. In this period, of course, those who had fought in the First World War and returned to civilian life were reaching the end of their careers. As they passed into retirement, perhaps their thoughts drifted back to the part they played. Whatever the cause, interest in Jutland was rekindled during this period, although much of what was written took the form of balanced but arguably straightforward and unchallenging narrative history.

Although many authors drew on the documentary evidence left by participants, usually of commissioned rank and often involved in the 'controversy', most were sensible enough not to try to reignite old arguments, although presenting the facts in such a way as to prevent elderly sailors from exploding into apoplexy must have been challenging. Foremost amongst the post-war literature was arguably the American historian Arthur Marder's magisterial five-volume work, *From the Dreadnought to Scapa Flow* (1961–70, London: OUP), but other histories emerged by authors such as Geoffrey Bennett, Richard Hough and Donald Macintyre, a former naval officer and prolific writer of Second World War naval history.

Of arguably far greater interest has been a wave of more recent works on the subject. First to appear, in 1986, was John Campbell's *Jutland: An Analysis of the Fighting* (1986, London: Conway Maritime Press), a highly technical examination of exactly which ship steamed on what course for how long, who they shot at and who shot at them, and far more besides. Based largely on contemporary damage reports, Campbell's book is not for the faint-hearted, but for the determined reader it would be hard to find a more clinical, objective look at exactly what happened.

In 1995 the historian V. E. Tarrant filled another gap in the literature with *Jutland: The German Perspective* (1995, London: Arms and Armour Press), essentially an unchallenging narrative but one which redeemed itself with the simple expedient of providing translated primary source material from the German Official History.

In 1996 Andrew Gordon published *The Rules of the Game* (1996, London: John Murray), a groundbreaking forensic examination of British command and control problems at Jutland and how they could be traced directly to the doctrinal and operational culture laid down in the nineteenth century. Gordon in part raked over the embers of the 'Jutland Controversy' but with such extraordinary attention to detail that it would be hard to find a better analysis of the senior command figures responsible for leading the Royal Navy at Jutland and during the First World War as a whole.

The kind of forensic analysis carried out by Gordon, Campbell and, to an extent, Tarrant, frees the author from the emotional baggage of personal testimony. However, when the subject is very close to their hearts as, for example, it clearly is to Gordon's, a former Royal Navy officer, it does carry the risk of substituting the historian's own prejudices for those of the veteran. This is, perhaps, an inevitable consequence of the passage of time.

Finally, in 2003, Nigel Steel and Peter Hart published *Jutland 1916: Death in the Grey Wastes* (2003, London: Cassell), based mainly on personal testimonies held by the Imperial War Museum. Many of the contributors were ordinary sailors from the 'lower deck', still more were only junior officers at the time, and this book more than any other explained Jutland as a human tragedy on an epic scale, not just a theoretical event for historians and former admirals to argue about.

So, in brief, Campbell gives the reader the technical analysis,

Tarrant the Germans, Gordon the Royal Navy's command and control, and Steel and Hart the men who were there, is there anything important left to say about Jutland?

Well, possibly not by authors. In recent years, new contributions have come from the world of marine archaeology. The relatively recent advances made in technical diving have enabled divers to find and explore historic wrecks in greater numbers than ever before, including those at Jutland. Further advances in underwater photography and video recording have meant that the evidence brought back has progressively improved in quality, and there is no doubt that new discoveries have been and will continue to be made. The importance of this material in increasing our understanding of the bigger picture of Jutland is perhaps debatable, although it has an undoubted fascination.

The increased accessibility of the wrecks has in turn led to greater interest on the part of film and television makers. Wrecks generally seem to have become a glamorous growth area for television, with entire series like *Wreck Detectives* (Channel 4), *Deep Wreck Mysteries* (ITV) and *The Sea Hunters* (National Geographic) devoted to them. The wrecks of Jutland have received their share of the attention, for example in a 2005 episode of the History Channel series *Battlefield Detectives*. Ironically this interest has come just at a time when actual participants have all but vanished. In a desperate attempt to maintain human interest, programme makers sometimes seem to resort to the desperate use of rather contrived 'moving' personal testimony even when two or three generations removed: 'weeping grandson' syndrome, perhaps another consequence of the passage of time.

Although some questions will, of course, always be a matter of interpretation, and complete consensus about Jutland will probably never come, over the years we have established almost beyond contradiction virtually everything we need to know to understand its causes, course and consequences. We have reliable sources for the operational history of the battle. We have first-hand testimony from both major and minor players, although as always it needs to be treated with a degree of caution. We have never been so well informed about the technology of the day and its strengths and failings.

In short, it is the contention of this chapter that, as far as the big questions are concerned, there really is nothing left to say. This does not mean, of course, that the last word on Jutland has been and gone. The story of Jutland is one of drama, action and intrigue, blow and counter-blow, a gigantic game of chess played out on a huge board with thousands of lives as the pieces. Each of those lives had their own story of Jutland; over time they will come to light in lost letters and diaries, and each new account will no doubt add something, however small, to the picture. New authors, too, will add their own 'spin' on the story, some more effectively or controversially than others, but each bringing the battle to a wider audience from time to time. Each big anniversary will doubtless continue to have its book.

Technology, handled appropriately, may perhaps offer the most exciting new possibilities. Computer-generation techniques might one day show the world what two dreadnought fleets actually looked like in action, bringing to the large or small screen images which have only existed in the minds of reader and author for nearly a hundred years. Were a big-budget producer to take on *Jutland: The Movie* this writer would shamelessly join the queue, just so long as they aimed for the standard set by *Downfall* or *Saving Private Ryan* rather than *Pearl Harbor* or *U571*.

Of course, however mouthwatering a prospect for those of us who love to be entertained as well as informed, such an epic would be unlikely to contribute anything to our knowledge. Neither would more wreck dives, or interviews with descendants, however moving. The contention of this author is that, as far as analysis is concerned, Jutland is finished. There is nothing more to say. We have all the answers we are ever going to get. Unless somebody thinks of a new question.

Chapter 7

The British Army on the Somme: July–November 1916

Trevor Wilson

The Battle of the Somme began in the early morning of 1 July 1916, a bright midsummer day. It continued until 18 November 1916, when only the grievous impact of winter and an alarming decline in the availability of trained manpower obliged the Allied command to close the offensive down.

Fortuitously, the Somme battle occurred right in the middle of the First World War. More fortuitously, it saw the British Army, for the first time in this conflict, occupying the predominant place in a great offensive against the principal enemy, Germany. It was doing so, moreover, in the crucial area of battle, the Western Front. The British, of course, had fought there already. Back in late 1914, the tiny British professional army had aided the French in thwarting Germany's attempt to overrun Western Europe in six weeks. And in 1915, while also deploying troops in futile efforts against the Turks (in Gallipoli) and Bulgaria (at Salonika), the British command had expended elements of their army in France's mighty but unsuccessful attempts to drive the Germans in the west into retreat.

But the Somme in 1916 was, for Britain, altogether another matter. Offensives against lesser adversaries had faded into well-merited insignificance. The Somme campaign was directed on the essential front against the essential enemy, and the British, faute de mieux, had become the major force in the assault.

Within Britain, the Somme endeavour was widely endorsed. Cabinet ministers had, after several weeks of contemplation, rejected any other area of assault. For example, they had concluded that British aid to the Russians, who after a year of retreat were promising an advance against the Germans, would best take the form of an Anglo-French attack in the west. Widespread support existed for the role to be played in it by Sir Douglas Haig, for the last six months British commander on the Western Front. And great expectations were held of the contributions of Lord Kitchener, organizer of the two million eager men who had enlisted in response to what they believed (not without reason) was German aggression; and even more of David Lloyd George, since May 1915 Britain's first-ever Minister of Munitions. The New Armies, and the new weaponry, were regarded as the combination which would end for good the stalemate – with Germany in control of most of Belgium and the northern section of France – which had obtained since late 1914.

The soldiers of Britain being sent into battle on the Somme were of three different groups, but with one large thing in common: they were all volunteers. The first group was the remnants of the pre-war regular army, volunteers who (apart from their largely upper-class officer corps) consisted of men decidedly of the lower classes, some of them seeking a life of adventure but most seeking an escape from unemployment and grinding poverty. The second group were the Territorials, men who before the war had usually been fully engaged in civilian employment but had been happy to spend their spare time – particularly at the weekend – in a bit of military training. The third were the men who made up the New, or Kitchener, Armies: that is, that great body of civilians who had never contemplated military life in peacetime but had hastened, usually eagerly but sometimes with a bit of pressure (by employers, families, girlfriends), to join the colours in response to the German offensive in the west. All of these three groups were represented in the Somme army, but the regulars and Territorials had been markedly or somewhat diminished by battles in the previous years. It was the volunteer enrollees who, having been trained and eventually uniformed by sometimes underqualified instructors with inadequate weapons, gave the British army of 1916 its peculiar flavour.

The course of the battle requires brief re-telling. It was conceived by the military leaders of the Allies as an element in grand strategy. That is, the Anglo-French offensive would coincide roughly simultaneously with assaults on the Central Powers by Russia and Italy. Together, these would exert pressure on Germany (and to a lesser extent on Austria-Hungary) on as many fronts as could be managed. Thereby the Germans, who had the advantage of internal lines, would not be able to switch forces from east to west and back again as circumstances required. The choice of the area in France on which to launch the assault has since been much criticized. It is said to have favoured the defender, both on account of the long period during which no battle had been fought on the Somme and, coupled with this, the accommodating nature of the soil for the construction of deep and formidable trenches. There was also the fact that the Germans occupied the higher ground here, and so would be more difficult to displace. So Churchill, after the war, felt entitled to call the Somme 'undoubtedly the strongest and most perfectly defended positions in the world'.

But these strictures against the Somme as a battleground were not decisive. Virtually anywhere on the Western Front, the Germans held the higher ground, because in the aftermath of the Allied counter-offensive on the Marne in September 1914 the enemy had deliberately halted their retreat at favourable points. So Messines Ridge, Passchendaele Ridge, Vimy Ridge and the Chemin des Dames were all German-held features against which, for lack of more enticing objectives, the Allies felt obliged to hurl attacks in the course of the war (not always unsuccessfully). The Somme, with its gradual slope and lack of industrialized areas, seemed a tolerable objective compared with these. And if the area had not been much fought over, and so facilitated German preparations, that had its advantages for the Allies also. The Somme was one of three regions where the Allies might hope that an attack on their part would lead to a large success over the enemy. Two of them had already, in 1915, been the subject of major offensives by the French, and in both instances huge numbers of French deaths and no significant advance into German-held territory had been the consequence. The Somme, by contrast, was virgin territory for a great offensive. And the majority of Britons chosen to fight there were virgin warriors, quietly confident of their ability to do it right.

In the months before the battle the British volunteers were trained for the struggle to come, in so far as weapons existed for their training. The territory lying behind the battlefield was provided with a water supply and hospitals and roads and all the other necessaries for a great attack. And at home the munitions industry, and its working class, laboured to supply the military forces with the huge volume of commodities they required. The army's tasks were various. In particular, the attackers must eliminate the barbed wire guarding the enemy trenches and drive the German trench-dwellers into their underground hiding-places where they would be imprisoned – at least until the British had crossed No Man's Land – by the collapse of their trenches on the exits.

What, once they had conquered the German front lines, the British were to accomplish had changed markedly in the weeks before the campaign. As originally planned, although the British constituted a large component of this assault, they were still engaging in a predominantly French endeavour. Joffre's force of 40 French divisions would assault alongside 20 British divisions. What invalidated this scheme was the action of Falkenhayn, the German commander-in-chief. Although claiming to hold the view that Britain constituted the main enemy, in February 1916 he launched a huge offensive against Verdun, a French-held stronghold well to the south of the Somme. His purpose – despite subsequent claims to the contrary – was to capture Verdun and so shatter French confidence beyond recall. That purpose he never accomplished, and his failure – followed by misjudgements when directing Germany's Somme defensive – ultimately destroyed his career.

Yet the maintenance of the German assault at Verdun did impose a grievous burden of casualties on the French – somewhat heavier, indeed, than that of the Germans – to the point where the French were driven to require that the British now become the major contributor to the Somme. So where initially the French had been intending to contribute 40 divisions to the Somme, by 1 July was 14 divisions the most they could manage. The British, meanwhile, were still employing the 20 they had promised. The length of front to be attacked in the southern (that is, French) sector was correspondingly reduced. And the purpose of the attack also changed. Initially the British, having struck east and severed the German line, were to turn southward and aid the French in driving the Germans back. Now the British were to be the principal element in the assault. They were to thrust east as far as Bapaume and then swing north-east in the direction of Arras and Douai, with the French on their right moving in the same direction. It was certainly by 1 July a predominantly British undertaking.

It proved also to be, on that day, a British catastrophe. All calculations by the British command had assumed a sufficiency of artillery ammunition and an abundance of skills on the part of the gunners. They intended to fire a preliminary bombardment of so devastating a quality as would accomplish three things: eliminate the barbed wire protecting the opposing trenches; render life so intolerable in the German positions that their surviving occupants would still be hiding in their deep dugouts while the British infantry crossed No Man's Land; and even commit some wreckage upon the German artillery to the rear of the enemy trenches. A few mathematical calculations would have provided cause for doubt that this could be accomplished.

Certainly the British Army on the Somme possessed more weaponry than had ever been its previous experience. But that, although the subject of much self-congratulation, signified little. The size of the rival army, and the defensive structures with which it had provided itself, were also unprecedented. The Germans, instead of a single line, were now sheltering in a repeated succession of trenches measuring thousands of yards. And in the accommodating soil they had dug deep dugouts which would only become ineffective if struck directly by a high-explosive shell or subjected to covering up by the collapse of the trench.

The British command could have known this. Its forces had attacked on the Western Front, if on a limited scale, on enough occasions in 1915 to provide warning of the problems they were facing. At Neuve Chapelle in March 1915, attacking on a much smaller scale but, relative to the numbers of men and yards of trench, with a bombardment twice the intensity of the Somme, they had captured and held the single-line front trench but had not managed to get any further. At Loos in September, with a level of bombardment significantly lower than Neuve Chapelle – in fact about the equal of that employed on the Somme – but with an element of poison gas added hopefully to reinforce the artillery, the British had suffered a setback so severe that it had led to the sacking of Sir John French, the Western Front commander-in-chief. These were not reassuring precedents.

In late 1915 and the first half of 1916, Lloyd George had made mighty efforts to speed the increase in shell production. But one device for this purpose was the abandonment of quality control, with lamentable results. Its consequence was that between a quarter and a third of British shells, when they did not explode in the guns that were supposed to be firing them, did not explode at all. And yet more disastrously, a majority of shells, even when functioning, were not at all to the point. In their preliminary bombardment, the British fired 1½ million shells, causing much discomfort to their enemies but only limited destruction. The reason was that two-thirds of the shells were shrapnel. These hurled a lot of bullets in the open and so might have severely damaged a force attempting to advance out of cover. They offered little threat to an army sheltering in trenches and dugouts. Only one-third of the shells were high-explosive, which was what was required severely to maul the German defences, and a good majority of these carried a pretty inadequate volume of firepower. That is, the shells gave the appearance of considerable weight, but did so only on account of the powerful casing which was deemed necessary to avoid an explosion inside the gun.

Even the really large shells with a lot of explosive, of which there were simply too few for the British attack to succeed, were not without disadvantages. The shells exploded usually upon contact with the earth, not after they had buried themselves. That provided a fine upward display, but effected limited destruction downwards which was where the Germans were usually sheltering.

The result for the British attackers was disaster. It was not, as has often been claimed, that the British troops attempted to cross No Man's Land shoulder to shoulder at a slow pace and burdened with supplies. Plainly, they responded to the perils of crossing the interval between the two armies by whatever means minimized danger. But the dangers proved prohibitive. Indeed so ineffective had the British bombardment proved that the enemy on much of the front opened devastating fire even before the British attackers had reached their own front line. So it is probable that as many as one-third of casualties on 1 July were sustained before British forces had ever entered – let alone attempted to cross – No Man's Land.

Overall, the consequences of that first day of the Somme were the most severe setback ever suffered by the British Army in any 24 hours of its long history: 20,000 killed and another 37,000 wounded. The rewards for these huge losses were trivial. On the southern part of the front the British overran the first German defensive line and advanced toward, but did not attempt to capture, the second German line. This constituted the capture of three square miles, hardly the accomplishment of even a moderate objective. But it was all that the great endeavour of 1 July had to offer the British Army or British people. On the left of the British front their artillery bombardment had proved a distinct failure, and such enemy territory as was early occupied had, at heavy cost, to be relinquished. But it was in the centre of the attack that the total failure to capture and hold enemy territory mattered most. For it was here, in Haig's scheme of things, that a powerful rupture was to be made in the enemy's lines and the way opened for a great cavalry sweep to Bapaume and beyond. Nothing of the sort happened, or appeared likely to happen. Here the problems confronting the infantry proved most formidable, and the artillery bombardment proved least effective. So the attack of III Corps, intended to clear the way for the cavalry, accomplished for the British 12,000 dead and wounded; 99 per cent of the German front line remained in enemy hands.

There was no contemplation in the Allied command of calling a halt at this point. The French at Verdun were not yet – but soon would be – free from unrelenting assault. And, far more important from the British viewpoint, the assault on the Somme was the consequence of almost two years of devoted preparation, which only now was producing the trained warriors and modern weaponry for a great campaign. So the assault would go on.

The only question was on which part of the front. Joffre, still imagining that he was in command, demanded a concentration on the previously key area in the centre, even though it had thwarted the best efforts at conquest on Day One. His notions were quite impractical, as Haig felt it necessary to tell him. The trenches in this region were still packed with Britain's dead and wounded. The only feasible area for a renewed offensive was on the right, where the British and French on 1 July had made some progress. Having on that day overrun the German first line, now they must go for the second, and hope for exploitation.

The effort was made on 14 July. In order to lessen the considerable distance an attacker would have to travel, the British moved into No Man's Land during the night and attacked at dawn. Success in this early stage was significant. The British overran the German second position and put to flight such of the enemy's infantry as had survived the bombardment. Much emphasis has since been placed on the supposed novelty of the decision to begin the operation in the dark. (Attacks in the dark had in fact been attempted before, and would be again, without success.) But the key to success lay elsewhere: in the amplitude of artillery fire. On 14 July the British employed two-thirds of the number of guns available on 1 July against one-eighteenth the length of trench. Consequently 660 pounds of shells fell on every yard of front attacked, an intensity five times as great as a fortnight earlier. That was sufficient.

But it was sufficient only for this opening stage. Attempts made the next day to press home the victory, first by cavalry (making their debut in actual Somme fighting) and then by infantry, were complete – and predictable – failures.

The problem with a success like 14 July was that its limited target attracted a disproportionate weight of resistance and counter-attack. So in the ensuing weeks the attack was spread more widely. On 23 July, in a series of encounters akin to a bloodbath, Australian troops and English Territorials captured and retained Poziéres in the centre of the 1 July front. Thereafter, throughout August and early September, the British continued the grim process of piecemeal advance along the blood-drenched crest of ground from which the Germans had once been able to overlook their opponents' positions.

To all appearances, the British (along with their French allies and the bold manpower of the Commonwealth) were simply acquiring one bit of French territory after another, paying an atrocious cost but at least imposing (anyway until late August) a mounting toll on enemy forces ordered to recover every inch of territory they had lost. Yet there was more method than this in Haig's madness. His attacks had a sort of purpose. With or without his knowledge and encouragement, his gunners and infantry were developing the 'creeping barrage', a coherent method of attack whereby British foot soldiers might advance behind the shelter of an advancing curtain of shells which gave them some chance of reaching the enemy trenches. And the piecemeal advances of his units actually had an overall objective. They were forming into a coherent line from which (by analogy with 1 July) a really powerful advance might be attempted.

Moreover, Haig had a new weapon to employ in this endeavour. When he had succeeded as commander of the BEF in December 1915, he had found correspondence about a metal box, powered by an engine and propelled on caterpillar tractors, which was being developed in Britain as a means of crossing No Man's Land unscathed and engaging enemy defenders at close quarters. Haig was instantly enthusiastic (contrary to a popular view that he opposed military innovation). He had ordered large numbers of these vehicles and made plans to use them in the opening stages of the Somme campaign. This enthusiasm proved premature. The 'tank', as it was code-named to suggest that it was only a water-carrier, could not be produced this early or in any sort of quantity. And when it did come into production, it proved to have limitations. The tanks were painfully slow-moving and cruelly susceptible to mechanical failure. And although they could resist most rifle and machine-gun bullets, they were both conspicuous targets and utterly susceptible to high-explosive shells.

Nevertheless, by 15 September Haig had a few score tanks to hand, and remained determined to employ them in his new, hopefully decisive, full-front attack. The tank should be able to transgress No Man's Land and engage enemy riflemen and machine-gunners at close quarters. Thereby the agonies of the offensive might be diminished and the way opened for the cavalry to convert forward push into breakthrough.

Reality proved otherwise. For one thing, the tank on its first appearance was inappropriately employed. The command was so concerned to protect these vessels from its own shelling that it was decided not to employ the creeping bombardment ahead of the infantry in areas where the tank was making an appearance (which happened to be the areas most safeguarded by the enemy and where British infantry would be most numerously employed). This was a misjudgement. The creeping bombardment was a far more important ingredient of infantry protection than the tank, and the failure to employ it in the key areas was a serious deficiency. The result may be simply put. On 15 September, although the British continued, at a heavy price, to push the Germans back, and although the tank made some progress in a few areas, the great turnaround anticipated by Haig in the Somme campaign was not remotely accomplished.

Quite strikingly, a more significant success was achieved ten days later. Tanks were barely employed, being for the moment nearly all out of action, and the cavalry was not held to hand. But the creeping bombardment was fully employed in what was strictly a 'bite and hold' operation. It achieved its objectives. But of course it did not bring the British infantry to open country, and opportunities for subsequent cavalry action were wholly wanting. Moreover the Germans were as quickly constructing fresh defensive trenches as the British were overrunning existing ones. So 26 September was the real revelation of how much, and how little, a British offensive could hope to achieve.

The Somme campaign should have stopped here. The weather was deteriorating and no meaningful objectives lay to hand. But

Haig still yearned for the mighty victory he had so long fore-shadowed, and even though he had never given a sign of accomplishing it and the weather had now turned decisively against him he would go on trying. So he did until mid-November, by which time the diminution of trained troops was becoming painfully apparent. On the rather neglected northern sector his forces achieved a moderate if costly success, and he found here the grounds for claiming a substantial victory. It was not. But it would have to do.

The cost of the whole campaign had been heavy. The British had lost, in casualties, 432,000 men, and the French around 200,000. The German figure was certainly smaller, despite many attempts to prove the contrary. Against the British, the Germans suffered around 230,000 casualties. The acquisition in territory for the Western Allies had been trivial – about seven square miles. And all that that had done was advance the British from the base of one crest of land to the base of another. The Germans, now under Hindenburg and Ludendorff, felt no obligation to retain every yard of French soil they had occupied, and were preparing to retreat to better positions.

So who had won? To a large extent, the answer depends on how one frames the question. If the query is 'Had the British pressed forward and made the enemy aware that the British Army was a new and death-dealing force on the battlefield?', then the campaign was certainly some sort of an Allied victory. If the question is 'Had the British and French ruptured the enemy line, or killed a larger number of Germans than they themselves had lost?', then the answer was no and the campaign was plainly an Allied setback.

But it is possible to ask another question. Even if at a heavier cost to themselves, had the Allies inflicted on the Germans a deprivation of manpower which the enemy were not able in the existing power situation to sustain? The answer is that at the time no one could tell, and that even in the present there is no agreed answer.

In one view (that, among others, of John Terraine), the Somme battle – despite its lamentable first day – was overall an Allied victory. It forced the Germans at heavy loss to relinquish territory they were determined to retain, and it revealed unequivocally that the British Army was now an unrelenting force in this war. In an opposite view, the British and French managed to squander casualties far in excess of those they inflicted on the enemy, and so entered the following year in a weakened condition and with no clear idea of how to proceed.

What is certain is that the Western Allies entered 1917 with no clear vision of how, in the light of their 1916 experience, to proceed better. The French, in the first half of 1917, embarked on another mighty offensive, although under different leadership and on a different part of the Western Front. Thwarted, the French Army soon collapsed into a widespread mutiny whose long-term cause was clearly the calamitous losses of Verdun and the Somme. So in mid-1917 the British Army, faute de mieux, took over the role of major offensive power on the Western Front. They did in the ensuing months manage to maintain an army in being and on the offensive. But they proved to have no more decisive way of proceeding than had been evident the year before, and achieved no more conclusive a result. As for the collapse in German morale, which Haig had been loud in proclaiming during the Somme and would continue to proclaim in the following year, it was no more evident in 1917 than it had been in 1916. And the manner of conducting battle advantageously, if at last being gradually devised, would not be comprehensively to hand until 1918. Even then, it would be accomplished not on account of the judgement of the British high command, but in spite of it. In this respect, anyway, the great endeavour of the British Army on the Somme in 1916 does not, certainly as far as its commanders are concerned, deserve high commendation.

Further Reading

Edmonds, Sir James and Capt Wilfred Miles (1938), *Military Operations France and Belgium 1916* Vols 1 and 2 (*The Official History*). Basingstoke: Macmillan.

Farrar-Hockley, A. H. (1970), *The Somme*. Basingstoke: Pan Macmillan.

Liddle, Peter (1992), *The Battle of the Somme: A Reappraisal*. Barnsley: Leo Cooper / Pen and Sword.

Middlebrook, Martin (1971), *The First day on the Somme*. London: Allen Lane.

Prior, Robin and Trevor Wilson (2004), *Command on the Western Front: The Military Career of Sir Henry Rawlinson 1914–1918*. Barnsley: Leo Cooper / Pen and Sword.

——(2005), *The Somme*. New Haven, CT: Yale UP.

Chapter 8

India and the First World War

Santanu Das

At the centre of Delhi, the capital of India, stands the India
Gate, a majestic colonial arch, 42 metres high. Originally known
as the 'All India War Memorial' – designed by Edwin Lutyens
and with the foundation stone being laid in 1921 – the monument is dedicated to the 'dead of the Indian armies who fell
honoured in France and Flanders, Mesopotamia and Persia, East
Africa, Gallipoli and Elsewhere in the Near and the Far East' in
the First World War, as well as to those killed in the North-West
Frontier operations and the Third Afghan War. The litany of
place names testifies not only to the 'world' nature of the Great
War but also to its far-flung theatres which summoned the
children of the Empire and often claimed their lives. Thus, along
the road from Estaires to La Bassée in France, lies a plot of land
that is forever India: this was where the Indian Corps first saw
action in October 1914 and incurred heavy losses and is now the
site of the beautiful Neuve Chapelle Memorial to the Indian war
dead. Memory also exists privately, stubbornly. A search through
our extended family and friends in Calcutta revealed the war
mementoes – several medals, a despatch commending his 'gallant and distinguished services' signed by Churchill, and other
documents – of Captain Dr Manindranath Das. A medical
doctor, he served with the Indian troops in Mesopotamia from
1915 to 1917 and received the Military Cross, the same award
that distinguished Siegfried Sassoon and Wilfred Owen, among
others.

India contributed more than one and a quarter million men,
including 827,000 combatants, the majority of whom served in
Mesopotamia. The exact number of Indian soldiers and non-
combatants involved in the conflict varies, but David Omissi has
put the figure at 1.27 million, counting some 49,000 Indian sepoys

among the 947,000 Imperial war dead. The summary of Indian casualties, according to *Statistics of the Military Effort of the British Empire during the Great War, 1914–1920* (1920), runs as follows:

Summary of Indian casualties:

Died from all causes	53,486
Wounded	64,350
Missing	2,937
Prisoners	302
Presumed prisoners	523
Grand Total	121,598

Fighting for the empire during the first stirrings of nationalist uprisings, these Indian soldiers have been doubly marginalized: by their own national history which has largely focused on the heroes of the Independence movement and by standard histories of war and modern memory which have remained largely Eurocentric.

In what is now widely known as the 'second wave' of First World War studies, ushered in by Jay Winter's *Sites of Memory, Sites of Mourning: The Great War in European Cultural History* (1995), two of the most exciting developments have been a comparative, interdisciplinary perspective and the recovery of hitherto marginalized voices, particularly of women, civilians, and of the colonial conscripts. As a black South African labourer in France noted, the most astonishing part of his experience was 'to see different kinds of human race'. Indeed, the colonial contributions to and experience of the war are increasingly becoming the focus of intense inquiry. The aim of this short chapter is to recover and examine the Indian experience of the war through a dialogue between archival, historical and literary evidence while respecting the specificity of each document. Such an approach, I shall argue, is important to recover a part of colonial history for which we do not have the abundance of diaries, memoirs and letters that delinate the European experience of the First World War. I shall focus on two lines of inquiry: first, an analysis of the reactions and responses the war elicited in India from the princes and the political and literary bourgeoisie; and secondly, an examination of the inner world of the semi-literate Indian 'sepoy' (from the Persian word *sipahi*, meaning soldier) as he encounters foreign lands and modern industrial warfare.

'Heart and Soul with Great Britain': Responses from India

On 8 September 1914, in a message to 'The Princes and Peoples of My Indian Empire', the 'King-Emperor' observed that 'nothing has moved me more than the passionate devotion to My Throne expressed both by My Indian subjects, and by the Feudatory Princes and the Ruling Chiefs of India'. Indeed, apart from certain isolated revolutionary activities, the support for the war in India was overwhelming. The native princes, heavily dependent on the Raj, almost started competing with each other with their extravagant offers. The Nizam of Hyderabad led with his offer of more than a million pounds while the Government of India, with the assent of Imperial Legislative Council, offered His Majesty's Government a lump sum of £100 million pounds towards expenses of the war. Vast sums of money flowed from the 700-odd native princes, in addition to offers of troops, labourers, hospital ships, ambulances, motorcars, flotillas, horses, food and clothes. Consider the following war speeches made by two powerful queens in India. The first is from a Hindu princess, Taradevi, in Calcutta on 25 December 1914, and the second from the queen of Bhopal, delivered at the Delhi War Conference in April 1918:

> Gentlemen, though I am a lady of such an advanced age yet I am *Kshatriya* and when my *Kshatriya* blood rises up in my veins and when I think I am the widow to the eldest son of one who was a most tried friend of the British Government I jump on my feet at the aspiration of going to the field of war to fight Britain's battle. (Princess Taraderi, Calcutta, December 1914)

> Is it not a matter for regret then that Turkey should ... join hands with the enemies of our British Government? All gentlemen like you have read, I suppose, in the papers, how the British Government is now, as ever, having Mohammedan interests at heart ... India will leave nothing undone to justify the confidence, the love, the sympathy with which the King-Emperor has always honoured us. (Queen of Bhopal, Delhi, April 1918)

In the first extract, we have the image of the Hindu warrior-queen invoking the caste politics – *Kshatriya* is the Hindu martial caste – of a feudal, hierarchical society for recruitment in the world's first modern war. The second quotation points to a more complex area. With the entry into the war of Turkey whose sultan bore the title of Khalifa or the religious leader of the Muslims, the English became extremely anxious about the possibility of a global *jihad*. In fact, special communiqués were issued assuring that 'the holy places' of Islam will be 'immune from attack or molestation by the British naval and military forces'. Here, the queen of Bhopal is seen ensuring the continuing loyalty of her Muslim subjects for a war against their religious brethren. Indeed it was a difficult choice for the Indian Muslims who comprised some 30 per cent of the Indian Army. Most Muslim soldiers from India continued to fight for the British Empire but there were isolated cases of mutiny, the most serious being that of the 5th Light Infantry at Singapore.

Within the Indian context, what is surprising is the widespread support from the educated middle classes and the political bourgeoisie, including the Indian National Congress, and the All India Muslim League. Meetings were arranged, fundraising was organized and pro-war pamphlets produced, one typical title being 'Why India is Heart and Soul with Great Britain in this War'. Even the anti-colonial and pacifist poet Rabindranath Tagore, who had received the Nobel Prize in 1913, offered war poems to *The Times*. Mahatma Gandhi, the father of the nation, raised an ambulance corps in London and pledged 'absolute unconditional and wholehearted cooperation with the Government', observing that 'not to help the Empire is to commit national suicide'. Like his Irish or Jamaican brethren, he believed – like the majority of Indians – that the present sacrifice would later be rewarded with greater political recognition and autonomy, with 'Swaraj'. But political shrewdness is not the sole explanation. One needs to delve deeper into the complexities of the colonial psyche, captured in a piece of doggerel verse: 'Who calls me now a coward base, / And brands my race a coward race?' It shows an internalization by the indigenous people of the insidious politics of the racial, physical and cultural inferiority of the ruled on which the colonial project is based. This position is stated more acutely in the Jamaican journal *Federalist*: 'As coloured people, we will be fighting to prove to Great Britain that we are not vastly inferior to the whites.' Being constantly made to feel small before the 'superior' civilization of the West and still smarting under the blemish of the Sepoy Mutiny of

1857, the majority of Indians saw the First World War as an opportunity to set aright the racial slur and prove at once their masculinity, courage and loyalty. Fighting alongside their European masters becomes the vindication of their *izzat*, a word roughly translated as 'honour', that occurs obsessively in the letters of the Indian soldiers.

Some of these ambivalences are captured in the wartime writings of Sarojini Naidu. Educated at London and Cambridge, Naidu was an internationally celebrated figure and was christened 'the Nightingale of India' for her poetry in English. A prominent nationalist and feminist leader, she became the president of the Indian National Congress in 1925. Involved in the war efforts, she observed: 'Let young Indians who are ready to die for India and to wipe from her brow the brand of slavery rush to join the standing army.' Imperial war service thus becomes a way of salvaging national honour. Consider her war poem 'The Gift of India', written in 1915 and published in *The Broken Wing*:

> Gathered like pearls in their alien graves,
> Silent they sleep by the Persian waves.
> Scattered like shells on Egyptian sands
> They lie with pale brows and brave, broken hands.
> They are strewn like blossoms mown down by chance
> On the blood-brown meadows of Flanders and France.

The sensuous vocabulary with its murmur of labials and sibilance links the poem with the verse of Wilfred Owen, looking back to Tennyson and Yeats, revealing the intimate processes of the colonial encounter. But the nation imagined here is India, not 'Britannia'. The emotive power of the poem is rooted in the war-bereaved consciousness of the mother who fuses with the powerful, indigenous trope of 'Mother India' suffering under colonialism. The poem is a plea to remember India's 'gift' to the Empire: 'Remember the blood of thy martyred sons'. The First World War catches the Indian consciousness at a fragile point between a continuing loyalty to the Raj and a burgeoning national consciousness.

'Red peppers and black peppers': Soldiers' letters from France and Mesopotamia

The first two Indian divisions – renamed Lahore and Meerut – arrived at Marseilles during September and October 1914 to the joyous cries of 'Vive la Hindus'. Drafted to fill in the gaps left by the heavy losses in the British Expeditionary Force, they initially totalled 24,000 men – of whom 75 per cent were Indian sepoys and 25 per cent British. They formed the Indian Expeditionary Force 'A', were re-equipped in Marseilles and put under the command of Lieutenant General Sir James Willcocks. The infantry privates were called *sepoys*, the cavalry troops *sowars* and the Indian officers held the commission of the Viceroy and were allowed to command only Indian troops. A total of 138,608 Indians served in France between October 1914 and December 1915. On the other hand, the largest number of Indians sent overseas – some 588,717 men, including 295,565 combatants and 293,152 non-combatants (often forming porter and labour corps) – served in Mesopotamia, in the three Ottoman cities of Baghdad, Basra and Mosul. The Mesopotamia campaign, culminating in the disastrous siege in Kut-al-Amara (December 1915 to April 1916) where many Indians lost their lives, is now blamed on the shortsightedness of its commander Charles Townshend who famously said, 'How easy the defence of Kut would have been had my division been an all British one instead of a composite one.'

Similarly, the military performance of the Indians in France has been marked by controversy. While historians such as Jeffrey Greenhut and John Keegan have depicted them as incompetent peasant-warriors, neither trained nor suited for industrial warfare or the long European winters, younger scholars such as George Morton-Jack have questioned such assumptions and stress their courage. Both views need to be accommodated. Thus, the immediate shock of mechanized warfare did prove too much for the freshly drafted Indian troops, and in the first two weeks – between 22 October and 3 November 1914 – 57 per cent of the sepoys were admitted to hospitals with hand wounds, largely suspected to be self-inflicted. But the hand-wound rate dropped sharply after Willcocks had five sepoys shot for cowardice that winter. The Indian sepoys took part in some of the severest fighting, including the battles at Neuve Chapelle, Festubert and Loos, incurring heavy casualties and earning the first Victoria

Crosses to be awarded to Indians. Among them, one of the most distinguished was Subedar Mir Mast VC, OBI, IOM who, in the Second Battle of Ypres, rallied the men and held his position after the unit had lost all British officers, and brought in the wounded including eight British and Indian officers. The Indian wounded from France were nursed at the hospitals in England, the most famous being the Royal Pavilion Military Hospital at Brighton.

While attention has been paid to the military performances, what I want to highlight briefly is the emotional world of the Indian sepoy. Recruited from the semi-literate peasant-warrior classes of north India in accordance with the 'martial race' theory – Punjab contributed the highest number of Indian troops – these men did not leave behind the extensive documents that we have in the case of the European troops. What we have instead are hundreds of censored letters. These letters, dictated or written in their native languages by the troops, were translated into English for the censors and the English extracts are what survive today. They are housed in the British Library, and a useful selection has been edited by David Omissi, titled *Indian Voices of the Great War: Soldiers' Letters, 1914–1918*. These letters open up a whole new world in First World War history, covering a whole range of experiences and emotions from an almost metaphysical wonder at the prosperity and modernity of France through comments on its educational system, gender equality, the warmth and hospitality of the people to occasional romance and sex. Consider the following two letters, available in the India Office collection in the British Library, London and extracted in Omissi's volume capturing the excitement and the tedium respectively:

The country is very fine, well-watered and fertile. The fields are very large, all gardens full of fruit trees. Every man's land yields him thousands of *maunds* of wheat ... The fruits are pears, apricots, grapes and fruits of many kinds. Even the dogs refuse them at this season. Several regiments could eat from one tree. The people are very well-mannered and well-to-do. The value of each house may be set down as several *lakhs* and *crores* of rupees. Each house is a sample of paradise.

As tired bullocks and bull buffaloes lie down in the month of Bhadon so lies the weary world. Our hearts are breaking ... Germany fights the world with ghastly might, harder to crush than well-soaked grain in the mill.

To the north Indian peasant-soldier, the wealth of France is registered through the hyperbolic narrative of wheat and fruit but soon realism gives way to the imaginative and the religious: 'a second Paradise'. Similarly, tedium and homesickness are conveyed through a set of local, evocative images, showing how cultural specificity shapes the processes of perception and representation. And these local images are also used to devise ingenious codes to hoodwink the censors, as in the following extract from a letter from Bugler Mausa Ram in the Kitchener's Indian Hospital: 'The state of affairs is as follows: the black pepper is finished. Now the red pepper is being used, but occasionally the black pepper proves useful. The black pepper is very pungent and the red pepper is not so strong.' In this letter, black pepper and red pepper refer to Indian and European troops respectively as the writer advises against further recruitment.

The social reality of these peasant-soldiers, uprooted from their local village and conscripted into modern industrial warfare in France, finds one of its most evocative accounts in Mulk Raj Anand's war novel *Across the Black Waters* (1940). Anand dedicated the novel 'to the memory of my father Subedar Lal Chand Anand, MSM, (late 2/17th Dogra)' who underwent training for the First World War. Though he possibly was not sent overseas, many of his friends fought in the war in France, and Anand drew on their memories. In comparison, much less is known about the Indian experience in Mesopotamia. There are fewer letters and very little personal documents. An invaluable and hitherto unknown source is the remarkable memoir of Captain Dr Kalyan Mukherji, titled *Kalyan-Pradeep*, written by his 80-year-old grandmother in Bengali after his death in Mesopotamia in 1917, interspersed with the letters he had written home. Mukherji, a Cambridge-educated doctor, served under General Townshend in Mesopotamia as part of the Indian Medical Service, and accompanied the prisoners of war after the fall of Kut. His letters chart his gradual disenchantment, as in the following one written after tending the horribly wounded on the battlefield:

England has been our main educator. The patriotism that England has so long taught us and other Western nations upheld as well, it is this patriotism which is responsible for all this bloodshed. All patriotism is about usurping other nations – and to build empire … And following England's example, misguided youths of our country are taking recourse to violence, bombing innocent people. Shame on patriotism! Unless this narrow vision is abolished, this bloodshed in the name of patriotism will continue. [My translation from the Bengali.]

Western imperialism, Indian nationalism and the First World War are all shown to be linked here in a vicious cycle of violence fuelled by patriotism. Mukherji's hatred of warfare and nationalism of all sorts and the level of intellectual sophistication and emotional poignancy place him not with the semi-literate sepoys of the Raj but more with the anti-war British soldier-officers such as Wilfred Owen and Siegfried Sassoon.

As we reach the ninetieth anniversary of the Armistice, there is a great need to recover hitherto silenced colonial lives and perspectives, and read them alongside European experiences. What were the levels of contacts, not only between sepoys and their British officers but between troops from the colonies and the dominions, especially in places where they fought together, as with the Australians and the Indians in Gallipoli? At the same time, we should also address the invidious distinctions within the colonial hierarchy: while Indians were allowed to fight in Europe, the West Indians and the Africans were not. Moreover, how were the thousands of labourers – a vast and crucial multiracial underclass comprising Chinese, Vietnamese, Maoris and West Indians, to name a few groups – perceived by the Europeans and by each other, and what do we know of their experiences? Interviewed on 4 April 1973, Abitisindon, a Malawian woman who worked as a courier, told Melville Page: 'I went there [to the war] to eat, that is all.' These are important, tantalizing aspects of the war which have just started to be recognized and they will provide new directions for First World War studies, making us think of the war in terms of race, empire and colonial participation. Responsible archival recovery of buried colonial lives and experiences by scholars working in different countries and with different approaches, and reading these materials alongside better-known European lives and documents will enable a fresh and more comprehensive understanding of the war not solely as a European tragedy or a military exercise but as a *World War* –

the multiracial and international catastrophe it was – and its still-continuing legacies in various communities and families around the world.

Further Reading

I am grateful to the son and daughter-in-law of late Captain Dr Manindranath Das for sharing his war mementoes and many anecdotes with me. Parts of the article are based on research conducted in the National Archives of India (Delhi) and the West Bengal State Archives; also the India Office Library, British Library and National Archives in London. I am grateful for the help of the staff in these institutions.

Anand, Mulk Raj (1940), *Across the Black Waters*. London: Jonathan Cape.

Corrigan, Gordon (1999), *Sepoys in the Trenches: The Indian Corps on the Western Front 1914–1915*. Staplehurst: Spellmount.

Das, Santanu (ed.) (forthcoming), *Race, Empire and First World War Writing*. Cambridge: CUP.

——'Sepoys, Sahibs and Babus: Reading and Writing about the Great War in India' in Hammond, Mary and Shafquat Towheed (eds) (2007), *First World War and Publishing*. London: Palgrave, pp. 61–77.

Ellinwood, DeWitt C. and S. D. Pradhan (eds) (1978), *India and World War I*. Delhi: Manohar.

Fussell, Paul (1975), *The Great War and Modern Memory*. Oxford: OUP.

Gandhi, M. K. (trans. Mahadev Desai) (1927 / 1982), *An Autobiography or, The Story of My Experiments with Truth*. Harmondsworth: Penguin.

Greenhut, Jeffrey, 'The Imperial Reserve: The Indian Corps on the Western Front, 1914–1915', *The Journal of Imperial and Commonwealth History*, 1983, Vol. XII, No. 1, 55–73.

India and the War (intr. Lord Sydenham of Combe) (1915). London: Hodder and Stoughton.

India and the War (nd). Lahore: Imperial Publishing Company.

India's Contribution to the Great War (1923). Calcutta: Government of India.

Merewether, J. W. B. and Frederick Smith (1919), *The Indian Corps in France*. London: Murray.

Morton-Jack, George, 'The Indian Army on the Western Front, 1914–1915', *War in History*, 2006, 13 (3), 329–62.

Naidu, Sarojini (1917), *The Broken Wing: Songs of Love, Death and Destiny 1915–1916*. London: William Heinemann.

Omissi, David (ed.) (1999), *Indian Voices of the Great War: Soldiers' Letters, 1914–1918*. Basingstoke: Macmillan.

—— (1994), *The Sepoy and the Raj: The Indian Army, 1860–1940*. Basingstoke: Macmillan.

Page, Melville E. (ed.) (1987), *Africa and the First World War*. Basingstoke: Macmillan.

Sarkar, Sumit (1989), *Modern India 1885–1947*. Oxford: OUP.

Statistics of the Military Effort of the British Empire during the Great War, 1914–1920 (1920). London: His Majesty's Stationery Office.

Strachan, Hew (2001), *The First World War*, Vol. 1: *To Arms*. Oxford: OUP.

Visram, Rozina, 'The First World War and the Indian Soldiers', *Indo-British Review: A Journal of History*, Vol. XVI, No. 2, June 1989, 17–26.

Willcocks, Sir James (1920), *With the Indians in France*. London: Constable.

Winter, Jay (1995), *Sites of Memory, Sites of Mourning: The Great War in European Cultural History*. Cambridge: CUP.

Chapter 9

Religion and the Great War

Michael Burleigh

Nowadays the churches of all denominational persuasions are so irredeemably identified with a moralizing pacifism that it takes a major leap of imagination to sympathetically comprehend how their forebears conducted themselves during the Great War. Talk of God was omnipresent in that conflict. When the French socialist novelist Henri Barbusse imagined a pilot flying over its trenches, the latter heard rising up cries of 'Gott mit uns' and 'God is with us', which in such respects, He certainly was.

In the early twentieth century Christianity was still a pervasive moral force and at the centre of rites of passage, although subject to change and challenge. The intimate relationship of throne and altar had been either severed or weakened in a number of countries. This was especially the case in France or Italy where anticlerical liberals and radicals were generously represented in the political classes, and which, de facto or de jure, waged a sort of Cold War against the Catholic Church throughout the late nineteenth century, whose apogee was the 1905 Separation Law in France. But it was also true in the Anglican Communion, where the Church had been disestablished in Ireland, and would be in Wales once legislation passed in 1914 was enacted in 1920, as well as Australia, Canada and Jamaica, where there was either concurrent endowment of all denominations or, in the last case, outright disestablishment in 1870.

In addition to these constitutional recessionals, a number of rival creeds – all heavily indebted to the Christian original – had become more visible by the 1900s, including liberalism, nationalism, socialism, as well as the tinier bands of positivists, atheists and secularists, whose impassioned tones suggest that fervency circulated as a finite quantity. None of this does more than qualify the assertion that in and around 1900, Christianity remained a powerful cultural and moral force which in the build-up to and bloody duration of the Great War played a considerable role, although the more ineffable aspects of God and the dying or terrified man necessarily elude us. That in itself is to touch on a secular trend which itself seemed to be reversed by the war. Many historians of nineteenth-century religion have remarked on its creeping feminization as males discovered the rival attractions of politics and the pub. For a brief time the war saw a reversion of men to religion.

Critics of 'the churches' invariably alight upon the infinite number of examples of, mainly Protestant, clergy saying and writing apocalyptic or hysterical things to justify sending their nation's lambs to the slaughter. Before pursuing that theme, it is well to enter a few advance qualifications. Firstly, this was not a sudden development, since clerics in Germany or Spain had earlier played a key part in mobilizing patriotic sentiment during the wars of liberation against 'diabolic' Napoleon, as well as during the Carlist wars in Spain, the struggle for Italian unification, and in the war between France and Prussia. Secondly, the fervent religious patriotism of British or German Protestants or the Russian and Serb Orthodox, was not characteristic of Catholic Irish Australians or Francophone Quebecoise, or the nationalist Catholic lower clergy of Bohemia, Croatia or Slovenia, whatever the allegiance of their hierarchs to the Dual Monarchy. Italy's abandonment of neutrality owed everything to nationalist opinion and next to nothing to the institution that claimed the deepest allegiance of most Italians. Much may have been made of France's 'sacred union', but significant sections of the Catholic Church regarded the war not as a verdict on the culture of Luther and Nietzsche but on the immoralism of the anticlerical Third Republic.

The Catholic Church was in an especially delicate position, as exemplified by the famous exchange between Hartmann of Cologne and Mercier of Malines as they gathered for the September 1914 electoral conclave: 'I hope we shall not speak of war' announced the emollient German; 'And I hope we shall not speak of peace' remarked the grim Belgian. The new pope they chose on this occasion, Benedict XV, sought to prop up Austria-Hungary (against Protestant Germany); the Ottoman Empire (against Orthodox Russia); and a neutral Italy so that victory would not strengthen the state's hand on the Roman Question – when he did abandon his alleged 'silence' regarding atrocities alleged by all sides so as to pursue the cause of peace, he immediately drew down upon himself charges of bias. More practically, the Vatican spent 82 million lire on relief efforts and aid to prisoners of war, thereby effectively bankrupting itself in the process. Finally, it is often overlooked that especially among Anglophone Protestants there were widespread hopes that in 1914 ecumenical contacts with Germany would avert a war altogether, hopes reflected in the $2 million which the steel magnate Andrew Carnegie dedicated to the Church Peace Union. By some bitter irony, a Protestant world peace conference was scheduled to convene at Constance on 3–4 August 1914, with a parallel meeting of German and French Catholics in Liège pencilled in for the following week.

Much cynicism has been vented against the clergy for their role in the war; some of this seems unfounded. Patriotic clergy played a major role in exercising various kinds of moral suasion, although in this respect they were no different from, say, the septuagenarian English Poet Laureate Robert Bridges who in 1915 published a bilingual Anglo-French anthology called *The Spirit of Man* which contrived to leave out any German contributions while including the Russians. Clergy often put their money (and their sons) where their mouths were. Between June 1915 and February 1917 six Church of England agencies subscribed £4.5 million to government war bonds, while in the enemy camp, the Prussian territorial churches poured 13 million Reichsmarks into similar ventures. Better known is the part played by clergy in recruitment, in the years before conscription by age cohort made fighting non-optional. Again, judging by the sheer number of sons of clerics as well as seminarians and the like who fought and died in the war, they were not asking others to make sacrifices they eschewed themselves, although Siegfried Sassoon recalled the clergyman who told departing recruits: 'Now God go with you. I will go with you as far as the station.' The only British soldier to win the VC with bar was Noel Chavasse, the bishop of Liverpool's son.

Both in Europe and beyond, where missionaries drummed up indigenous coolies and native soldiers, clergy were prominent in reminding young men of their patriotic duty. Bishops, like Hensley Henson of Durham, were already lynchpins of their local county communities, at a time when the British Army was still organized on a territorial basis. He was acutely conscious of the need not to preach anti-Christian sentiments, writing the following:

The Christian preacher ought to strive so to preach that in the retrospect of a later time, he shall be able to recall his words without shame. For the War will not last for ever. Sooner or later peace will return, and the passions of the conflict will begin to die down in the most exasperated minds. The work of the Christian preacher will again become normal. ... His influence for good will not be helped if his people have associated him with the very violences of thought and speech of which they themselves are growing ashamed.

Such fastidiousness was not always evident. Bishop Arthur Winnington-Ingram of London was not averse to preaching in uniform and standing on a Union Jack-bedecked wagon or surrounded by arrangements of martial drums: 'We would all rather die, wouldn't we, than have England a German province?' Much was at stake in what he dubbed 'a Holy War' against the Hunnish 'anti-Christ'. His view of things has been rendered almost incomprehensible by a line of satire stretching from Joan Littlewood to Lindsey Anderson. The war literally became a holy one on the southern front when in 1914 the Germans succeeded in persuading their Ottoman ally to proclaim a pan-Islamic jihad against the Entente powers whose empires contained half the world's Muslim population. When Jerusalem fell to Allenby in 1917, papers talked of avenging Richard the Lionheart, which may have contributed to Turkish suspicions of such Christian minorities as the Armenians, Jacobites, Maronites and Nestorians.

Clerics and theologians were heavily involved in converting the war into a clash of antagonistic spirits. This was not so much a matter of warring heavenly hosts – although they were often said to hover like clouds over sodden battlefields – but of inimical 'cultures', the shopkeeper materialism of the British, the Mongol savagery of the Russians and the frivolity of the French all arrayed, in German eyes, against the honest, stolid German Michael, who became a baby-bayoneting fiend in a Pickelhaube when viewed from the other side. Adopting his characteristically homely tones, the American evangelist opined: 'If you turn Hell upside down, you will find "Made in Germany" stamped on the bottom.'

Rival theologians vied to invest the conflict with missionary purpose. Preaching on the theme of Romans 8.31, the Kaiser's chaplain, Dr Ernst Dryander, claimed that the war was being fought to preserve 'German faith and German piety' against the frivolous-savages of Paris and St Petersburg. The distinguished theologian, Adolf von Harnack, averred in 1916 that Germany's war aims were noble because of the sacrosanct end they would bring about, namely the extension of German influence and therefore of the kingdom of God which it embodied. This was dangerously like the claim: 'God is what the God-inspired people do'. The evidence for His presence being calculated by the intensity of emotion was revealed in August 1914 without any countervailing room for manipulation of opinion as clinically anatomized by the Viennese satirist Karl Kraus. The eminent theologian Ernst Troeltsch wrote:

> We fight not only for what we are, but also for what we will and must become. .... Our faith is not just that we can and must defend our state and homeland but that our national essence contains an inexhaustible richness and value that are inexpressibly important for mankind, a value that the Lord and God of history has entrusted to our protection and development.

This road led to the publication of a manifesto by prominent Protestant theologians, refuting German responsibility for the outbreak of war, and claims that militarism was integral to German national greatness. This came as a great shock in England, where since the days of George Eliot, liberal theologians had lionized the higher critical scholarship whose flagships were so many *Jahrbücher* and *Zeitschriften* arrayed on the shelves of Oxbridge or rectory libraries.

Clerics did more than simply mobilize patriotic sentiment while literally demonizing their respective opponents. In Britain they were exempted from military service, so some 6,000 of them moved into crucial civilian occupations so as to indirectly circumvent the ban on them fighting. Another 3,500 became military chaplains, of whom 172 died on active service, four of whom received the Victoria Cross for outstanding bravery under fire. While German clergy were similarly forbidden to fight, laicizing laws meant that nothing prevented French or Italian priests from joining up. This did much to detoxify some of the worst anticlerical suspicions, especially since there was a simultaneous convergence of Catholic and republican messianisms regarding France's universal civilizing mission. The clergy abandoned the scowling apartness that had been their lot, and their stance, since the advent of the Third Republic. Some 32,699 clerics, 23,418 seculars and 9,281 regulars joined the armed forces, while a further 12,000 laboured in field hospitals. Even 841 Jesuits, the bugaboos of arch-secularists, volunteered to fight, of whom 20 per cent expired on the battlefields. The cleric soldiers distinguished themselves whether as leaders or in undertaking near-suicidal missions so as to spare their married comrades this unenviable choice. Like their counterparts in other armies, the military chaplains afforded spiritual solace to the quick, the dead and those in the purgatory of serious injury, including men sentenced to execution for cowardice or desertion. More casually they played the piano at rear area bases and staging posts, lent their literacy to those unaccustomed to use of a pen, or simply shared sweets and cigarettes. Appropriately enough the British chaplain Geoffrey Studdert Kennedy was nicknamed 'Woodbine Willie' by his men; a packet of these cigarettes was buried with him in 1929.

For while it is almost inevitable that historians have concentrated on the exhortations to war, the organizational structures of chaplaincies and the like, or how the churches as institutions were favoured or disadvantaged by their political stances during the war, we know surprisingly little about God and his soldiers in that conflict. Men facing the ultimate existential crisis quickly rediscovered the power of prayer. Huntly Gordon was a Scottish gunner who had grown up in a manse, before going to the same school as Field Marshal Douglas Haig. He favoured the Psalms since 'they were written by a fighter who knew what it was like to be scared stiff'. At the Ypres Salient he jotted down:

I stick fast in the deep mire, where no ground is [Psalm 69]

The earth trembled and quaked: the very foundations also of the hills shook [Psalm 18]

Our heart is not turned back: neither our steps gone out of thy way; No, not when thou hast smitten us into the place of dragons: and covered us with the shadow of death. ... For our soul is brought low, even unto the dust: our belly cleaveth unto the ground [Psalm 44]

God was not far either from those who had the responsibility
of millions of lives on their shoulders. Haig himself was a Pres-
byterian by upbringing, although according to the young chaplain George Duncan whose services Haig favoured, he hardly
mentioned God either in private or public. Letters to his wife
were another matter:

> I feel that every step in my plan has been taken with Divine
> help – and I ask daily for aid, not merely in making the plan,
> but in carrying it out, and in this I hope I shall continue to
> do so until the end of all things which concern me on earth.
> I think it is this Divine help which gives me tranquillity of
> mind and enables me to carry on without feeling the strain
> of responsibility to be too excessive. I try to do no more
> than 'do my best and trust to God' ... as you know, I don't
> talk much on religious subjects.

His sister Henrietta, who was in contact with their dead sibling
George, let the Field Marshal know that in the spirit world at
least, Napoleon was hovering by his side, a reminder that other
forms of religiosity – from rabbits' feet to ghosts – were active
during the war.

While the home fronts saw a brief upsurge in church attendance, with a more enduring growth of religious burials in such
atheistical strongholds as Berlin or Hamburg, on the fighting
front divine agency was often detected on Marne and Mons,
while soldiers from rival armies anxiously watched for three
whole years as the 'Golden Virgin' of Albert threatened to topple
from a spire overlooking the Somme. The French Army also
discovered the martial virtues of such saints as Martin, Maurice
and Michael, as well as Joan of Arc. But then again, the Catholic
clergy were in touch with their lower-class brethren in ways that,
inevitably, were wanting in the case of the C. of E.

The British Army's religion was the subject of a detailed
survey which was published in 1919. Perhaps its most striking
conclusions were encapsulated by the comment that although
'The soldier has got religion, I am not sure that he has got
Christianity'. There was much remembered sentimental religiosity from childhood, as expressed in bits of John Bunyan's
Pilgrim's Progress or martial hymns, but in general the churches,
and especially the Anglican Church, had failed to connect with
the lower classes despite the efforts of progressive clergy to do

little else for the previous five decades. As a Scottish chaplain reported: 'The men are not hostile, only indifferent. We have been speaking a language that has lost all meaning for them, and ourselves too.' Efforts to transfigure the fighting man into the suffering Christ, as epitomized by the Christmas 1914 illustration of 'The Great Sacrifice', competed with the dulling effects of mechanized warfare in which, as one soldier reported, 'I stopped thinking, I now do just what I am told, and in between think about eating, drinking and sleeping.'

A sort of geo-strategic audit of how the churches fared at the end of the war would favour Catholicism in the sense that the Holy Places had been delivered from the Turks, the Russian Orthodox Church had been virtually extirpated, while the advent of the Weimar Republic terminated the old alliance between defunct throne and Protestant altar. Internationally the Church could say it had stood for peace, while no French or Italian nationalists could claim that the patriotic fervour of the clergy was wanting. A vengeful German Protestantism went into the potent mix that would produce National Socialism.

Finally, the Christian churches ably endeavoured to canalize mass grief and incomprehension at the Holocaust that had been visited on the nine million young and middle-aged males in Europe. Across the Continent, churches became key sites of mourning, whether in the form of votive altars within or the crosses and pietàs in the squares without. Ninety years later the Bishop of London and the choir of the Chapel Royal remain integral to Britain's annual service of Remembrance, arguably the only residual occasion on which the Church of England impinges on the post-Christian national consciousness. Paradoxically, amidst so much death, religion seems in retrospect to have been positively vibrant.

Chapter 10

Forgotten Film-Makers: Britain's Official Wartime Film Propaganda

Nicholas Reeves

Remembrance Sunday is Britain's annual opportunity to remember those who gave their lives in the service of their country and, while the commemoration is not limited to any one war, it is the First World War that still occupies a very special place in the national consciousness. Hardly surprising then that, in 2007, the BBC supplemented its live television coverage of the Cenotaph ceremony with *Wilfred Owen: A Remembrance Tale*, a half-hour film examining the work of Britain's most celebrated First World War poet, killed in action just days before the end of the war. It was through a 1931 edition of his poems that his work first found a large audience.

Even greater public recognition came in the 1960s when Owen's poems first started to demonstrate their ability to keep the First World War at the centre of the popular imagination. In 1962, Benjamin Britten's *War Requiem* juxtaposed some of his poems with the Latin Mass for the dead, and Decca's recording the following year brought the music (and Owen's poems) to a mass audience with unprecedented sales of over 200,000. And in exactly the same year, a new edition of Owen's poems was published. From that point onwards, his ability to provide his readers with unmediated, direct access to the soldier's frontline experience was assured, and it is probably the muscular, uncompromising character of his poetry that has ensured that so many schools throughout the United Kingdom have used, and continue to use, Wilfred Owen as their poet of choice to introduce teenage students to poetry's particular ability to record and comment on the human experience.

In *Wilfred Owen: A Remembrance Tale*, Jeremy Paxman makes

a powerfully persuasive case that this attention is entirely appropriate, and it is no part of the purpose of this essay to challenge his conclusions. But Paxman's film provides compelling evidence that poetry was not the only medium through which the unique character of the British experience of the war was recorded. Thus, early in the film Paxman reads one of Owen's poems but, as the poem develops, images of Paxman are replaced with images drawn from contemporary factual film shot on the Western Front, a technique that is deployed a number of times in the remainder of the film.

In using contemporary film in this way, the film draws directly on a method first established by the BBC at almost the same time that Owen's poetry was reaching a mass audience. For it was in 1964 that the BBC broadcast its groundbreaking documentary series *The Great War*. Released in no fewer than 26 40-minute episodes, each episode was transmitted twice a week from May to November; the whole series was broadcast again in 1975. While much attention focused on the portentous commentary delivered by Ralph Richardson and a memorable musical score by Wilfred Josephs, it was in fact the power and immediacy of the factual footage that gave the series much of its real power. And it is on precisely that same footage that the makers of *Wilfred Owen: A Remembrance Tale* drew; it is on precisely the same footage that almost every other television programme about the First World War has drawn throughout the more than 40 years since *The Great War* was first screened. The end result is that a number of sequences from wartime British factual films have been shown again and again, and one of the most famous is used in the sequence described above: as we hear Owen's words, we watch a soldier stumble down a trench towards the camera, carrying a wounded comrade over his shoulders. The images are immediately familiar.

Yet only very few people have ever seen *Battle of the Somme*, the feature-length film from which this sequence was taken, and none but a handful of scholars and their students know anything of the achievements of the small group of official film-makers who overcame extraordinary odds to film on the Western Front in 1916. The reasons why this should be so are far from clear. It may be that for all the success of the visual arts, British culture remains essentially literary. It may be that in the more narrow field of film culture, the fact that the British documentary film first achieved significant recognition in the 1920s meant that the wartime films, in which the raw images were left largely to speak for themselves, were disregarded as the naive expressions of a film culture that had not yet come of age. It may simply be that with the onset of the talkies, so-called 'silent' films were rarely screened and, when they were, the circumstances almost totally failed to do them justice. Thus, they were invariably projected at the wrong speed (with the consequential jerky, speeded-up movements with which we are all too familiar), and without the live music that had always been an essential part of the audience's experience of film before the talkies.

Whatever the explanation, it does not lie in a lack of knowledge. I was privileged to be part of a small group of scholars working in the 1970s and 1980s who, drawing extensively on the extant film and documentary records, reconstructed the detailed history of official film-making in Britain during the First World War. By 1914 cinema was already firmly established as the dominant medium of popular entertainment and, very soon after war broke out, individuals in both the film industry and government were arguing that there was every reason to enlist this newest mass medium in the battle to win hearts and minds that was to become such an important aspect of the war. Significantly, they recognized the huge potential of what the British ambassador in Bucharest described as 'real British war films, as distinct from faked war dramas'. His opposition to the fiction film that (then as now) dominated commercial film culture, derived from an understanding that the staged war films that had been made in earlier wars would no longer be accepted by the audience. But this very commitment to the factual film made the production of such films problematic, because it would of course require the agreement of the service departments – and that proved enormously difficult. Key decision-makers at the Admiralty and the War Office shared with their peers across Whitehall a profound distaste for cinema, which they regarded as a second-rate, disreputable form of working-class entertainment which could not possibly make a contribution to the serious business of winning the war. Moreover, it was a medium of which they had no direct knowledge. Cinema had established itself by pricing its product low enough to attract an almost exclusively working-class audience, and as one middle-class film manufacturer admitted in 1914, 'The cinemas are not for people like ourselves, we do not go to them; the poor people go to them.'

If social conservatism was one source of their hostility to film propaganda, a more modern preoccupation with news manage-ment provided the other. Drawing lessons from the Russo-Japanese War of 1904–05, the government decided that it would impose strict censorship on all information related to the con-duct of the war and, as a result, even accredited war corre-spondents were not allowed anywhere near the front until May 1915. In such a climate, it was remarkable that the service departments ever agreed to allow movie cameramen access to the front and, even after that agreement, those who initially supervised their work were so cautious as to make it extremely difficult for the cameramen to do their job. But, in the end, the cameramen who worked on the Western Front did work out a modus vivendi with the intelligence officers who supervised their work, albeit one in which GHQ remained firmly in control – not only did they determine precisely what could be filmed but all their footage was subject to rigorous military censorship, at home and at the front. Yet in spite of all this, by the time the war was over, some 240 films has been released, together with 152 issues of an official newsreel. Films of the army predominated, shot mainly on the Western Front, but other theatres of war – including the Middle East – featured as well. There were films of the navy and the newest of the services, the Royal Flying Corps, and wartime audiences were also given unprecedented access to the great and the good, including a remarkably intimate film of a visit by the King to the army in France. Finally, the film-makers also explored the impact of war on life at home, with an espe-cially strong emphasis on the changing role of women.

All of that constituted a significant achievement in itself, but what is much more remarkable is the way in which the official films avoided the hysterical and deeply chauvinistic 'propaganda of hate' that dominated the press and other unofficial forms of propaganda. This other propaganda routinely portrayed the Germans as barbaric Huns who routinely mutilated children, raped women and indiscriminately slaughtered all who crossed their path, and it would have been easy enough to use the fiction film for propaganda of this kind – indeed, cinema's ability to construct 'realistic' narratives made it especially well-suited for such a task. But not only did the official propagandists resolutely refuse to indulge in invented atrocity stories, their factual films were in fact characterized by ideological restraint and a mea-sured, unemotional, almost objective approach.

Nowhere is this more clear than in the inter-titles which, in silent films, are the equivalent of the spoken commentary in the sound film and, as such, often carry the ideology of the film – almost without exception, the titles are short, sparse and factual. Thus, a typical example is provided in a short, early film released in March 1916: *Ypres – The Shell-shattered City of Flanders* contained just seven inter-titles: 'General panorama of the City'; 'The remains of the Grande Place (City Square)'; 'All that remains of the Cloth Hall'; 'The exterior of the Cathedral'; 'The Western Door'; 'The Interior of the Cathedral – the broken organ'; 'Left amidst the ruins'.

'General panorama of the City' – how often had those words been used in travel films before the war, yet here they introduce scenes of the unprecedented wartime destruction of the city. In stark contrast to the hysterical hyperbole of other wartime propaganda which left audiences in absolutely no doubt what conclusions they should draw, the official films leave it to the audience to construct those conclusions for itself.

All of that would be reason enough to pay attention to the official wartime film-makers, but the real nature of their achievement is even more remarkable than this. In the summer of 1916 they released a film that occupies a unique position in the history of British cinema. Up until then, footage shot behind the front line on the Western Front had been released in very short films, but when the Topical Committee that supervised their work saw the first rushes of the footage that Geoffrey Malins and J. B. McDowell had shot with the British Fourth Army north of the river Somme in the days leading up to the advance on 1 July and in the early days of the Somme offensive, they quickly recognized its unprecedented potential. They made the audacious decision to draw the footage together into a single feature-length film, and *Battle of the Somme*, with a running time of 77 minutes, opened in no fewer than 34 cinemas in London on 21 August 1916; a week later a further 100 prints were made available for national distribution. The film received wildly enthusiastic reviews and won huge audiences which broke through cinema's traditional class barriers for the very first time. Nicholas Hiley has calculated that it was seen by 20 million people at home in its first six weeks and, given that it went on playing in British cinemas for many months, it may well have been seen eventually by the majority of the population, making it probably the most successful British film of all time.

So why did it make such an enormous impact? Why were the

contemporary audiences so large? What was it about the war on the Western Front in the summer of 1916 that the official cameramen were able to share with their audiences? Notwithstanding the powerful images of military hardware in the opening sections, it is above all else the ordinary soldier who is at the heart of this film. The war was being fought by hundreds of thousands of ordinary working men, and this is their film. It is *their* faces which confront us on the screen – jokey and smiling as they 'perform' for the camera en route to the front; fixed and immobile, staring through and past the camera as they wait to go into action; exhausted, shattered, staring once more as they return from the front line. These are ordinary men enduring the unendurable; these are men who, in the face of apparently impossible odds, retain their dignity, their self-respect, their humanity even. This is the nature of war to which *Battle of the Somme* gave audiences direct access, and it did so to an extent without parallel in any other cultural product of the period.

Of course the film does not tell the whole story – above all else, it makes no attempt to give its audience any sense of the catastrophic scale of the casualties which the British suffered on these early days at the Somme. But for an official propaganda film, its extended sequences of the physical devastation of war, the battlefield landscape, the prisoners of war, the wounded and, above all else, its images of the dead, construct a remarkable, and remarkably powerful, representation of war. Indeed, the very characteristics that have led some to criticize the film are at the very heart of its unique appeal – the lack of a strong narrative structure, the roughness of some of the editing, the sparse, factual character of the inter-titles, the remarkable cinematography, all combine to construct a very particular authenticity.

Certainly whenever *Battle of the Somme* has been screened since, it has continued to engage and move audiences. For many years I showed the film to undergraduate audiences, and time and again I was startled at its ability to move them, even when, as in the early years, the absence of a print with a soundtrack meant that they viewed the film in the wholly artificial environment of silence. More recently, on 22 October 2006, a packed audience at London's Queen Elizabeth Hall attended a screening at which a newly restored print of the film was accompanied by a live performance of a new orchestral score by Laura Rossi, specially commissioned by the Imperial War Museum for the film's 90th anniversary. This remarkable screening gave a twenty-first century audience the opportunity to see the film as its film-makers intended, and the event itself closely mirrored the major public screenings of 1916 – a prestigious venue, a packed audience, all the intensity and power which only music performed by a live orchestra can bring to so-called 'silent' film. And just like audiences 90 years before, they watched and listened, engrossed, engaged and deeply moved. 'I have been twice to see these films and was profoundly struck by the emotion, and almost reverence with which they were followed' – the words were written in 1916, but they could have described that South Bank audience 90 years later. An emotional piece by the editor of the *Regiment* in September 1916 reiterated a view very common in journals of this kind that civilians were woefully ignorant of the reality of war, but argued that this film might perhaps shake them out of their complacency, claiming it would teach 'millions ... the true meaning of war'. Notwithstanding the extent of our greater knowledge of the brutal realities of war, *Battle of the Somme* retains its ability to force us these many years later to confront those realities once more.

So for all these reasons it is surely time to accord the official British film-makers of the First World War the recognition they so clearly deserve. The nature and extent of their achievements has long since been identified in the scholarly literature – it is surely time that the nature of their extraordinary achievements is brought to the attention of a wider audience; it is surely time that television audiences who are so familiar with tiny fragments of their work come to understand something of the character and extent of the body of work from which those sequences are taken; it is surely time that we all recognize the key role that these films have played in the popular culture of the First World War, not just for people at home and around the world who saw the films during the war but for all those who, through the medium of television, have also caught glimpses of this work.

Two years after the war was over, the most famous of the wartime film-makers, Geoffrey Malins, wrote an account of his wartime achievements:

In all the pictures that it has been my good fortune to take during the two and a half years that I have been kept at work on the great European battlefield, I have always tried to remember that it was through the eye of the camera, directed by my own sense of observation, that the millions of people at home would gain their only first-hand knowledge of what was happening at the front.

Time and again in the book Malins overstates and exaggerates the nature of his personal achievement but here, at least, his claims were entirely fair. What even he could not have known, however, is that through the medium of television, millions of people all over the world would, these 90 years later, continue to acquire some of their 'first-hand knowledge of what was happening at the front' through the footage that he and his fellow cameramen shot. It was, without question, an extraordinary achievement.

Further Reading

Badsey, S. D., 'Battle of the Somme: British war-propaganda', Historical Journal of Film, Radio and Television, Vol. 3, No 2, 1983.

Haste, Cate (1997), Keep the Home Fires Burning. London: Allen Lane.

Hiley, Nicholas, 'The British Cinema Auditorium' in K. Dibbets and B. Hogenakamp (eds) (1995), Film and the First World War. Amsterdam: Amsterdam UP.

——'Hilton DeWitt Girdwood and the Origins of British Official Filming', Historical Journal of Film, Radio and Television, Vol. 13, No. 2, 1993, 129–48.

Malins, Geoffrey H. (1920), How I Filmed the War. London: Imperial War Museum (reprinted with an introduction by Nicholas Hiley, 1993).

McKernan, Luke (1992), Topical Budget: The Great British New Film. London: BFI Publishing.

Reeves, Nicholas, 'Cinema, Spectatorship and Propaganda: Battle of the Somme (1916) and its contemporary audience', Historical Journal of Film, Radio and Television, Vol. 17, No. 1, 1997.

——'Film Propaganda and Its Audience', Journal of Contemporary History, Vol. 13, 1993, 463–94.

——(1986), Official British Film Propaganda During the First World War. London: Croom Helm.

——'The Power of Film Propaganda – Myth or Reality?', Historical Journal of Film, Radio and Television, Vol. 13, No 2, 1993, 181–201.

——(1999), The Power of Film Propaganda – Myth or Reality? London: Cassell.

Sanders, M. L., 'Wellington House and British Propaganda during the

First World War', *The Historical Journal*, Vol. XVIII, No 1, 1975, 119–46.

——'British Film Propaganda in Russia 1916–1918', *Historical Journal of Film, Radio and Television*, Vol. 3, No 2, 1983, 117–29.

Sanders, M. L. and Philip M. Taylor (1982), *British Propaganda During the First World War*. London: Palgrave Macmillan.

Smither, R., '"A Wonderful Idea of the Fighting": The Question of Fakes in *The Battle of the Somme*', *Historical Journal of Film, Radio and Television*, Vol. 13, No 2, 1993, 149–68.

Chapter 11

'Peace could not give back her Dead': Women and the Armistice

Jane Potter

In May Wedderburn Cannan's poem 'The Armistice: In an Office in Paris', the women speakers quietly mark the moment 'the War was won', both reflecting on the men who would now be 'safe' and lamenting those who had been killed:

'It's over for me too ... My man was killed,
Wounded ... and died ... at Ypres ... three years ago ...
And he's my Man, and I want him,' she said,
And knew that peace could not give back her Dead.

Vera Brittain, nursing at Queen Alexandra's Hospital at Mill-bank in London on the morning of the Armistice, was well aware of the crashing of the maroons outside that signalled the end of the war, but carried on methodically washing dressing bowls, because 'It's come too late for me.' 'Not one remained to share with me the heights and the depths of my memories,' she wrote. 'Too late' is a phrase that resonates in many women's recollections.

An overwhelming sense of loss marks both Cannan's and Brittain's descriptions of the moment of the Armistice and it characterizes their respective memoirs. Yet these two women espoused very different views of 'the war to end all wars'. Vera Brittain's memoir *Testament of Youth* (1933) is a heart-rending and embittered condemnation of the Great War and the losses it inflicted on her generation. It also charts Brittain's awakening internationalism, which in 1937 culminated in her formal commitment to pacifism. May Cannan, by contrast, never subscribed to the belief that the war was futile, asserting she was 'not coming home with Sassoon'. 'Someone must go on writing for those who were still convinced of the cause for which they had taken up arms,' she wrote in her posthumously published memoir *Grey Ghosts and Voices* (1976), a reason perhaps that it enjoys less canonical status than *Testament of Youth*. Grief – articulated so movingly by writers such as Brittain and Cannan – even at 90 years' distance still colours our perception of what the Great War meant for women, especially those who mourned husbands, fiancés, sons and brothers.

The raucous celebrations, characterized by flag-waving, communal singing, kissing and cheering, supposedly engulfed everyone in what the anonymous author of *WAAC: The Woman's Story of the War* (1930) described as 'the frenzied melting-pot of Armistice night'. Yet numerous writers who recorded 11 November 1918 were also acutely aware of what had been lost. Maude Onions recalled how despite the 'deafening roar' of church bells and sirens let loose in celebration of the end of 'hostilities' in Boulogne, 'not a sound, not a movement, came from the hundreds of human beings who thronged the streets. The stricken soul of France seemed to have lost even the desire to rejoice.' The American Mary Roberts Rinehart was saddened by the 'mad processions of *poilus* and girls dancing, and kissing' that she witnessed on that day in Paris when set in contrast to the tragic 'procession of the *multiples* . . . men with one leg stumping along and singing. It broke my heart.' Like Vera Brittain, Rinehart knew that for 'too many women shrouded in black ... the victory has come too late'. Mrs C. S. Peel, working as an assistant newspaper editor in Fleet Street, 'longed to go out into the streets, but could not because there was a great deal to do'. As she tried to correct proofs, she could not stop crying as she also thought of those 'for whom peace had come too late': 'Naturally there was rejoicing, and yet what pain there was underneath it.'

The Armistice, therefore, was a paradox. It marked both an end and a beginning; it was at once celebration and commemoration. It was an end to the carnage and, concurrently for women in particular, signalled the end of years of agonizing waiting and worry. But for many women it also meant an end to the myriad active-service roles they undertook – and to the comradeship they had formed. While they were barred from soldiering and, so popular fiction tells us, often lamented this state of affairs with cries of 'Oh, if only I were a man!', women had many opportunities for work in 1914–18. They took the places of men in business, in the police force, in transport, in retail and on farms. They were munitions workers and they were ambulance drivers. In the aftermath of the war, a significant number of women, many of whom were members of the First Aid Nursing Yeomanry (FANY) or the Women's Army Auxiliary Corps (WAAC), helped in the 'great clean-up' and the tending of graves on the Western Front. Nursing, the obvious and much-romanticized outlet for women's desire to be involved, was carried out under the auspices of numerous organizations from Queen Alexandra's Imperial Military Nursing Service (QAIMNS) to the Voluntary Aid Detachments (VADs). Women's active service memoirs, scores of which were published between 1914 and 1918, attest to the vast gulf between the sentimental vision and the realities of wartime nursing with uncompromising, graphic and even sickening descriptions of wounds. The idea that women had no sense of the suffering endured by men, that they were all advocates of Jessie Pope's much-condemned patriotic verse, is challenged again and again when one reads the testimony of female witnesses both during and after the war. Even if they were not among those who bravely argued against militarism at the time, such as Catherine Marshall or Mary Sargant Florence, or came to espouse pacifism in the interwar period like Vera Brittain, women were no less appalled and indelibly marked by their experiences.

The return to domesticity for women of all classes was not an easy transition. With very few exceptions, women who returned from active service bore no physical, outward signs of injury or trauma. Yet their 'post-traumatic stress', as we would now call it, went largely unrecognized. They came back to a world in which a duty of care towards returned soldiers was expected of them. The men who came home were very different to the ones who left, being wounded in body and / or traumatized in spirit. As Irene Rathbone remarked, 'There were men whom the war made. There were a far greater number whom it ruined.' Like returned soldiers, women were never really 'demobbed'. Some 160,000 women lost husbands in the war and pensions did little to allay financial hardships. Working-class women who left domestic service to make munitions returned to it with increased demands for pay and autonomy. Marie Barten, a pupil at St Mary's Higher Grade School, Folkestone, astutely remarked in her essay entitled 'War Work for Women' in July 1918 that 'Many girls have left offices and shops to do some kind of war-work, and when the war is over, I do not think some of the girls who have got used to outdoor work will like going back to indoor occupations.'

The franchise was granted to women in Britain over the age of 30 in 1918 and universal female suffrage became reality in 1928, but not as a reward for women's wartime efforts, 'rather like a chocolate is given to a child who has behaved unexpectedly well under trying circumstances', wrote Irene Rathbone. It was the result of a sustained effort by campaigners throughout 1914–18. (Other countries such as Austria, Germany and Russia (SFSR) also granted the vote to women in 1918, while the United States Congress ratified the Nineteenth Amendment to the Constitution in 1920. French women did not get the vote until 1945, Italian women until 1946.)

The negative image of the 'surplus women' – those who never married because so many men had been killed – has been challenged by scholars. While it is true that the spinster was a suspect individual in society, at once a sad old maid and a dangerous influence, such 'surplus women' pre-dated the carnage of 1914–18, with debates about them being particularly acute at the end of the nineteenth century. Moreover, many of these 'sad old maids' revelled in their independence and *chose* to remain single in the aftermath of the war for a whole host of reasons that had very little to do with the lack of eligible men.

Just as they had done during the war years themselves, women in the wake of the Armistice 'got on' with life. It would be a mistake to suggest that the grief that characterizes so much of women's experience of the Great War and its aftermath somehow resulted in a generation that 'felt sorry for itself'. It would be wrong to see women solely as 'victims'. Indeed, another salient feature of much of women's writing is that however horrific the war was, however much it marked their youth and haunted their mature years, it was an experience that was an enduring part of their lives. Kate Finzi wrote in her memoir *Eighteen Months in the War Zone* (1916) that 'although no sane person would go through it a second time', the experience of the war was 'something one would not have missed'. Joan, the heroine of Irene Rathbone's novel *We That Were Young* (1932), asserted that

Youth and the war were the same thing – youth and the war were us ... Yes, we hated it, and loved it, both. Loved it only because we gave so much to it, and because it was bound up with our youngness – rather like an unhappy school. It was *our* war, you see. And although it was so every-dayish at the time, and we were so sickened with it, it seems, now, to have a sort of ghastly glamour . . . Our hearts are there – unwillingly – for always. It was our war.

The post-war world was one of opportunity for women, with better employment and education, however slowly these developed, but it was bound up with the ghosts of the dead and it is true that many wanted simply to forget. 'Yes, I am glad I went through the war,' declared the author of WAAC. 'But never again. Never. Never. Nor do I care to dwell upon its memory, as I have had to do while writing this book.'

Writing was a form of expiation and it is this written legacy, whether published or unpublished, that even now has much more to tell us about women and the Great War. Women of all classes undertook work that went beyond prescribed gender roles. Class barriers may have only broken down for the duration and women may have returned to a highly stratified society, but the war nonetheless provided opportunities for active service, better wages and a sense of independence. Those that point to these 'positives' as evidence of women relishing war, have continually neglected to temper such experience with that of the overwhelming loss. The opportunities came at a price and women continued to pay that price well after the Armistice.

Future Directions

While numerous studies of women in the First World War remain key texts in our understanding of their roles and experiences, including Angela Woollacott's *On Her Their Lives Depend: Munitions Workers and the Great War* (1994), recent scholarship has sought to broaden and redefine our perceptions by challenging both the canon of literature and historical representation. In the same way that military historians are questioning the 'lions-led-by-donkeys' notion, so too are women's historians and literary scholars reassessing the female legacy of 1914–18 through previously untapped and unanalyzed diaries, letters, memoirs and popular fiction. Carol Acton in *Grief in Wartime: Private Pain, Public Discourse* (2007) extends the analysis put forward by Jay Winter (*Sites of Memory, Sites of Mourning*), examining how women both are perceived as and perceive themselves to be the archetypal figures of mourning. Katherine Holden (*The Shadow of Marriage: Singleness in England 1914–60* (2007)) and Virginia Nicholson (*Singled Out: How Two Million Women Survived Without Men After the First World War* (2007)) both debunk the notions of the lonely spinster, bereaved and embittered by the losses of the Great War, while in *Suffrage Discourse in Britain during the First World War* (2005), Angela K. Smith demonstrates the ways in which the campaign for women's suffrage was carried on in fiction and non-fiction, challenging the idea that the movement was silenced for the duration. Janet Lee's *War Girls* (2005) brings into focus the personal stories of the women of the First Aid Nursing Yeomanry, while Yvonne McEwen highlights not only the trauma faced by nurses but the medical practices they helped to pioneer in *It's a Long Way to Tipperary: British and Irish Nurses in the Great War* (2006). Numerous literary studies have examined the novels, memoirs and poetry of canonical writers, such as Virginia Woolf, Rebecca West, H. D. and Katherine Mansfield, whose texts are often considered 'high literature'. My own work, by contrast, explores popular and middlebrow fiction as well as active service memoirs to challenge the stereotypic characterization of women (often gleaned through the canon of soldier poets or modernist novelists) as either sorrowful pacifists such as Vera Brittain or war-mongering versifiers such as Jessie Pope. Moreover, studies of women and the Great War are now increasingly international and interdisciplinary, as Alison S. Fell and Ingrid Sharp's collection, *The Women's Movement in Wartime: International Perspectives, 1914–19* (2007), demonstrates.

Writing in the 1930s shortly before *Testament of Youth* was published, Vera Brittain, in an article entitled 'War-Book Women', lamented 'the completely inadequate representation in war literature of the part that women played in the Great War'. Men's literature negatively categorized females and their experience, she argued – and in many ways it continues to do so, at least in so far as this literature continues to be privileged over others. Brittain answered her own question, 'Who will write the epic of the women who went to the War?', when she published *Testament of Youth* in 1933, but it is not the only source. We do as much of a disservice to 'the part women played in the Great War' if we focus solely on Brittain's testament as we do if we focus only on that of male soldier poets, such as Owen and Sassoon. Writing is an essential element in catharsis, in coming to terms with grief and loss, and this is attested to by hundreds of novels, memoirs and poetry collections that were published throughout the war and the interwar period. As May Cannan wrote:

> I suppose most of us have the desire to leave something behind us when we go into whatever there is (or is not) beyond the void. I don't think I ever treasured any extravagant hope of leaving anything that would be remembered, but as the years have gone by and times changed I have been glad to think that at least I wrote a salute to my generation.

Such salutes, which exist also in the unpublished letters, diaries and sound recordings of survivors in the archives and collections of museums and libraries, provide rich sources of accumulated memory that still have much to tell us about women and their part of history.

Further Reading

Acton, Carol (2007), *Grief in Wartime: Private Pain, Public Discourse*. Basingstoke: Palgrave Macmillan.

Brittain, Vera (1933 / 2004), *Testament of Youth*. London: Virago Classics.

Cannan, May Wedderburn and Bevil Quiller-Couch (2000), *The Tears of War: The Love Story of a Young Poet and a War Hero*. Upavon, Wilts: Cavalier Paperbacks.

Cohen, Debra Rae (2002), *Remapping the Home Front: Locating Citizenship in British Women's Great War Fiction*. Boston: Northwestern University Press.

Fell, Alison S. and Ingrid Sharp (eds) (2007), *The Women's Movement in Wartime: International Perspectives, 1914–19*. Basingstoke: Palgrave.

Grayzel, Susan R. (1999), *Women's Identities at War: Gender, Motherhood and Politics in Britain and France during the First World War*. Chapel Hill: University of North Carolina Press.

Gregory, Adrian (1994), *The Silence of Memory: Armistice Day 1919–1946*. Oxford / Providence, RI: Berg, 1994.

Holden, Katherine (2007), *The Shadow of Marriage: Singleness in England 1914–60*. Manchester: Manchester UP.

Lee, Janet (2005), *War Girls: The First Aid Nursing Yeomanry in the First World War*. Manchester: Manchester UP.

Marlow, Joyce (ed.) (1999), *The Virago Book of Women and the Great War*. London: Virago.

McEwen, Yvonne (2006), *It's a Long Way to Tipperary: British and Irish Nurses in the Great War*. Dunfermline: Cualann Press.

Nicholson, Virginia (2007), *Singled Out: How Two Million Women Survived Without Men After the First World War*. London: Viking.

Ouditt, Sharon (1994), *Fighting Forces, Writing Women: Identity and Ideology in the First World War*. London & New York: Routledge.

Persico, Joseph E. (2004), *Eleventh Month, Eleventh Day, Eleventh Hour: Armistice Day, 1918 World War I and Its Violent Climax*. New York: Random House.

Potter, Jane (2005), *Boys in Khaki, Girls in Print: Women's Literary Responses to the Great War 1914–1918*. Oxford: OUP.

Smith, Angela K. (2005), *Suffrage Discourse in Britain During the First World War*. Aldershot: Ashgate.

Tate, Trudi (1998), *Modernism, History and the First World War*. Manchester: Manchester University Press.

Todd, Selina (2005), *Young Women, Work, and Family in England 1918–1950*. Oxford: OUP.

Tylee, Claire with Turner, Elaine and Cardinal Agnès (1999). *War Plays by Women: An International Anthology*. London & New York: Routledge.

Weintraub, Stanley (1985), *The Stillness Heard Round the World: The End of the Great War: November 1918*. New York / Oxford: OUP.

Winter, Jay (1995), *Sites of Memory, Sites of Mourning: The Great War in European Cultural History*. Cambridge: CUP.

Woollacott, Angela (1994), *On Her Their Lives Depend: Munitions Workers and the Great War*. Berkeley, CA: University of California Press.

Lines from May Wedderburn Cannan's poem *The Armistice – In an Office in Paris* used by kind permission of James Cannan Slater.

Chapter 12

'A Museum of Man's Greatest Lunatic Folly': The Imperial War Museum and its Commemoration of the Great War, 1917–2008

Terry Charman

On 5 March 2007, the Imperial War Museum marked its 90th anniversary. On the intranet that day, the Museum's staff were reminded that in the years of its existence, 'it has seen two World Wars, three main London sites, four branches, five director generals and nearly 60 million visitors'.

From its inception, the Imperial War Museum was seen, as King George V said in his opening address on 9 June 1920 at the Museum's first site at the Crystal Palace, not only as 'a store-house of material for the historian ... and an inspiration for future generations' but also as 'a lasting memorial of common effort and common sacrifice'. But more than that, it was hoped that the Museum would demonstrate, according to the IWM's 21st Annual Report, published on the eve of the Second World War, 'the futility of war, and that heroism is brought at all too dear a cost. [The Museum] was to make an historical record of the war "that was to end war", and not the first of a series of world wars, each more terrible than the last.'

Sadly of course, this was not to be, and starting in October 1939 and on subsequent occasions, the Museum's terms of reference were expanded so that it now attempts to record all aspects of international conflict since August 1914. And as the 90th anniversary of the Armistice approached in 2008, an active effort of acquisition was being pursued by all the Museum's collecting departments with regard to the conflicts in Afghanistan and Iraq. But the First World War continues to exert an interest, indeed fascination, with the Museum's visitors for whom the Somme and Jutland are now as remote as Waterloo and Trafalgar must have seemed to both the IWM's founding fathers and the original members of its staff, all of them veterans of the Great War.

For the first three years of its existence, the Imperial War Museum had no 'home' as such, but there were ambitious plans for a purpose-built museum building to be located on the Embankment at the site of the present day Ministry of Defence. However, financial constraints and lack of public support and political will meant that these plans came to nothing, and thus it was at the well-established Crystal Palace at Sydenham that the Museum, on a four-year lease, found its first home. So great was public interest in the new museum, that in its first nine months at the Crystal Palace the IWM received 1,433,891 visitors, with an incredible 94,179 visiting over the 1920 August Bank Holiday alone.

Although spacious and a proven attraction for visitors, the Crystal Palace was, in the long term, an unsuitable site for many of the large exhibits, and in 1924 the IWM moved to galleries at the Imperial Institute in London's museum quarter, South Kensington. Again, the lease was only temporary, this time up until 1940, and so the search still continued for a larger and permanent home. In today's conservation-conscious world, it is sad to recall that in the move to South Kensington many of the Museum's larger objects, including aircraft, tanks and guns, were either destroyed or donated to other institutions. Those objects were rather airily dismissed at the time as being 'either redundant, or of no historical or technical interest'. One can only feel that, despite the rather extravagant claims made in that year's Annual Report, the models commissioned to replace many of them, fine and accurate as they may have been, were to prove no substitute for the real thing. The policy of disposal of 'unwanted' items continued throughout the interwar period with, for example, the Headquarters Mess of the Malay States Volunteer Regiment receiving a whole collection of breastplates, swords and bayonets, and the British Legion 24 German steel helmets to be sold at the May 1930 Empire Fair.

The Imperial War Museum's role of being 'a lasting memorial to common effort and common sacrifice' was amply illustrated by observations in those same Annual Reports. On Armistice Day 1924, wreaths were deposited by the Prince of Wales (later King Edward VIII, and later still the Duke of Windsor), the Board of

Trustees and ordinary members of the public on many of the guns and other exhibits in the galleries at South Kensington. At 10.50 a.m., a short prayer was recited by a former Royal Navy chaplain, Reverend F. C. Horan, and students from the Royal College of Music sang the national anthem. More surprisingly perhaps, one of the Museum's prize objects, the field gun of 'E' Battery, Royal Horse Artillery, which on 22 August 1914 had fired the first British round on the Western Front, was wheeled out and used for firing the last rounds of the salute at Field Marshal Earl Haig's funeral in February 1928.

In the year before Haig's death, the Museum attendance fig-ures had dropped to below 200,000, a reflection perhaps on the social and cultural climate of the hedonistic 'Roaring Twenties', the era of 'the Bright Young Things'. But the following year showed a significant increase in visitors, and the Annual Report noted 'a very marked revival of interest in the War, as exhibited in newspapers, dramatic representations and cinematographic films ... '. This increase only served to highlight the cramped and unsatisfactory accommodation at South Kensington. Nor indeed was the IWM exempt from natural disaster, as when on 28 July 1928, 'in consequence of a violent thunderstorm', the basement was flooded and many exhibits had to be rescued from the water.

A solution to the IWM's accommodation problem presented itself not long after the flood, when, in 1929, the building that had housed the Bethlem Royal Hospital, 'Bedlam' – which had moved to Beckenham, Kent, in 1926 – looked to be available. Newspaper magnate Lord Rothermere, who had been Air Min-ister in 1917 when the IWM was established, had bought the building and wished to replace it with a children's playground in memory of his mother, Geraldine Mary Harmsworth. Owing to financial reasons, Rothermere was forced to halt the demolition of the building, and asked instead for bids to take it over from interested organizations and institutions. In the event, Rother-mere, two of whose sons, Vere and Vyvyan, had been killed during the war, strongly supported the IWM's bid, to which, in 1930, the London County Council and the Office of Works also agreed.

Britain's political and economic crisis in 1931, and the ensuing cutbacks in public spending, meant that the IWM's move from South Kensington had to be postponed until 1935. As it was, the conversion costs amounted to £50,000, a not inconsiderable sum in those days, and when the Museum's total financial estimates for a year were £11,745. And it was not only this that brought home the effects of the Great Depression to the IWM. The Annual Report for 1933–4 noted that 'many ex-Servicemen in straitened circumstances have brought in treasured souvenirs which they wished to dispose of to obtain a few necessary shillings. It is often painful to have to refuse these appeals.' Happily, in the case of one unemployed boiler-maker, who had served as a Lewis gunner in France, and had walked from the North to London to find employment, the Museum was able to oblige. He had built from odd scraps of material 'a small but vivid and detailed model showing a section of the German and British front-line trenches ... and had drawn on his memory to introduce many accurate touches ... The Trustees were pleased to be able to buy it on its merits, and it has proved,' the Report concluded, 'an attractive exhibit.'

August that year marked the 20th anniversary of the outbreak of war in 1914, and again the IWM witnessed an upsurge in interest, not only with visitors but with heavy demands on its archival resources. The photographic department was especially in demand with such best-selling part works as *I Was There: Undying Memories of 1914–1918*, edited by Sir John Hammerton, and *Twenty Years After*, which was edited by Major General Sir Ernest Swinton and which included a pictorial essay on the IWM which makes for fascinating reading today.

The following year, on 11 November 1935, after what had become the usual observance of Armistice Day at the IWM – prayers in front of Sir Edwin Lutyens' original 1919 Cenotaph and the relaying by the BBC of the ceremony in Whitehall – the Museum closed its doors at South Kensington, preparatory to the move to Lambeth. This was completed in March 1936, and the Museum was formally opened by the Duke and Duchess of York (very soon to become King George VI and Queen Elizabeth) on 7 July 1936. The Duchess, whose elder brother Fergus had been killed at the Battle of Loos in September 1915, and who had also lost two close cousins, remarked of the new museum, 'It is a very good thing that people should know and realize how horrible war is.'

Barely three years would pass before Britain would again experience those horrors. The IWM had first faced the prospect of a new world war as far back as November 1933, the month after Hitler's Germany had left the League of Nations, with plans to evacuate the large exhibits and works of art. The Sudeten crisis of 1938, which culminated in the Munich Agreement, had provided the IWM with a dress rehearsal for the 'real thing' with, in one emergency measure, an assistant and seven attendants, equipped with German steel helmets, gas rattles, picks and shovels, acting as an air raid patrol. During the crisis the IWM had found itself much in demand from 'large numbers seeking guidance and information for the future from the study of the relics and records of the last war'.

Rather smugly, but with complete justification, the Annual Report for 1938 concluded: 'The wisdom of having preserved the records of the last war has already been amply proved by the use that has been made of them, not only by those whose duty is now to organize the passive defence of their homes and localities, but also by officials of the great service departments.'

On 23 August 1939, with the threat of war very real, the IWM, in common with other public buildings, closed to the public in order to facilitate the evacuation of certain exhibits and paintings. Earlier that month the archives show that the IWM indulged in its own appeasing of Nazi Germany by returning Field Marshal von Hindenburg's chair, 'as a sign of eternal friendship between our countries', in time for the ceremony to mark the 25th anniversary of the Battle of Tannenberg, which in the event Hitler cancelled.

After being closed to the public for the first four months of the 'Phoney War', the Museum reopened on 29 January 1940 and remained open until 9 September that year, when the Blitz forced its closure. Already, after Dunkirk, 'when the shortage of war material was acute', the armed forces had selected 18 guns from the IWM's collection to be taken back into service; steel helmets and trench clubs went to the Home Guard; veterinary instruments to the Royal Veterinary College; and gun sights and optical instruments to the Ministry of Supply. However, the Trustees remained resolute in refusing to hand over both the gun from HMS *Lance* which had fired the first naval shot of the Great War, and that served by Boy Jack Cornwell VC in HMS *Chester* at the Battle of Jutland.

In the course of the war, the IWM was badly damaged both by conventional bombing and by the V weapons (41 'incidents in all'), and it was in no condition to be reopened to the public until 27 November 1946. The IWM's war history sombrely concludes, 'There was no formal opening … In any case, lack of space prevented any form of ceremony.' Those austere words were to be symptomatic of the next 15 years of the IWM's existence, during the latter part of which there were real and genuine fears that the Museum would 'simply wither away and die'. That this did not happen is due almost entirely to the efforts of Dr Noble Frankland, director of the IWM from 1960 to 1982, who masterminded the Museum's renaissance during those years and turned it into the world's premier museum of international conflict.

When Dr Frankland, a wartime Bomber Command navigator with the Distinguished Flying Cross, first visited the IWM in September 1955 he found that, 'the galleries had a dingy and neglected air ... crowded with masses of mostly quite small items arranged in congested groups and unrelated each to each other and disconnected from any discernible historical themes'. Five years later, Dr Frankland was back as director and confronted with the same 'dismal state of decay' and also with 'the staff heavily demoralized'.

Dr Frankland found that his predecessor, Mr L. R. Bradley, a Great War veteran, had an 'empathy ... almost wholly with the First World War ... to him the Second World War was a nuisance which deposited masses of material in the Museum, squeezing its already restricted space and disrupting such order as its exhibitions had earlier had'. Mr Bradley, who was one of the original members of the IWM staff in 1917, was of the opinion that the usefulness of the IWM was now diminishing with the passing of the years since the end of the First World War, and indeed its very significance, not to mention appeal and interest to the public, had now been both overshadowed and overtaken by the later conflict. In his memoirs, Dr Frankland wrote that his predecessor 'gave the impression of hoping, as he approached the grave, that the Museum, which he had served for so long, would do the same'.

Under Dr Frankland, this air of defeatism was swiftly banished; properly qualified staff were recruited and a much more professional approach adopted throughout the IWM. Major exhibitions like 'Colditz' (1973–4) ensured that attendances rose, and the IWM achieved a high public profile with its participation in the award-winning television series *The Great War* and *The World at War*. Since his retirement in 1982 after 22 years as director, Dr Frankland's successors, Dr Alan Borg (1982–95) and Sir Robert Crawford (1995–2008), have continued to build on the foundations laid by him, and the IWM's five sites in the first years of the twenty-first century have had a total attendance in the region of two million visitors a year.

Of course the IWM has not been to everybody's taste. Cecil Beaton, visiting it on 12 March 1974 to view his wartime photographs, described it in his diary as 'a place I loathe'. (In view of that remark, there is a nice touch of irony in the fact that the Museum's Lower Board Room now bears the name the 'Beaton Room' in his honour.) Mr Tim Daly's reaction to the IWM was even more violent when, on the night of 13/14 October 1968, he tried, unsuccessfully, to burn the Museum down. He had done this 'because he had seen children being taken round the Museum. He believed that the Museum taught them that war is glorious.' This was a naive view then, and is even more so today. The IWM permanent displays, such as the award-winning Holocaust Exhibition (seen by nearly 2,250,000 visitors since 2000), show only too graphically the horrors of war of which Queen Elizabeth spoke back in July 1936.

As the 90th anniversary of the Armistice approached, Mr Bradley's fears about the usefulness and purpose of the Imperial War Museum fortunately proved to be unfounded. Nor too has the First World War been overshadowed by the Second or subsequent conflicts. The 'Trench Experience', modelled on a dugout and fire bays held by the 1/10th Battalion The Lancashire Fusiliers in the autumn of 1916, is one of the Museum's most popular attractions: 'much better than a collection of display stands in a stuffy museum' opined one teenage visitor. The temporary exhibition 'My Boy Jack', telling the story of Rudyard Kipling's son John who was killed at the Battle of Loos, proved an enormous crowd-puller in the winter of 2007–8. This was especially true of younger visitors who, on Remembrance Sunday 2007, had seen *Harry Potter* star Daniel Radcliffe play John in the TV drama of the same name which attracted 5.7 million viewers.

The IWM's collecting departments still deal with a mass of enquiries from the public, scholars and the media concerning all aspects of the First World War. And the staff of the Department of Printed Books are still fielding questions on the same subjects as their predecessors in the 1920s and 1930s: the Angels of Mons, Nurse Edith Cavell, the Unknown Warrior, the Two Minutes' Silence, and Lawrence of Arabia. In recent years, the memorial aspect of the IWM has also come to the fore again when, on 11 November, the Last Post is sounded, a two minutes' silence observed, evocative music played on the Western Front Violin, and visitors have the opportunity of meeting and paying homage to the last surviving British veterans of the Great War.

At the beginning of 2008 plans were well advanced for the IWM's major exhibition 'In Memoriam' which was to mark the 90th anniversary of the Armistice of 11 November 1918. Previous anniversaries marking the Battle of the Somme in 2006 and Third Ypres in 2007 had generated massive media and public interest and the Museum anticipated an equal if not increased interest in 2008. For, as outgoing Director General Sir Robert Crawford wrote in 2001, 'We are compelled yet again to acknowledge how the world we live in today was shaped by the events of the First World War.'

Chapter 13

Anthologies of Great War Verse: Mirrors of Change

Dominic Hibberd

British poets and versifiers, civilians and soldiers alike, wrote so much during and after the First World War that most readers will always have to approach the war's poetry through anthologies. The anthologies themselves have been extraordinarily numerous and varied; only a few can be mentioned here, but they deserve more attention from researchers than they have as yet received. They have tended to appear in groups, many during the war itself, a few in the early 1920s, another batch during the Second World War, and then another during Vietnam; since then they have come out in a fairly steady flow. Taken together, they form a vivid record of changing attitudes to the war and its values: with so many poems to choose from, compilers have been able to present the conflict as anything from futile waste to glorious victory.

In 1914 R. M. Leonard was actually assembling his *Patriotic Poems* for the Oxford Garlands series when war was declared on 4 August. There was no time to change the contents, but he rewrote his preface and followed it with the Poet Laureate's new 'August, 1914' (*Times*, 8 August). Other anthologists were quick to follow. E. V. Lucas 'hastily brought together' a collection of old patriotic poems, added a new one by John Drinkwater, and made the book topical by entitling it *Remember Louvain!* (1914, London: Methuen). The preface to John Fawside's *The Flag of England: Ballads of the Brave and Poems of Patriotism* (1914, London: Nash) is dated 14 October: by that time there were several new poems to set among old favourites.

It would have been unthinkable to put anti-war poems into these and the many other 1914–15 collections. A few poets did attack the war from the start, but their work got no further than the left-wing press. The great majority of British people were certain the German invasion of Belgium had to be resisted, and they wanted to help: the idea that poets should write about what Wilfred Owen was to call 'the pity of war' would have seemed absurd. One obvious task for older men of a literary bent was to collect up patriotic poems or write new ones in the hope of encouraging younger men to volunteer. In his introduction to Charles Seddon Evans's *Our Glorious Heritage: A Book of Patriotic Verse for Boys and Girls* (1914, London: Heinemann), the Dean of Norwich said that a poet's duty in wartime was to celebrate heroic deeds and give voice to love of country and freedom, as well as to express any 'special idea' such as respect for a nation's pledged word or the protection of the weak against the strong (references to the famous 'scrap of paper' and brave little Belgium).

The first anthology to consist entirely of poems written during the war was *Songs and Sonnets for England in War Time* (1914, London: Bodley Head), sold in aid of the new National Relief Fund for soldiers' families. The anonymous compiler was confident that in 'the stress of a nation's peril, the poet at last comes into his own ... Prophet he is, champion and consoler ... here to strengthen, comfort and inspire'. Poets had certainly been working hard: all 51 poems in the book had appeared in the press between August and September. Already there was a sense that the poetry of this war was going to be something special: the publisher, John Lane, claimed in a note that the book was the first-ever anthology of poems actually written while a conflict was in progress. That uniqueness was short-lived: *Poems of the Great War* (1914, London: Chatto & Windus), all new work, was soon published in aid of the same charity. 'This collection of War Poems ... represents the free offering of English poets to the cause of National Relief.' Nearly all the contributors were eminent in the world of letters, but even in 1914 their efforts were not universally appreciated.

Despite mockery from some reviewers, the market for anthologies of 'War Poems' boomed for a while: more than a dozen were published in 1915, probably the highest total for any year. Many were sold in aid of charity: profits from H. B. Elliott's *Lest We Forget* (February 1915, London: Jarrold) went to the Queen Mary Needlework Guild, Baroness Orczy explaining in a preface that the book was dedicated to British women who were doing their bit by making warm clothes for their absent menfolk. Elliott's contributors were noticeably less distinguished than those in the 1914 anthologies, but they included a number of women and some of the war's most ubiquitous early versifiers. Profits from Mabel C. Edwards' and Mary Booth's *The Fiery Cross* (1915, London: Grant Richards) went to the Red Cross. Modern members of that organization might be horrified by the anti-German tone of much of the contents, but one striking new poem contained neither hatred nor anger, Rupert Brooke's 'The Soldier', making perhaps its first appearance in an anthology. It is difficult now to imagine the early impact of Brooke's sonnets: here at last was what seemed a genuinely poetic response to the war, by a soldier who had seen action. The compilers said in their preface that a poet's duty was to 'inspire' and 'console', and Brooke's sonnets did that in a way that no civilian verse could hope to emulate. Civilian poets were left with little more to do than honour the dead.

Not all the 1915 anthologies were in aid of charity. Galloway Kyle, Hon. Director of the Poetry Society, was watching the market with his usual shrewdness. He must have been the brains behind *A Crown of Amaranth: Being a collection of poems to the memory of the brave and gallant gentlemen who gave their lives for Great and Greater Britain* MCMXIV–MCMXV (late 1915, London: Erskine Macdonald). The preface to the 1917 edition is signed by Macdonald and S. Gertrude Ford, but 'Mr Macdonald' was a secret alias for Kyle himself, who had found ways of making a comfortable living out of other people's poetry by accepting commissions and by using the Poetry Society, the *Poetry Review* (which he controlled from 1913) and the Erskine Macdonald imprint, which was to appear on volumes by many young aspirants during the war. *A Crown of Amaranth* contained an elegy to Brooke by Gertrude Ford and two more to that other dead hero-poet of 1915, Julian Grenfell, as well as Grenfell's already-famous poem 'Into Battle'.

Kyle may not have been alone in exploiting the wartime market. It is difficult not to suspect an element of vanity publishing in three large compilations by Charles Forshaw, *One Hundred of the Best Poems on the European War* (2 vols, 1915, 1916, London: Elliott Stock) and *Poems in Memory of the Late Lord Kitchener, K.G.* (1916, Bradford: Institute of British Poetry). The names of almost all Forshaw's contributors are, and probably always were, entirely unfamiliar, and all were limited to one poem each. He had produced similar books before the war. Most of the verse was feeble stuff, but his 1915–16 volumes can claim two distinctions: his second hundred poems were all by women, the first of only two such wartime anthologies (the second being Alys Macklin's *The Lyceum Book of War Verse* (1918, London: Erskine Macdonald), another of Kyle's ventures); and his Kitchener collection had 176 contributors, more than any other Great War anthology until very recently.

Far fewer anthologies were published in 1916 than in the previous year. The introduction of conscription put an end to recruiting verse and helped to silence the 'old men'. And again Kyle understood the market: his warmly received *Soldier Poets: Songs of the Fighting Men* (September 1916, London: Erskine Macdonald) was the first anthology to consist entirely of work by serving soldiers, mostly volunteers, each shown with rank and regiment. Many of them had not been heard of before, but the book included work by Grenfell, Charles Sorley, W. N. Hodgson and Sergeant J. W. Streets, a former miner whose fervent patriotism had attracted middle-class approval. It was the right moment to publish such a book: the public was still being told the Somme offensive was going well, yet casualty lists were growing fast. Kyle's preface claimed that all his chosen 'war poems' expressed 'a unity of spirit, of exultant sincerity and unconquerable idealism': descriptions of death and gruesomeness could be left to 'the neurotic civilian who stayed behind to gloat on imagined horrors and inconveniences'. In due course the war's verse was going to be 'an illuminating index and memorial' of the period, giving poetry a new significance.

A year later Kyle's success was followed up – without the slightest acknowledgement – by E. B. Osborn's *The Muse in Arms: A collection of war poems, for the most part written in the field of action, by seamen, soldiers, and flying men who are serving, or have served, in the Great War* (November 1917, London: Murray) – 'the first coherent picture of the British warrior's moods and emotions ... painted by himself'. Osborn claimed the poems were far more valuable than the innumerable 'high-explosive canticles' fired off by civilians in 1914–15, most of which had already been consigned to oblivion. When 'the British warrior' glimpsed 'the ultimate significance of warfare', he showed 'a singular capacity for remembering the splendour and forgetting the squalor', for 'infinite cheerfulness', that 'open and sunny joyousness which is eternally expressed' in Grenfell's 'Into

Battle'. He disliked talk of patriotism and felt no hate for the enemy: his underlying motive was intense comradeship, 'the secret of our victorious warfare'. Osborn believed there had never been anything like this poetry in any previous literature.

The list of poets in the first edition is exclusively of servicemen, almost all of them officers, none higher in rank than captain (the two women contributors are not mentioned). For the first time poems are grouped by theme: 'School and College' and 'Chivalry of Sport' both contain more poems than 'The Christian Soldier', and there is plenty of 'sunny joyousness'. Nothing in the book hints that Passchendaele is in progress or that one of the poets, Siegfried Sassoon, had recently made a public protest. Sassoon is represented by his idealistic 1915 poem 'Absolution' and his more recent 'The Rear-guard', a grim description but not a poem of protest.

In December 1917 Kyle produced *More Songs by the Fighting Men / Soldier Poets: Second Series*, having apparently not known that Osborn's book had been imminent. His preface stated grandly that 'No literary work of our day has possessed so much genetic force or been of greater influence' than the first *Soldier Poets*. But he never brought out a third series.

In 1918 the German March offensive made the British public fear defeat for the first time, a dramatic change reflected in Bertram Lloyd's *Poems Written During the Great War 1914–1918* (July 1918, London: Allen & Unwin). Published even before the Allies had made sure of victory on the Western Front, this was the first anthology to be squarely aimed at 'the cant and idealization and false glamour' with which war had been masked. Lloyd chose work by British and foreign writers, men and women, civilians and a few soldiers: the leading contributors were the civilian socialist and conscientious objector W. N. Ewer, with seven poems, Sassoon, with five (including some of his angriest satires), and Lady Margaret Sackville, another strong opponent of the war, with four. A year later Lloyd went further with an entirely new selection, *The Paths of Glory* (1919, London: Allen & Unwin), stating that all his poets were united in regarding war as 'an execrable blot on civilization', and this time he was able to recruit work from at least a dozen men who had served in the forces.

A few more conventional anthologies appeared just after the war. E. R. Jaquet's *These Were the Men* (1919, London: Marshall) was intended as a memorial to 'our splendid men'. Jacqueline T.

Trotter's *Valour and Vision* (1920, London: Longmans, Green; revised and enlarged edition, 1923, London: Hopkinson) was as heroic as its title suggests, and like its predecessors four or five years before it was published in aid of charity. Trotter tried to present the war poet as 'historian' by arranging poems in a supposedly (but in fact highly inaccurate) chronological order. Sassoon was allowed only one mild poem in the first edition, but Trotter added two harsher ones in 1923, as well as two by Wilfred Owen, whose *Poems* had come out in 1920. But the public was growing tired of war poetry – even Owen's aroused only limited interest. Among the 'war books' that came in a sudden flood at the end of the decade there was only one anthology of verse.

Frederick Brereton's *An Anthology of War Poems* (1930, London: Collins) had an introduction by Edmund Blunden. As critic, editor and academic, Blunden has probably had more influence than anyone on the modern view of 1914–18 verse. His introduction to Brereton names only five poets: Brooke (whose poems had become 'difficult to read'), Sorley, Robert Graves, Sassoon (the first poet to describe war 'fully and exactly') and Owen, by implication the greatest of them. Sassoon is again the leading contributor to the book, with seven poems, followed by Owen with five; Brereton also chooses three by Isaac Rosenberg, probably the latter's first appearance in an anthology, as well as two by Ivor Gurney. The modern canon is beginning to take shape, in a very different pattern to anything that might have been foreseen in 1914–15.

Silence fell again until the Second World War, when four or five anthologies of 1914–18 verse appeared, intended not to undermine the war effort but to illuminate the courage and suffering of soldiers. One of these books even included Owen's 'Dulce et Decorum Est', although that poem did not appear in Robert Nichols' *Anthology of War Poetry 1914–1918* (1943, London: Nicholson & Watson). Nichols preferred Owen's studies of comradeship, such as 'Greater Love', a major theme of his own war poems. His selection and enormous preface reinforced the canon, except that he omitted Rosenberg and Gurney: he chose only 14 poets, all of them familiar from later anthologies and all but two of them infantry volunteers. Sassoon again leads, with 13 poems, followed by Blunden with nine, the first time Blunden had taken so prominent a place. Owen gets only four, but the preface makes very high claims for him.

After 1945 war weariness set in again, and there were no more anthologies for almost 20 years until Vietnam began to disturb the public conscience. Fifty years after 1914, Brian Gardner's *Up the Line to Death: The War Poets 1914–1918* (1964, London: Methuen) was the first of many modern selections, of which there have been at least 25 to date – an extraordinary number, partly explained by the discovery that 'war poetry' is excellent classroom material. Gardner's book set the anthology pattern for 20 years or more and is still in print, but it belongs to its time: it is not based on thorough research, and it organizes poems by theme without regard to date or context. One of Gardner's assumptions is that all poets, even Kipling, turned against the war after the Somme – so, for example, Wilfrid Gibson's little poem 'Breakfast' has to be a relatively late wartime work by, as a biographical note asserts, a soldier who had been at the front. Actually Gibson never served abroad, and his poem, written in October 1914, long before he joined the army, is one of the very first attempts to imagine front-line conditions. Gardner's book was a moving introduction to war poetry for many people, but it contributed significantly to what is now often seen as the 1960s 'myth' of the Great War.

Several variations on Gardner culminated in Jon Silkin's *The Penguin Book of First World War Poetry* (1979, Harmondsworth: Penguin Books), which reinforced the myth with a densely argued introduction and a selection from British and foreign poets that made no pretence of being representative of anything except the war's true poetry – and Silkin believed that no genuine poetry could say anything positive about war. He felt he had to include 'Into Battle' and a few other standard anthology pieces, but he marked them with an asterisk to indicate disapproval. His views were deeply felt but relatively narrow and not always soundly based.

Like Gardner, Silkin included no women, an omission soon challenged by Catherine Reilly's *Scars Upon My Heart* (1981, London: Virago), the first anthology of women's 1914–18 verse since 1918. After that, women poets could no longer be ignored. Eleven were included in Dominic Hibberd's and John Onions' *Poetry of the Great War* (1986, Basingstoke: Macmillan), a selection which attempted to confront the myth by giving a more accurate and wide-ranging cross-section of the war's poetry, correcting facts and quoting many poems that had never been reprinted since 1918. Martin Stephen's *Never Such Innocence*

(1988, London: Buchan & Enright) made a similar attempt, with more poets but rather less accuracy (Stephen seemed unaware of our own book). Since then there have been two more anthologies of women's verse, as well as two highly original selections, Martin Taylor's *Lads: Love Poetry of the Trenches* (1989, London: Constable) and Vivien Noakes's *Voices of Silence: The Alternative Book of First World War Poetry* (2006, Stroud: Sutton). *Voices of Silence*, with many more poems than any previous anthology, avoids all the standard authors in favour of unknown work from many sources; one thing that emerges is the irrepressible cheerfulness, if not quite 'sunny joyousness', of many soldiers.

The 1960s myth is fading at last under repeated assaults from historians, biographers and anthologists such as Vivien Noakes. The most recent anthology to date happens to be Dominic Hibberd's and John Onions' *The Winter of the World: Poems of the First World War* (2007, London: Constable). We made our new selection before we knew of *Voices of Silence*, which has 18 poems in common with ours, but the two books can perhaps be seen as complementary, together giving a very wide range of representative material. We include famous poems – even 'Into Battle' – as well as many lesser-known ones, and arrange them, for the first time in any anthology, as accurately as possible in chronological order, so that the development of the war's poetry can be followed. Our aim is to show the poetry as it was – but, like all our predecessors, we have had to select. No anthology can ever be final or, despite our publicity, definitive. There will be more.

Further Reading

Catherine Reilly's invaluable *English Poetry of the First World War: A Bibliography* (1978, London: Prior) lists 131 anthologies between 1914 and 1970, but some of these are revised editions or volumes in a series such as Georgian Poetry which happen to contain a few war poems. Reilly omits collections of consolatory or patriotic verse where the contents are pre-war, although some of those books do in fact contain wartime work. Apart from the obvious histories, biographies and critical studies, the most revealing commentaries are the introductions to the anthologies themselves, starting perhaps with W. A. Knight's *Pro Patria et Rege* (1915, London: Bennett) with its fantastical nonsense about the enemy.

Chapter 14

Disenchantment Revisited

Brian Bond

Charles Edward Montague published *Disenchantment* in February 1922. The book consisted almost entirely of articles written for the *Manchester Guardian* in 1920 and 1921. It anticipated the outpouring of what has widely been regarded as anti-war memoirs and fiction in the late 1920s but was not really part of it. As Keith Grieves has pointed out (see Further Reading section following this essay) the place of *Disenchantment* in the historiography of the Great War has been complicated by the captivating simplicity of Montague's title, which has taken on a significance largely independent of the text. The author differed from most other soldier-writers by being much older and much more idealistic at the outset, hence his more intense anger at the frustration of his hopes. By contrast Charles Carrington's memoirs, *A Subaltern's War* (1929) and *Soldier from the Wars Returning* (1965), provided a more down-to-earth and graphic account of the combat experience of the junior officers and other ranks, and their difficulties in adjusting to an alien, unwelcoming post-war world.

A brief account of Montague's pre-1914 career and wartime experience is essential to appreciate the mentality and political assumptions which permeate the pages of *Disenchantment*. Montague was born in London of Irish parents on 1 January 1867. After graduating in classics from Balliol College, Oxford, in 1889, he joined the staff of the *Manchester Guardian*, becoming Chief Leader Writer in 1896 and marrying a daughter of the distinguished editor (and later Liberal MP) C. P. Scott. Austere, somewhat puritanical and with wide literary interests, Montague espoused all the major liberal causes championed by the *Guardian* in the 1900s (including women's suffrage and Home Rule for Ireland) but disagreed sharply with Scott on the outbreak of war. Despite strong Christian convictions, Montague decided at once that war with Germany was necessary to defeat 'Prussian militarism', and through all the destruction, tragedies and siren calls for a negotiated peace without victory he never wavered from this stance. He also believed that the war must be conducted by Britain on high moral standards in order to lay the foundations for a better world.

Given his completely unmilitary background and that in 1914 he was 47 years old with a wife and seven dependent children to support, Montague's determination to serve in the ranks testifies to his idealism and spirit of self-sacrifice. He dyed his prematurely grey hair yellow and by stressing his physical fitness (he was a cyclist, tennis player and mountaineer) he gained admittance, in December 1914, to the 24th (Service) Battalion Royal Fusiliers, a unit recruited from elderly sportsmen in which he felt completely at home. A serious accident in training delayed his departure for France until the end of 1915; and after only three weeks of defensive duties in the front line in March 1916 (in a dreary sector between Bethune and Lens) he was evacuated to hospital with trench fever, never again to return to the battalion.

In June 1916 he was commissioned and posted to the Intelligence Branch of General Headquarters in France where his role was initially to escort visiting dignitaries and VIPs to witness conditions as near to the front as they cared to go. Later he additionally became a conductor and guide to the accredited war correspondents with the duty of censoring their reports. Although he appreciated the opportunity to see far more of the war than he would ever have done in a battalion, he was discontented with these non-combatant roles and comparatively comfortable life in a chateau. But he performed his duties very efficiently and never complained or queried his orders. George Bernard Shaw remarked that there was nothing soldierly about him except his uniform. Stoical and reserved, he seemed to court danger in the front line, displaying no fear of shellfire. Shaw thought he was more distressed by war's waste and futilities than its horrors, and this perception is supported by Montague's remark in a letter to his wife that he had seen nothing which did not fall within what he had always expected: 'To me carnage isn't a revelation at all – it's only a verification.' War was simply a detestable thing to be avoided by all honourable men. To the very end of the war Montague hoped to return to front line service, but he was deemed to be too old and more useful as a staff officer.

On demobilization, Montague returned to the staff of the *Manchester Guardian* but he was never restored to the coveted position of Chief Leader Writer. He was writing at a particularly grim time – a period of strikes, high unemployment and even fear of revolution which made the wartime sacrifices seem to have been in vain. While he was undoubtedly angry and disillusioned about several important aspects of the war, and even more by the peace negotiations, by publishing his *Guardian* articles with scarcely any modification or linking passages he produced a scattergun effect which made his criticisms seem harsher, more sweeping and partisan than he had intended. As early as April 1922, in a letter to a friend, Montague admitted that in his book he had got the balance wrong. He had intended to give equal weight to national failures ('miserable sinners') and positive hopes of pulling through the present crisis. But he had put too much stress on negative aspects and this impression was strengthened by the one-sided title which ought to have been *A Near Thing* or *A Warning* rather than a suggestion of irreparable failure. His apprehension was justified because his title was seized upon by numerous later authors to associate him with the school of thought which held the Great War to be a ghastly and costly mistake. As Keith Grieves aptly remarks, 'One might be forgiven for expressing surprise that *Disenchantment* was not a prime source for *Oh What a Lovely War!*'

In discussing Montague's main criticisms of British conduct in the years 1914–21, which he saw as a coherent period, it needs to be underlined that he was a very intelligent, literary journalist (with a special interest in the theatre), and a man of sincere Christian and Liberal beliefs, but he was neither a professional soldier nor a historian. He brought these qualities and principles to bear on the harshest period of attrition in what approximated to a total war on the Western Front. He combined criticism of general shortcomings in moral standards, professional competence and integrity in politics, the press, the Church and the army, illustrated with anecdotes, analogies and reflections, but displayed little interest in the tactical and strategic problems and how they were tackled. In sum, his choice of themes was highly selective and personal in an episodic book which did not attempt to provide a comprehensive commentary on the war.

For the idealistic volunteers of 1914 it was a crucial

assumption that the war would be short and decisive. Montague was one of a vast number who bemoaned the fact that the war went on for far too long with the result that ideals were compromised and hopes were thwarted so that staleness and tedium set in long before the anti-climax of eventual victory. Like Siegfried Sassoon he satirized 'Base Details' to which there gravitated 'most of the walking wreckage and wastage, physical and moral, of active warfare ... men found too old or too young for trench work ... and malingerers triumphant and chuckling'. Whereas in 1914 it was a safe assumption that men behind the lines wanted to get at the enemy as soon as they could, now in 1916 or 1917 the presumption was that such men wanted to stay out of danger for as long as possible. 'Faith has fallen lame; generosity flags; there has entered into the soul as well as the body the malady known to athletes as staleness.'

Montague idolized and idealized the New Army of keen volunteers like himself but came to feel that its potential to offer vigour and fresh ideas had been smothered by the old regular army which feared being overrun by hosts of amateurs, including some of the best brains of the country, lacking 'professional habits' of mind but 'almost indecently ready to use new and outlandish means' for new problems. The old army won, retaining all the high commands like personal property or livings, while the Territorials and New Army 'toiled at the coolie jobs of its household'. Never, he noted (inaccurately), had senior commands been retained so triumphantly in the hands of the cavalry and the Guards.

He was on firmer ground in asserting that conscription (to which he was deeply opposed on principle) brought dilution and lower standards to the originally superb New Army battalions. Nine out of ten conscripts might be sound but the tenth would have the effect of a rotten apple in a barrel. As he correctly pointed out, as did later writers like Charles Carrington, the better battalions were thrown into battle again and again, losing their original members several times over. This attritional process was bound to result, he felt, in reduced combat efficiency and lower morale.

Although he adopted a very tolerant and charitable view about alleged German atrocities, taking delight for example in exposing the propaganda story of human 'soap factories' as a myth, he deplored the general decline in chivalry as the war progressed. Always championing the basic decency of the ordinary Tommy, he argued that the inculcation of blind hatred of the enemy and rumours of atrocities were mostly generated by the press and by propaganda originating far from the front. He was nauseated by stories of officers who condoned or even encouraged the murder of enemy prisoners or of men trying to surrender. But he had to acknowledge that the British did commit atrocities and that 'the chivalrous temper had had a set-back'. His overriding concern throughout the war was that the eventual Allied victory would be fatally tarnished if it was achieved in part through the brutal methods which propaganda attributed to the Germans.

Montague was very critical of certain civilian groups and institutions who, he felt, were behaving shabbily and letting down the moral standards which should characterize British society in wartime. What he termed 'your virilist chaplains', for example, employed bloodthirsty phrases which outshone any actual combatant, regretting that the killing was not to go on until a few German towns had been smashed and 'our last thing in gas had had a fair innings!' He allowed that the chaplains did many good turns and handed out tobacco, but they failed to provide any spiritual inspiration: he quoted Milton to the effect that, 'The hungry sheep looked up and were not fed.'

As for the press and its reporting of the war from France, he knew from personal experience what a difficult time the correspondents had had: in getting anywhere near the action, understanding what was happening, and, most difficult of all, reporting the truth as they saw it. Treated like pariahs by GHQ in the first year or so of the war, a select number were then transformed into privileged favourites of the staff but then found it virtually impossible to criticize senior commanders. Most journalists, he admitted, did their best and behaved with integrity, but a few reported imaginary events or blandly described 'the most bloody defeat in the history of Britain' (that is, 1 July 1916) as quite a good day, indeed almost a victory. What most infuriated the troops was 'a certain jauntiness of tone' which suggested that they enjoyed nothing better than going 'over the top', and that a battle was just a 'rough, jovial picnic'. He concluded this section with the remark that millions of ex-servicemen had completely lost their trust in the press and took the line, 'You can't believe a word you read.'

When applying the word 'disenchantment' to the Houses of Parliament and British statesmen generally, Montague found nothing to say in defence or mitigation. Too many politicians of military age had demanded the forced enlistment of others while evading military service themselves. Statesmen had utterly forfeited the trust of soldiers by their false promises of creating a 'land fit for heroes to live in'. Quite the contrary, 'every disease which victory was to cure he sees raging worse than before: more poverty, less liberty, more likelihood of other wars, more spite between master and man, less national comradeship'.

In a remarkable rant which completely ignored the myriad problems (many of them intractable) facing the peacemakers at Versailles, he described it as the meanest of treaties. He believed that by adopting a vindictive and punitive attitude towards the beaten enemy we had 'won the fight and lost the prize; the garland of the war was withered before it was gained'. Hundreds of thousands had died in vain in the belief that their monument would be a new Europe 'not soured or soiled with the hates and greeds of old'. However, the spirit of Prussia was blowing anew from strange (that is, English) mouths: 'Beaten out of the field, Prussia had won in the souls of her conquerors' rulers; they had become her pupils.'

Montague seems to be at his angriest and least objective in his tirade against the pre-war deficiencies of British officers' training and education which had completely unfitted them to cope with the abattoir of trench warfare. Instead they had ushered herds of the 'common people' down narrowing corridors of barbed wire into some gap that had all the German machine guns raking its exit. He admitted that 'all of ourselves' must share responsibility because of our boastful chatter about the public school spirit and our gallant contempt for 'swats', but had he or his fellow journalists at the *Manchester Guardian* taken any interest in the size and professional standards of the pre-war army? Historians might accept that there was an element of truth in these charges but would point to the enormous, unavoidable problems caused by the rapid expansion of the peacetime force of 200,000 to the vast continental army of more than two million men. They might also ask whether, faced with the new challenge of mass industrialized warfare, the generals of the much larger European armies had performed markedly better. Montague had allowed that Britain had produced a few good generals, such as Plumer, but the majority were 'asses' who had failed to give decent leadership to the 'lions' of the rank and file. In the end victory had only been achieved under a foreign Commander-in-Chief (Marshal Foch) supported by America's inexhaustible numbers.

Although there was some truth in most of Montague's criticisms, his newspaper articles constituted an extreme, one-sided case for the prosecution. As a very intelligent soldier-journalist he had observed many aspects of the war from a privileged vantage point between 1916 and 1918. He had witnessed directly the enormous problems of adapting to an unexpected form of static siege warfare by a rapidly expanded Expeditionary Force far greater than Britain had ever mobilized before. Moreover Britain had had limited room for manoeuvre, in every sense, as the junior partner in an alliance. Montague chose to stress that victory had come too late from an idealist's viewpoint, but he must have known that as late as mid-1918 it was still uncertain that victory could be secured at all against so formidable an opponent as Imperial Germany. At the time of writing, in 1920 and 1921, he had cause to be thankful that, for all the disappointments he had emphasized, Britain and her Western Allies had not been defeated. In lamenting the disappearance or degradation of many pre-war liberal (and Liberal party) ideals and practical advantages, Montague at times adopted a shrill tone which, as even his friend and biographer Oliver Elton hinted, was less effective than the 'plain stuff' of his diaries and letters. Indeed in 1921 Montague 'knowingly occupied a marginalized stance on the war' in presenting the viewpoint of an angry and depressed but by no means hopeless liberal idealist. His 'disenchantment' related much more closely to his wartime hopes and expectations and to disappointment with the post-war world than to later and very varied 'war literature' with which the term has often been too closely associated.

In 1929 Charles Carrington published, under the pseudonym 'Charles Edmonds', memoirs of his experiences in the First World War which had been written ten years earlier. With his former comrades in mind he sought to counter 'the uniform disillusion of most authors of war books'. Readers needed to be reminded that among the millions who had served there were other types than 'Prussian militarists' and the equally conventional 'disillusioned pessimists'. In his account there would be no disenchantment: 'No corrupt sergeant majors stole my rations or lodging. No casual staff officers ordered me to certain death, indifferent to my fate.'

In 1965 Carrington returned to the subject in *Soldier from the*

Wars Returning, surveying Britain's role in the war from a much broader perspective and providing a much fuller account of his own military career. He remained convinced that Britain's cause had been just, that the nation had reason to be proud of the army's achievement.

Charles Carrington was born at West Bromwich in 1897 but moved as a young boy to New Zealand where his father became dean of Christchurch. His family background was cultured and upper middle class. He achieved literary distinction with his biography of *Rudyard Kipling* (1955); two of his brothers and a sister would also publish scholarly books; and his eldest brother became archbishop of Quebec, primate of All Canada. Charles was educated at Christ's College, Canterbury, but returned to England shortly before the outbreak of the First World War to prepare for taking a scholarship examination for Oxford or Cambridge.

Although under age he at once enlisted in the ranks of a service battalion of the Royal Warwickshire Regiment but soon began to fear that the war would be over long before his unit would be ready for active service. He eventually sailed to France in December 1915 with the 5th Battalion, Royal Warwicks. He was still under 19 years old and, on his own admission, a somewhat romantic and innocent young man. Full of excitement and eager to experience the real war after more than a year of dreary training and disappointments in England, Carrington was fortunate to spend six months in a comparatively 'cushy' part of the line opposite the formidable enemy fortified stronghold of Gommecourt before being plunged into the very centre of the Somme offensive in July 1916 at La Boisselle and Ovillers.

Shortly after demobilization in 1919 he wrote a concise account of his part in this battle and in that of Passchendaele in October 1917. Using war diaries and other confidential battalion papers, as well as his personal journal and letters, he strove to recapture the vivid personal experience while it was still fresh in his memory, realizing, most perceptively, that in ten years' time recollections would have faded and later considerations would inevitably creep in. He aimed to be completely honest, ridding himself alike of modesty and shame. He was too diffident to hope that the two essays were publishable, but changed his mind when the sudden spate of war books began to appear in the late 1920s. In the epilogue to *A Subaltern's War* Carrington launched a bold counter-attack against what he took to be the characteristic theme of disenchantment in the current outpouring of war books. He entitled this vigorous riposte 'An Essay on Militarism', using the word not pejoratively but rather to mean the soldiers' viewpoint and their patriotic pride in the army and its achievements in a necessary and just war.

Carrington felt strongly that his generation of young soldiers was being misunderstood and misrepresented. They had not gone to war gaily in 1914 in the spirit of Rupert Brooke only to lose their faith amid the horrors of the trenches and to return in a mood of anger and despair. On the contrary, though loath to speak of their experience and to do so – if at all – with a sort of rough cynicism, they were not disenchanted. War could indeed deal terrible blows but these, he argued, fell more on the group than the individual. Fighting side by side created a sense of being initiated and of a shared inner life. Moreover, not only unpleasant emotions had to be borne; courage and comfort could also be fostered by the shared experience of the company. It was also dishonest to deny that war could yield moments of intense happiness. The unluckiest soldiers, whose leave was always stopped, who never had a 'Blighty wound', still spent only a comparatively few days in combat of the most horrible kind. These intense episodes sharpened the senses and made the intervals correspondingly delightful. Young men, he pointed out, like adventures and could experience the thrill of excitement even amid the dangers at the front. There was above all the special bond of comradeship 'richer, stronger in war than we have ever known since'.

Which authors, in Carrington's opinion, had introduced the legend of 'disenchantment'? C. E. Montague with his 'charming' book of that title had clearly popularized the key term, but Henri Barbusse's *Under Fire* (1916) had already set the agenda with his unremittingly bleak account of meaningless suffering 'which would not allow any redeeming features in a soldier's life'. Also he briefly mentions Erich Maria Remarque whose hugely popular best-seller *All Quiet on the Western Front* had only appeared in English translation a few months earlier in March 1929.

Carrington reserved his sharpest criticisms for H. G. Wells whose topical novel *Mr Britling Sees It Through* (1916) ought, he wrote, to have been called 'Mr Wells does not see it through'. The anti-hero, Mr Britling, had welcomed the advent of war in a heroic spirit but had lost his nerve in the calamities of 1916 and become a flabby, verbose defeatist. Carrington suggested that

Britling's loss of confidence and change of stance reflected H. G. Wells's own volte-face.

He was clearly very angry with writers who denounced war on account of the discomfort in the trenches, who 'gloat over the mud and the cold, the filth and the disease, making them the principal charges against the decency of a soldier's life'. War's trinity of horrors – discomfort, fear and death – had to be endured: 'those who bear the greatest suffering survive, and it is this which supplies the heroic element even in modern war'. He becomes rather shrill in denouncing comfortable folk who hate war because it shakes them out of their routine and who can only imagine its negative aspects of suffering and destruction.

Although he does not name him in this context, he clearly has C. E. Montague and similar idealists in mind when rebutting the charge of disenchantment on the soldiers' part. At the outset he and his comrades knew that they had a simple duty and a Herculean task. At the end the game seemed to have been hard and the prize small. 'No golden age of virtue triumphant and vice defeated rewarded our toil, but then I do not remember that we ever expected such results.' At the lowest ebb in 1917 British soldiers were not disillusioned but simply 'fed up'. As they grew war-weary so their doggedness hardened, and there was no widespread loss of belief in the cause. He rightly predicted that if a similar challenge arose in the future, as indeed it would a decade later, the great majority of British citizens would fight and endure all over again.

Perhaps the most important point in this epilogue was his perception that 1919 was 'the maddest year of all', the real moment of disenchantment. The spell which had bound him and his comrades for such a long time was suddenly broken; an illusion came crashing down about their ears and left them in an unfamiliar world. Millions of soldiers keyed up to an unnatural pitch of determination found the tension relaxed so suddenly as to throw them off balance. Because the future was so uncertain, soldiers had learnt to live for the present, grasping avidly at any transient pleasure. Suddenly they were living 'after the war' with a very uncertain future; friends had dispersed and they had to earn a living in a world where a huge gulf was opening up between wartime hopes inflated by propaganda and the harsh realities of life on 'civvy street'. Hundreds of thousands of young men like Carrington had suffered hardships and borne responsibilities scarcely imaginable to non-combatants, but they had known no other adult life. Consequently, he concluded, 'Dis-illusion came in with peace, not with war, peace at first was the futile state.' In war there had been a clear, overriding objective, but peace seemed to lead nowhere: it was anticlimax. He con-cluded with a rhetorical question: if the war had been such a disastrous and, ultimately, futile event why had he and his fel-lows been such fools as to take part in it? His answer, simple enough at the time, though not so obvious in retrospect, was because there was absolutely no other course open to a plain, honest man.

Carrington concluded his later reflections, *Soldier from the Wars Returning*, with an epilogue which was bold and opinio-nated. He reminded his readers that the national mood in Britain had been exhilarating and idealistic because strategic necessity and the highest principles of combat pointed the same way: 'For once in life the plain practical issue coincided with the moral issue.' There was no doubt about what ought to be done and -- to his generation -- the prospect of danger and discomfort gave an additional spur. Neither the government nor the people had wanted war with Germany but the latter's barbarous conduct had been critical. But in taking on the character of a crusade, British conduct of the war had assumed another characteristic of the original Crusades, as 'a squalid series of confused episodes' in which it was hard to perceive that one side's conduct was more virtuous than the other's.

The intransigence of the German High Command had ruled out a negotiated peace so Britain had had no alternative to fighting on until victory was eventually won. The author admits that in 1919 he held political views which many would find indefensible (but which find considerable endorsement from historians now), namely that far from being too harsh on Ger-many, the terms of the Treaty of Versailles had been too mild. In particular, her war leaders should have been prosecuted and publicly humiliated as were their successors after the Second World War at Nuremburg.

Carrington also made an important distinction between win-ning the war and disappointment with its political legacy that is still not generally understood, or not accepted, to this day. The British war effort had, in essentials, achieved the original political objectives: Belgium and the occupied provinces of France had been liberated; Germany's military tyranny removed; and the threat to Britain and her Empire apparently ended. If Europe in general was in a worse state after 1918 than before that was not the fault of the British forces and people who had won the war.

These two eloquent, reflective volumes reveal Charles Carrington to have been very much a man of his time: born into a devoutly Christian family and temperamentally more a scholar than a career soldier, he was also an unashamed patriot and imperialist. He remained proud of his military service in both world wars and convinced that Britain had had no honourable alternative but to enter them and keep fighting until victories were achieved. For a generation which may not share his values Carrington's memoirs nevertheless deserve to be read for their depiction of the character of the British Army and the profound, positive influences which military service exerted on a generation of volunteer civilians in uniform.

Montague's memorable title, *Disenchantment*, and his strongly expressed conviction that the British Tommies were 'lions' led by an incompetent officer corps of 'donkeys', have profoundly affected critical views of the First World War as badly mismanaged and ultimately futile. Carrington and other authors in the 1920s and 1930s, whose approach was more sympathetic towards the army (or more precisely towards their old battalions), have perhaps been less influential with the general public but much better regarded by historians such as the late John Terraine, Gary Sheffield, Hugh Cecil and the present writer.

More importantly, it is now better understood than in the 1930s, or even the 1960s, that labels like disenchanted, disillusioned or anti-war are simplistic and unhelpful. Nearly every author of war memoirs or war fiction was 'anti-war' in deploring destruction and heavy losses, but most, including Siegfried Sassoon, had been gallant officers and were certainly not pacifists. They were also imaginative, skilful writers who had reacted more sensitively than the vast majority of ordinary soldiers. Consequently, they cannot safely be assumed to represent the latter's reactions either to the war itself or the post-war world.

Further Reading

The literature of the First World War, in the widest sense, remains of continuing interest to both historians and literary critics. Their approaches and interpretations, particularly as regards the war on the Western Front, differ sharply. Correlli Barnett raised some critical issues in *The Collapse of British Power* (1972, London: Eyre Methuen) by his vigorous argument that middle-class officer-authors had greatly exaggerated the discomforts and horrors because, in contrast to the other ranks, they had led pampered and sheltered lives. He also suggested that the defeatist tone of much of the literature had contributed to the disastrous spirit of appeasement in the 1930s. Hugh Cecil, in a brilliant pioneering book, *The Flower of Battle: British Fiction Writers of the First World War* (1995, London: Secker and Warburg), and in several contributions to edited volumes, including P. Liddle's (ed.) *Home Fires and Foreign Fields* (1985, London: Brassey's Defence Publishers), showed that fiction could be very valuable to historians both for descriptions of combat and for revelations about the imaginative mental life of soldiers. He also demonstrated the remarkable variety of the genre, stressing that the tone of the majority of publications continued for several decades to be upbeat and patriotic rather then bitter or pessimistic. Brian Bond in *The Unquiet Western Front* (2002, Cambridge: CUP; paperback edition 2007, Cambridge: CUP) argued that historical interpretations taking a positive line about Britain's role in the war had been overshadowed by the literary and cultural approaches which emphasized appalling conditions, unacceptable casualties and suffering, and the 'futility' of the outcome. He concluded that there was still a disturbing gap between the views of most military historians and those purveyed by the media as evidenced by the stage entertainment and film *Oh What a Lovely War*, the *Blackadder* television series and overemphasis on the poetry of Wilfred Owen. More recently these controversies have been impressively surveyed from a different angle by Dan Todman in *The Great War: Myth and Memory* (2005, London: Hambledon and London).

Although uneven in its treatment of war literature and historically unreliable, Paul Fussell's *The Great War and Modern Memory* (1975, New York: OUP) has deservedly been influential, especially for his perceptive discussions of some of the best-known writers, including Robert Graves, Siegfried Sassoon and Edmund Blunden. Also recommended for their literary and cultural insights in an international setting are Modris Eksteins' *Rites of Spring* (1989, London: Bantam Press) and Samuel Hynes' *A War Imagined* (1990, London: Bodley Head). Andrew Rutherford's *The Literature of War* (1978, London: Macmillan) contains an excellent discussion of Frederic Manning which illustrates the inappropriateness of labels such as 'anti war'. C. E. Montague's career was the subject of an early *Memoir* by Oliver Elton in 1929 (London: Chatto & Windus), a year after his death, but the modern authority is Keith Grieves who contributed his entry in the *Dictionary of National Biography* and published a scholarly article about his book *Disenchantment* in *War in History* (Vol. 4, Number 1, 1997). Hugh Cecil, Brian Bond and Keith Grieves all contributed relevant essays to Hugh Cecil and Peter H. Liddle's (eds) *Facing Armageddon* (1996, Barnsley: Pen and Sword). Finally, Brian Bond has discussed Charles Carrington's books at greater length with other First World War memoirs in *Survivors of a Kind*, to be published by Continuum in 2008.

Chapter 15

Life-Writing and Fiction in First World War Prose

Max Saunders

The received view of the literature of the First World War is that it is essentially about truth-telling. The representative writers were the poets and memoirists: the poets writing anti-lyrics during the war, blasting what Charles Hamilton Sorley called 'the sentimental attitude' of writers like Rupert Brooke or the authors of patriotic magazine verse glorifying sacrifice; the writers of memoirs returning to the war with bitter irony and disillusion, often after a long silence, and from the period of another crisis which seemed to give the lie to liberal assurances: the Depression.

According to this view, both types of writer were bearing witness to the war's sufferings and offering their testimony to counter any attempts to justify war, whether in the past or the future. Even when a novelist of our day returns to the war – such as Pat Barker in her *Ghost Road* trilogy – it is Wilfred Owen (iconic First War poet) and Siegfried Sassoon (both a major war poet and writer of a key war-memoir) who are the central literary figures. I don't by any means dispute the achievement of writers like Owen and Sassoon, but I want to suggest that the map of First World War literature becomes much more complex when one asks what happens when fiction is admitted.

From one point of view if the function of the literature is to bear witness, fiction is a scandal. It becomes a particular kind of scandal when a book ostensibly recording autobiographical testimony turns out to have been faked – as in the case of Binjamin Wilkomirski's purported Holocaust memoir *Fragments: Memories of a Wartime Childhood 1939–1948* (1995), subsequently exposed as a fraud. Yet even when not presented fraudulently, the

fictionalization of massive cultural trauma can seem objectionable. It might be judged tactless or tasteless; it might be considered disrespectful towards the victims; impious or even
blasphemous. It is again the Holocaust that has generated most
such arguments: not just arguments about the representability of
such mass inhumanity, but about the ethics of trying to represent
it at all. One way of describing such responses – the way chosen
by Peter Novick in his book *The Holocaust in American Life*
(1999) – is to see a shift in the cultural construction of the event,
as it passes from the 'historical' to the 'sacred'. This is a controversial position to take over the Holocaust. Though Novick is
explicit that his work should not be taken as aligning him with
those denying the Holocaust took place, he does critique the
forms of institutionalization, and especially what he calls
'sacralisation' of it in contemporary American cultural life.

While such ideas might seem a distraction from the literature
of the First World War, in fact the major shifts in thinking about
that literature have come about precisely as a result of post-
Holocaust theory. Indeed, Holocaust studies and trauma studies
have revolutionized how we think about the First World War.
This is visible in four related areas: trauma; representability;
memorialization; and sacralization.

The view of the First World War as propagated in the 1960s
and 1970s – exemplified in works such as the play *Oh! What a
Lovely War* (1963) or Paul Fussell's *The Great War and Modern
Memory* (1975) – was essentially one of the literature as political
protest: protest against what was seen as the betrayal of the
young and the socially docile by their elders and leaders, through
either deceit or stupidity. In many ways this view was a product
of the 1930s and 1940s, combining the position of many intellectuals between the wars who were disillusioned by the
Depression and drawn towards Marxism to counter the rise of
fascism, with the post-Second World War socialist-leaning
consensus.

Since the 1970s this view of the war as political tragedy has
largely been replaced by one of it as psychological trauma. From
one point of view this is indicative of our predominantly psy-
chotherapeutic times, which prefer counselling to political acti-
vism or the 'stiff upper lip'. But from another point of view, this
shift has itself been influenced by the Holocaust. The belated
appearance of Holocaust memoirs repeated the pattern whereby
the celebrated First World War memoirs – Edmund Blunden's

Undertones of War (1928), Robert Graves's *Goodbye to All That* (1929), Siegfried Sassoon's *Memoirs of an Infantry Officer* (1930) – didn't appear until at least a decade after the war had ended. Clinical opinion shifted from speaking of 'shell shock', and understanding it as a result of physical blast and concussion, to diagnosing 'post-traumatic stress disorder' – very much as a result of the treatment of traumatized veterans of both wars. The Holocaust was a different kind of atrocity from the trenches of the Western Front. But what has emerged more clearly from considering them together has been the agonizing double-bind the survivors find themselves in: compulsively re-living what they would much rather forget; compelled to bear witness to the sufferings they saw, but unable to find a register that seems to do justice to the enormity of the horror; alienated from their dead friends and family, and overcome with survivor's guilt; but equally alienated from the living, who can never know their experiences.

The aftermath of the Holocaust has also caused a reappraisal of thinking about the memorialization of historical tragedy. Memorializing the Holocaust has become an ethical imperative, adding the hope of preventing future catastrophe to the traditional rationale for memorials, of honouring the dead 'Lest we forget'. The designing of Holocaust museums, civic monuments and memorial works of art has become an intensely contested postmodern field. This has in turn shifted the attention of historians of the First World War to the ways in which that conflict was memorialized – not only in the form of war memorials and war graves but in terms of how historical events pass into cultural memory. A representative example is Jay Winter's book *Sites of Memory, Sites of Mourning: The Great War in European Cultural History* (1995).

While it may have taken World War Two and its aftermath to reappraise World War One, the process also reveals how partial the protest-theory of the First War was. It enables us to see how, to a large extent, the post-World War Two trauma-theory view, and culture of memorialization, was in fact prepared by the aftermath of World War One. When we look again at the literature of the First War, we can now see in it qualities that have been neglected. For example, Pat Barker's trilogy seems a document of the late twentieth century, placing at the heart of its story the experience of trauma; the psychoanalytic treatment pioneered by W. H. R. Rivers; and sexuality. Yet if we turn to one of the best fictional works of the war – the series of four novels by Ford Madox Ford, known collectively as *Parade's End* (1924–28) – we find a traumatized protagonist, Christopher Tietjens, whose shell shock has produced amnesia as well as haunting visions of the soldier O Nine Morgan who dies bleeding in his arms. In Tietjens' mind the World War is tangled up with the war that his marriage has become. His glamorous wife Sylvia is one of the most striking characters in modernist fiction, and pursues Christopher to his base depot in France to taunt him and humiliate him with her adulteries with other officers.

For Ford, the crisis of memory is not only personal; it is about the memory or amnesia of a whole culture. Another of *Parade's End*'s brilliant characters, Valentine Wannop, a suffragette who eventually becomes Tietjens' lover, is teaching in a school on the day of the Armistice, as the teachers worry that people will get out of control during the celebrations. She thinks of the war and its ending as 'this crack across the table of History' – an event which doesn't only separate historical periods but disintegrates the medium of history itself. For an experimental writer like Ford, this also means that the medium of fiction can never be the same. One of the curious features of *Parade's End* is that its style develops through the course of the series, as the old modes of the historical novel and classic realism are abandoned in favour of chronological disruption (Ford developed with his friend Joseph Conrad what he called the 'time shift' in narrative), surrealism, stream of consciousness and interior monologue.

Where a novel like Richard Aldington's powerful *Death of a Hero* (1929) reads as a more discursive diatribe against the madness of the war, Ford's tetralogy is profoundly ambivalent. Though Tietjens' patrician, ironic intellect is cynical about politicians and their motives, he believes in the need to defend France, in patriotism, and in honour. One reason for *Parade's End*'s relative neglect until recently is perhaps that these things made it look anachronistic. It is an attempt to represent and understand the war, and to write its elegy, rather than to protest. Yet we can now see that Ford is truer to the spirit of his times, truer to the motives of the millions of men who enlisted.

Parade's End and *Death of a Hero* are both revealing about the forces that make for sacralization too. The war dead are conceived in terms of a vast blood-sacrifice, akin to Christian sacrifice for some writers (like Ford) or to the bloodshed of ancient Greek tragedy (for Aldington). Instead of redemption, however, the blood-letting brings blood-guilt. Where Ford sees regeneration as requiring a return to the natural world (which had also been disfigured and devastated), Aldington writes of the need for atonement. He rails against the official, institutionalized forms this takes – Remembrance Day, the two minutes' silence – because for him the scale of the disaster is too immense for any such rituals to be adequate forms of atonement.

Though Aldington doesn't use the term, his book is a critique of an already sacralized memorialization of the war; and he offers his protagonist George Winterbourne's story of sexual complications, mental disturbance, despair and ultimate futile suicide as a counter-story to the rhetoric of the unknown soldier and heroic sacrifice. To read such books now – when so few participants are still alive, the need for personal mourning has largely passed and the event has passed from personal to cultural memory – is to wonder about the survival of the rituals and ceremonies (what Ford calls 'parades'). For as the ideas of trenches and their battles, 'No Man's Land' and 'going over the top' have passed into our mythology, so the places – the sections of preserved or overgrown trenches in Flanders, or those reconstructed in museums or for 'reality' television programmes; and the war cemeteries and memorials – have become sacred sites: places schoolchildren are taken on pilgrimages. It would be pushing the argument too far, perhaps, to suggest that some of the war poems have become sacred texts. But they are certainly more widely taught and known than any others, and widely venerated.

If the sacralization of the First World War has tended to privilege testimonial writing over fictional treatments, nevertheless fictions such as these show the origins of that process of sacralization. And that in turn casts a new light on other literary works from the war. Even the most bitter and angry of the war poems – Owen's 'Anthem for Doomed Youth' or 'Dulce et Decorum Est', say – turn on these questions of the sacralization of horror. Certainly such works rage against warmongering patriotic cliché. But their point isn't to denounce the idea of sacrifice or heroism or sacralization but to denounce false versions of them. When Owen writes 'What passing bells for these who die as cattle', it is clear that conventional religious and pastoral forms of elegy won't suffice any more than the discourse that claims all death in war as 'glorious', or 'heroic'. What he isn't saying, though, is that these men who die inhuman and incomprehensible deaths shouldn't be memorialized; merely that a proper memorialization will bear witness to the atrocities and inhumanities they endured, and will express grief and pity for horror rather than producing redemptive aestheticizations. In a sense, all these writers reverse the process by which losses in battle are claimed to be redeemed through sacralization. Instead of glorifying the military in conventional terms of sacredness, they redefine the truly sacred as appalling suffering in battle – both physical and mental.

If the post-traumatic version of the war has led to neglect of the novels of the war, it has also caused us to disattend to the fictionalizations of memoir itself (and arguably even poetry). It is surprising how some of the best-known First World War memoirs engage with the question of fiction, and emerge out of attempts to fictionalize war experiences. Vera Brittain explains in the Foreword to *Testament of Youth* (1933) how she had originally planned to write 'a long novel', but to her 'dismay it turned out a hopeless failure', because 'the people and the events' she was writing about 'were still too near and too real to be made the subjects of an imaginative, detached reconstruction'. Robert Graves, too, describes how 'In 1916, when on leave in England after being wounded' he began writing his account of his first few months in France in fictional form: 'Having stupidly written it as a novel', he said, he had in *Goodbye to All That* 'to re-translate it into history'.

A comparable commerce between fiction and autobiography can be seen in Sassoon's *Memoirs of an Infantry Officer*, which gives its account of Sassoon's life as 'George Sherston', who shares Sassoon's war experiences but not his poetic vocation. In it Sassoon quotes from his diaries written in the trenches. The effect is to ground the narrative in immediate testimony. Yet Sassoon's own diaries, which have since been published, reveal something arresting. He often describes himself in the third person, as if he needed to view himself as a character in a novel, in order to write about his experiences. The diary is thus already fictionalized. The diary extracts in the *Memoirs* have then been rewritten – re-fictionalised; retranslated into history – in order to make them sound more autobiographical. Not all life-writing plays such complex games with intertextuality and inter-generi-ity, but most examples of war memoirs do something of the sort.

Ford went through a comparable, tortuous process of becoming able to write about his experiences on the Somme and the Ypres Salient. He too began a novel, then abandoned it. Then he produced a curious fusion of memoir and fiction. *No Enemy* (written before *Parade's End* but not published until 1929) is disconcertingly oblique about the horrors of war, instead screening them behind intense visual impressionism, whereby traumatic memory is dissolved into a sequence of landscapes and interiors. He is more concerned with the after-effects, and what he calls 'the painful processes of Reconstruction', splitting his narrative between the personae of a poet called 'Gringoire' (who has had many of Ford's war experiences) and an anonymous 'Compiler', who interviews him.

The experience of modern total war was so unlike anything in everyday life that it not only provoked disturbances in psychology, society and history but troubled the categories of their representation, whether in autobiography or fiction. In *Goodbye to All That* Robert Graves tells how he was erroneously reported as killed in action. This fictional death allows him to create an ironic myth of his immortality, while paradoxically writing goodbye to his pre-war self. In her extraordinary book *The Forbidden Zone* (1929), Mary Borden (who had set up a mobile field hospital in France) produced a heavily stylized and aestheticized set of modernist vignettes, which read like short stories. Of course the best prose of the war is profoundly autobiographical. R. H. Mottram's *The Spanish Farm Trilogy* (1924–26) and Frederic Manning's *Her Privates We* (1930) should be added to the novels already discussed. But for creative writers it was as if war's surreal qualities demanded fictionalization to begin to capture them.

Further Reading

Linda Anderson's *Autobiography* (2001, London and New York: Routledge) gives a good account of what trauma studies has brought to the theory of life-writing. *Cultural Memory Studies: An International and Interdisciplinary Handbook,* edited by Astrid Erll and Ansgar Nünning (2007, Berlin / New York: de Gruyter), is a useful reference work on the field and includes my essay on the relations between autobiography and cultural memory. For a further discussion of the idea of sacralization, and also of Mary Borden, see Saunders, 'Autobiography and World War: Pleasure, Sacralization, and Testimony: the case of Mary Borden' in *Memories and Representations of War: The Case of WW1 and*

WW2, edited by Vita Fortunati and Elena Lamberti (forthcoming, Rodopi). A good anthology of war prose is *The Penguin Book of First World War Prose*, edited by Jon Glover and Jon Silkin (1990, London: Penguin). Two of Samuel Hynes' books are indispensable on this topic: *A War Imagined: The First World War and English Culture* (1990, London: The Bodley Head) and *The Soldier's Tale* (1998, London: Pimlico). For the developments in psychological theories of war trauma, see Simon Wessely and Edgar Jones, eds, *Shell Shock to PTSD: Military Psychiatry from 1900 to the Gulf War* (2005, London: Psychology Press). Daniel Pick's *War Machine: The Rationalisation of Slaughter in the Modern Age* (1993, New Haven and London: Yale UP) and Trudi Tate's *Modernism, History and the First World War* (1998, Manchester: Manchester UP) are both excellent cultural and critical studies, as is Vincent Sherry's *The Great War and the Language of Modernism* (2004, Oxford: OUP).

Chapter 16

Oral History and the First World War

Lyn Macdonald

The First World War has left a unique legacy of oral recollection, for large numbers of the men who had fought and returned survived well into the age of technology when their words could be recorded, preserved and heard by future generations.

But it was many years before they spoke at all. In the years immediately following the Great War there was no lack of information in the form of memoirs and novels, but they were mainly written by officers and frequently by professional writers (Blunden, Sassoon, Sheriff, Erich Maria Remarques, Ernst Renn et al.). The 'ordinary soldier' contributed little to the mass of published material, although many wrote private memoirs which only came to light years later. They were not necessarily less literate than their 'superiors' who had been commissioned, for with five million men serving sequentially in the fighting forces a significant proportion of middle-class and professional men were in the ranks. It was furthermore the age of universal education and even those who had left school at fourteen after an elementary education had received a thorough grounding in the three Rs. But in the aftermath of the war, through the hard years of the 1920s and slowly-recovering 1930s the energies of most ex-soldiers were concentrated on holding down a job, building a career, providing for a family.

And then the Second World War erupted when those very young men who had served in the first were still in their prime, and if they were not directly involved in a military capacity (and many of them were), they were absorbed in other ways. 'Their' war had been overtaken and no one, it seemed, was interested. The monster Hitler out-monstered the Kaiser and, in the popular mind, the unimaginable obscenities of the extermination camps far outstripped the horrors of Passchendaele and Verdun.

Over the next 20 years the image of a 'good' and heroic war was reinforced by a torrent of reminiscences, books, plays and films, fictional and otherwise.

The revival of interest came in 1964, when the BBC marked the 50th anniversary of the outbreak of the First World War with its magnificent television series *The Great War*, in which, for the first time, veterans were seen and heard describing their experiences. The elderly do not tend to talk in the 'sound bites' beloved by the modern media and their words were extracted from much longer versions which, to the shame of the BBC, were later discarded.

But the series sparked renewed interest in the First World War and as it burgeoned and grew, the veterans, now in retirement, began to talk and discovered, to their modest surprise, that people were eager to listen. In 1974 when I trawled for First World War veterans to take part in a radio documentary and also to contribute to a book, there were literally thousands of replies. It was the start of a career-change and 30 years spent talking to old soldiers, recording their experiences and writing about their war. It was not the war as recorded in history books, or the honed and polished political or military memoirs written in hindsight and with one eye on the judgement of posterity. In all its warts-and-all reality this was the raw experience of war.

Old soldiers have always told tales of battle. As Shakespeare famously put it in the words of Henry V, 'He that shall live this day, and see old age will yearly on the vigil feast his neighbours, and say "Tomorrow is Saint Crispian." Then will he strip his sleeve and show his scars, and say "These wounds I had on Crispin's day." Old men forget: yet all shall be forgot, But he'll remember with advantages what feats he did that day.'

So, did they 'remember with advantages'? Not many did. I can recall few cases of bombast, little exaggeration and hardly a tale of personal derring-do. On the contrary, when one scented a story it often had to be patiently drawn out, and if one enquired about a medal, the response was likely to be that it 'came up with the rations' or, 'I suppose it must have been my turn.' But the vividness and detail of these memories recorded long years later is striking. One old soldier remarked, 'In a way I lived my whole life between the ages of 19 and 23 and everything that happened after that was merely an anticlimax.' Coming from a man in his late 70s who had led a successful and interesting life it is a chilling thought – but perhaps it accounts for the clarity of recollection.

But how far can you trust testimony of that kind, knowing that it is all too easy to 'misremember'? Not many people can put their hands on their hearts and swear that they have never caught themselves repeating a personal anecdote for the umpteenth time and suddenly remembering (though probably not confessing!) that it actually happened to a friend. After all, it makes a better story to tell it in the first person and after many years of repeating an anecdote one can actually come to believe it – even when it is only based on rumour. I lost count of the number of spy stories I was told, all of them virtually identical, of French civilians signalling information to the enemy by various devious means: a farmer putting a horse of a different colour in a field behind the trenches; someone altering the hands of a clock on a church tower; a woman hanging out washing as a battalion passed on its way to the line. In the early part of the war when civilians were still close to the battle line such stories went round the army and were still being repeated as gospel truth 60 or 70 years on. Do you believe them? Of course you don't – but you do look for the explanation and sometimes something interesting emerges. It was a fact that frequently when a battalion came into the line, a placard went up in the German trenches, 'WEL-COME THE 7th SUFFOLKS' – or whatever battalion it was. How did they know? Spies, that was it! It wasn't, of course. It was the simple fact that, early in the war, the Germans had better radio communication based on ground induction which enabled them to overhear every order telephoned between brigade and front line, right down to the last signal: 'Relief complete. Signed C.O. 7th Suffolk'. So the historian, whether recording or listening to oral history, must be constantly vigilant; never be entirely dismissive but, equally, avoid being gullible.

Oral history by its very nature can only be anecdotal and subjective. Excluding staff officers and those in senior capacities, no soldier of the line knows what is happening beyond his immediate vicinity. The former tend to pick their words with care and while they may be privy to the situation as seen by the command it so seldom coincides with the situation as seen by the man at the sharp end that it is frequently quite the opposite. One soldier told me with indignation that had rankled for 70 years about a comrade who was put on a charge and punished for the seemingly trivial offence of leaving half a biscuit on the fire step of a trench when they were being relieved. It is tempting to share his indignation, and it was not until I had the account of a

Captain McQueen who was sanitary officer of the Highland Division that the importance of cleanliness became clear. Captain McQueen was not much interested in the war; what he cared about to the point of obsession was sanitation. McQueen's enemies were not the Kaiser and the Germans. His belligerence was reserved for flies and, most of all, for rats. There were rats everywhere, and rats carried disease. Foodstuff could not be left lying around and empty food tins thrown over the parapet not only encouraged scavenging rats but could clink dangerously if a party went through the wire to patrol No Man's Land, and possibly alert the enemy.

So every battalion was ordered to take its rubbish with it when it left the trenches and bury it neatly behind the line. Quite often when roads are being widened on the one-time battlefields of France and Belgium you can spot a cache buried by some long-ago battalion and newly exposed where an embankment has been sliced away. There are usually some flattened condensed milk and bully beef tins, a few scrunched up sweet packets, tattered brown wrapping paper that had enclosed a parcel from home, an empty Bovril jar or a metal box marked Kendal Mint Cake – homely and poignant reminders of the men who once marched these roads. And it is the existence of oral history, the spontaneity of the words of individual soldiers multiplied many times, that enable you to enter into the experience, get under the skins of the men who were there, and possibly set the record straight.

Of recent years the popular view of the First World War has been governed by cliché and 'received ideas' of mud, blood and futile slaughter, haunted by those pale ghosts of the Great War, the poor benighted Tommies driven to their doom by remorseless authority. It is an image forcefully perpetrated by the Great War poets – and great they were. But they were poets and not reporters, and it is a sad fact that, particularly since they have been studied in schools, large numbers of people have formed a view of the First World War based almost exclusively on these powerful images.

Of course we need literature, and of course we need poetry and heroic images, but we need balance as well, and the words of survivors who lived through momentous times 'tell it like it was' and, at the very least, provide food for thought. In our cynical and iconoclastic age it can be hard to sympathize with the ideas and philosophy of people born almost a century ago into a generation still governed by the principles of disciplined Victorian morality and nurtured in the ideals of duty and patriotism. But it is worth the effort. Their experience is the very stuff of history. It cannot replace academic analysis or recorded fact. It cannot alter the ebb and flow of events. It cannot answer 'Why?' (though it might usefully prompt that question). What it can tell you is, 'How it was'.

Can oral history always be taken at face value? Not necessarily. In listening to any recording it is important to apply certain criteria. It goes without saying that one should first check out facts, usually a simple matter. If it is a recorded conversation or interview, who is the interlocutor? Is he imposing his own thoughts or putting words into the mouth of the speaker? If it is not an interview, it has almost certainly been scripted or at least edited.

In the natural course of events, the voices of those people of the First World War have fallen silent, but the treasure trove of their spoken memories remains to illuminate our history and enrich our understanding. But conflict continues and the importance of recording the history of very different aspects of the experience of war will not diminish. For it is that history which touches us all.

The main archives of sound recordings of participants in the First World War are held at the Imperial War Museum, Lambeth Road, London; at the National Army Museum, Royal Hospital Road, Chelsea; and at Leeds Metropolitan University in Yorkshire.

Chapter 17

Memorials

Gavin Stamp

The Memorial to the Missing of the Somme, that red-brick
ziggurat or tower of arches at Thiepval designed by Sir Edwin
Lutyens, can be regarded as the finest work of British architecture of the twentieth century even if it lies across the English
Channel, in France. Incised with the names of over 73,000 men
whose bodies were never found or identified after the Battle of
the Somme in 1916, it stands as a memorial to what Sir John
Keegan has described as, for the British, 'their greatest military
tragedy of the twentieth century, indeed of their national military history'. These two superlatives are not incompatible;
indeed, they are functionally and appropriately complementary.
Yet there has long been a reluctance in Britain to write about
war memorials as works of art and, in fact, to write about
memorials at all. Even today, the bibliography for war memorial
architecture is not very extensive. Perhaps this reflects the wider
modern British tendency to avoid confronting or discussing the
subject of death, exacerbated by the complacency induced by
the enjoyment of half a century of comparative peace since the
Second World War.

Some 30 years ago, in 1977, I was responsible for an exhibition
at the RIBA's Heinz Gallery called 'Silent Cities' about the
architecture of the cemeteries and memorials of the Great War.
In reviewing my recent book on *The Memorial to the Missing of the
Somme* (if this seems solipsistic, I must plead that these are my
qualifications for contributing this chapter), Margaret Richardson wrote that 'I remember that it was not particularly welcomed
at the time as many people felt that it was wrong to focus on the
"art" of the memorials. It is very different now . . .'[1] That such an
attitude once prevailed might seem odd, for not only did the
process of providing every town, every village, every church and

institution with a war memorial in the 1920s require the employment of large numbers of sculptors, designers, architects and craftsmen but in its work in France, Belgium and elsewhere the Imperial War Graves Commission in France had consciously and deliberately aimed at a high and consistent aesthetic standard.

Rudyard Kipling, the Commission's literary adviser, called it, 'The biggest single bit of work since any of the Pharaohs – and they only worked in their own country.' Perhaps the largest programme of public works ever carried out by a British government agency – for there are some 970 British cemeteries in France and Belgium alone – the design of these cemeteries and memorials was overseen by members a team of distinguished architects recommended by the Director of the British Museum, Sir Frederic Kenyon. This emphasis on excellence was a response to a wide debate in Britain about the suitable artistic and architectural response to commemorating the war and its casualties if and when it finally ended, an interest reflected in many contemporary wartime publications on the history of funerary monuments and war memorials.

The achievement of the IWGC under Sir Fabian Ware was unprecedented in Britain. Not only had no official attempt been made before to give fitting burial to or to commemorate every single casualty sustained in military conflict, but the artistic quality of most memorials to, say, the South African War, is largely indifferent. Now, after considerable debate over religious symbolism and uniformity of treatment, both war cemeteries and memorials to the missing were constructed which can today be regarded as standing among the finest creations of the Commission's Principal Architects: Lutyens, Sir Herbert Baker, Sir Reginald Blomfield, Charles Holden and others. This achievement is also represented by the Cenotaph in London, again designed by Lutyens.

But here is part of the problem, for the consistent style of these creations was classical. All these architects drew upon the European Renaissance tradition for inspiration, interpreting it with a greater or lesser degree of originality. As such, however, they do not fit into the conventional twentieth-century canon, for so much writing about the architecture of the last century has been concerned almost exclusively with the advent and triumph of modernism. The Menin Gate, the Thiepval memorial, and – not least – the Cenotaph were not easily accommodated into this standard interpretation of twentieth-century architecture. (Even more problematic are the memorials erected by the Commission after the Second World War, for the available literature completely ignores the existence of these distinguished designs by Philip Hepworth, Louis de Soissons and Hubert Worthington, who continued the approach and the classical manner established after the First World War.)

It is, of course, important not to regard war memorials in purely aesthetic terms; that is, ignoring or minimizing their terrible significance and their historical and social meaning. Many of the smaller war memorials – and a few of the larger – erected in Britain after the Great War are of no artistic merit at all, but that is scarcely the point. Some, indeed, may be repellent in their imagery. (Well did the architects of the IWGC eschew sculpture; as Blomfield recalled, 'many of us had seen terrible examples of war memorials in France and were haunted by the fear of winged angels in various sentimental attitudes'.[2]) Perhaps this problem is presented most acutely by two of the war memorials now concentrated at Hyde Park Corner in London, for here are presented two very different artistic responses to the industrialized slaughter of the Great War.

There is the Artillery Memorial with its representation in stone of a howitzer and sculptured friezes and bronze figures by Charles Sergeant Jagger (surely the greatest British sculptor of the last century), searingly unsentimental in their monumentalized realism. They include the recumbent figure of a dead artilleryman, added at the sculptor's own wish and expense, in 'A Royal Fellowship of Death' to emphasize the horror of war. Close by is a very different response to the war: the Machine Gun Corps Memorial, topped by a sensuous naked youth holding a sword, modelled by an older sculptor, Derwent Wood (who, unlike Jagger, had not served), and flanked by bronze machine guns garlanded with wreaths, as if to sanctify what such weapons did to the unprotected flesh of thousands of youths. The coy sentimentality of this creation is exacerbated by the Old Testament quotation chosen for the pedestal: 'Saul has slain his thousands, and David his ten thousands'. Today, the Artillery Memorial seems of infinitely greater artistic merit than the Machine Gun Corps Memorial, yet it was much criticized when unveiled in 1925. But both are of historical value as representing different responses to the conflict, even if Jagger's masterpiece now seems a more humane and intelligent statement. These are aspects of war memorial design which still need much more investigation. What is needed, perhaps, is a wider cultural study of the architectural and sculptural consequences of the war analogous to Paul Fussell's pioneering study of the literary responses, *The Great War and Modern Memory*, published in 1975.

A further reason for the comparative neglect of war memorials as a subject may be the modern compartmentalization of knowledge. Architectural historians have tended to treat war memorials in purely aesthetic terms when they write about them at all, but when, in my recent book, I attempted to put Lutyens's astonishing creation at Thiepval in its wider context, military as well as historical, the only critical reviews it received came from professional military historians, suggesting to me that military history seems to be quite as introverted and jealous as architectural history.[3] Surely war memorials need to be discussed objectively, in terms of political and social history as well as design, architecture and sculpture, and not just as an after-thought, as the necessary or didactic consequence of a particular military campaign or conflict. Part of the appeal and enduring nobility of the memorials erected by the Imperial War Graves Commission is that they do not vaunt British triumph and vic-tory but visibly commemorate profligate loss, thus encouraging reflection on the tragedy of human conflict. In view of this, it seems to me a pity that some military historians still seem to wish to fight the battles and maintain the hatreds and lies of the Great War rather than to understand the events in the widest possible context.

As it happened, the 1977 'Silent Cities' exhibition seems to have coincided with a low point in morale at the Commonwealth War Graves Commission. During my research, I became aware of what seemed to be a lack of confidence in the future at the Commission, owing to a fear that, when the generation that fought in the Great War had disappeared, nobody would be interested in visiting the war cemeteries in France and Belgium. This loss of confidence was possibly reflected in the lamentable fact that, when the Commission had moved from Grosvenor Gardens in London to Maidenhead a few years before, a large number of original files about the design of cemeteries and their architects had been discarded – a major loss for any detailed architectural study of the Commission's work. There was also, it must be said, a certain lack of appreciation of the quality and subtlety of the monuments and structures in its care, however well the war cemeteries continued (and today continue) to be maintained.

The Commission need not have worried. Since the 1970s, the number of people interested in and visiting the cemeteries and memorials has steadily increased – so much so that those wanting to attend the 'Last Post' ceremony at the Menin Gate are now advised to arrive early as large crowds assemble. Indeed, the growth in the number of visitors today is such that there has been a demand for visitor centres at the most popular monuments. New structures, combined with large car and coach parks, have been built at Thiepval and at Tyne Cot, outside Ypres, and one is threatened at the Australian memorial at Villers-Bretonneux. The design of such buildings presents new problems and the solutions are not always satisfactory (that at Thiepval is discreet and practical, but the new work at Tyne Cot has been ineptly planned and gravely impairs understanding of the memorial and cemetery). What is certain is that these melancholy relics of the Great War continue to haunt and fascinate generations born long after the Second World War.

This phenomenon may reflect the wider growth of interest in family history and the apparently ubiquitous presence of the two world wars on school history syllabi, for parties of schoolchildren are conspicuous among visitors to the cemeteries. It may also be a product of the continuing and disturbingly self-justifying British obsession with the Second World War which, in the last two decades, has given rise to so many campaigns for erecting new war memorials in London and elsewhere. In comparison to the architectural solutions that emerged after 1919, these are generally, to say the least, disappointing. A happier expression of this interest was the foundation of the Friends of War Memorials (the War Memorial Trust) in 1995, 'dedicated to the protection and conservation of our war memorial heritage', in response to neglect and vandalism (both freelance and official). That this may be a reflection of a wider appreciation of the artefacts of death is suggested by the foundation of the Mausolea and Monuments Trust, with similar aims, two years later. But what, from an architectural point of view, is cheering is that the increased interest in the Great War memorials and cemeteries has been accompanied by a recognition of their artistic merit. A large model of the Thiepval memorial took pride of place at the Lutyens Exhibition at the Hayward Gallery in 1981–82 and, even though comparatively little has been written about it, there is a wide acceptance that it is the supreme executed expression of that extraordinary architect's transcendent genius.

This changed climate of opinion has generated a larger literature on the subject of war memorials. Given that, as David Cannadine has written, 'inter-war Britain was probably more obsessed with death than any other period of modern history',[4] it is scarcely surprising that the process of grieving and finding ways to express the huge human loss after 1918 should have interested political and social historians. A political angle was present from the beginning, as shown by the fierce debates in Parliament and elsewhere over whether religious or secular symbolism was appropriate that resulted from the building of the permanent Cenotaph in Whitehall and the formulation of the policies of the IWGC. These, and the many debates at a local level over what form a war memorial should take, were examined by Alex King in *Memorials of the Great War in Britain: The Symbolism and Politics of Remembrance* (1998, Oxford: Berg). Perhaps the most influential of these modern studies is Jay Winter's *Sites of Memory, Sites of Mourning: The Great War in European Cultural History* (1995, Cambridge: CUP). In this book, Winter deals with the question of the style and nature of war memorials and makes the crucial point that although the Great War can be seen as making a caesura between traditional forms of artistic expression and modernism, 'the war gave a new lease of life to a number of traditional languages expressed both conventionally and in unusual and modern forms'. This was supremely true of the work of the Imperial War Graves Commission although most art and architectural historians remain largely impervious to the idea.

These historical studies are largely concerned with the phenomenon of war memorials and their meaning rather than their actual appearance.[5] When it comes to the design of war memorials, the literature remains rather thinner. In 1991, Alan Borg, then director-general of the Imperial War Museum, published his book on *War Memorials, from Antiquity to the Present* which put British memorials of the Great War into a wider historical context. Even wider in scope, both geographically and chronologically, is the earlier book *A Celebration of Death* (1980, London: Constable; republished as *Death and Architecture* in 2002, Stroud: Sutton) by James Stevens Curl, an author who has tackled this unfashionable subject with particular enthusiasm. More recently, the war cemeteries have been discussed in Ken

Worpole's book, *Last Landscapes: The Architecture of the Cemetery in the West* (2003, London: Reaktion). Nevertheless, it remains true that although cemeteries, funerary monuments and memorials of earlier centuries have been well covered, 'the subject of death in modern architecture has been largely avoided', as Edwin Heathcote remarks in his recent book on *Monument Builders: Modern Architecture and Death*. It may also be true that it is a subject which still repels publishers; this at least is suggested by the fact that the two exhaustively detailed studies of *British War Memorials* and *Remembrance* by Mark Quinlan (2005, Authors Online Ltd) had to be privately published.

The handful of war memorials dependent on figures by that very great sculptor C. S. Jagger – notably the Artillery Memorial – are discussed in the Imperial War Museum publication *Charles Sergeant Jagger: War & Peace Sculpture*, edited by Ann Compton (1985), but few of the many, many individual war memorials in Britain have received serious study by art historians. The design and embellishment of the National War Memorial of Scotland, that late, resonant expression of the Arts and Crafts movement on the top of Edinburgh rock has, however, been examined by Elizabeth Cumming.[6] Even so, although Lorimer was also one of the Principal Architects to the IWGC, his rugged cemeteries high up in the mountains of north Italy and his remote Memorial to the Missing by Lake Doiran in Macedonia remain largely unknown and unacknowledged.

Among the other architects who were employed by the Commission, Lutyens, so very influential on its approach, has been the subject of many studies in recent decades which have given due weight to his memorials and cemeteries, while a new monograph on Charles Holden by Eitan Karol (2007, Donnington: Shaun Tyas) includes a detailed and revealing study of his powerful and thoughtful designs for cemeteries and two of the New Zealand memorials, in Belgium and France. But there is no modern study of the work of Sir Herbert Baker, who designed so many memorials both on the Continent for the IWGC and back home for public schools, nor of that of Sir John Burnet, the great Scots architect who was Principal Architect for Gallipoli and Palestine. The one posthumous book about Sir Reginald Blomfield, whose Cross of Sacrifice appears in almost every British war cemetery, naturally discusses his memorial designs, but it is surely significant that the only modern study of his Menin Gate, the best known and most visited of all the memorials to the missing, should be written by a Belgian: *Menin Gate & Last Post: Ypres as Holy Ground* by Dominiek Dendooven (2001, Koksijde: de Klaproos), a book which examines its wider cultural significance. As for the several younger Assistant Architects who were responsible for the detailed design of most of the smaller cemeteries, they remain largely unknown and unresearched – although one of them, Gordon Leith, went on to have a distinguished career in South Africa. For who has heard of J. Reginald Truelove, designer of the memorials to the missing at Vis-en-Artois and Le Touret and architect of Stoke Newington Town Hall; or of H. Chalton Bradshaw, the Rome Scholar who designed the memorials at Ploegsteert and Louverval and who was also secretary of the Royal Fine Art Commission?

It is also important that the study of war memorials is not confined to British examples, for the different national approaches to commemorating the losses of the Great War are very instructive. The monuments erected in France by the American Battle Monuments Commission (in which the ratio of volume of stone to casualties is far higher than for any other nation) have been studied by Elizabeth G. Grossman. Stimulated by the 90th anniversary of the Battle of Vimy Ridge, Canadian historians are now taking a serious interest in the extraordinary expressionist monument (so different from all the others erected by the IWGC) at the eponymous site designed by the sculptor Walter S. Allward.[7] Although ignored in general histories written in English, the impressive abstract semi-modernist monuments erected by the Italians in north Italy in the 1920s are taken seriously by Italian historians who have a broad-minded and relaxed attitude to the remarkable architecture which was produced under Mussolini. France is more of a problem, as the artistic quality of the memorials, chapels and cemeteries created by the French is usually indifferent and very conservative in conception. It is as if France was so traumatized by the scale of her loss that a considered artistic response was impossible. On the other hand, a structure like the huge ossuary at Douamont at Verdun is so brutal in its streamlined, art deco character that historians seem to find it difficult to come to terms with it. However, the illustrated survey of the memorials erected by the French and the other fighting powers in France by J.-M. De Busscher, called *Les Folies de l'Industrie* and published in 1981, deserves mention.

The memorials raised by the defeated Germans are also problematic, but for quite different reasons. Although many of them were conspicuously accomplished and inventive in design, because of the associations and implications they bear they remain somewhat of an embarrassment to the Germans and have attracted little attention from English-speaking historians.[8] Particularly impressive are the war cemeteries in Belgium created by the Volksbund Deutsche Kriegsgräberfürsorge, designed in a sombre, rugged Teutonic Arts and Crafts manner by its chief architect, Robert Tischler. To judge by these and by the fortress-like memorials he created elsewhere after the Second World War, Tischler was a brilliant and imaginative architect, yet there is no monograph about him in any language and he remains largely unknown.[9] Much better known are the 'Mourning Parents', the grieving figures in granite by Käthe Kollwitz which are now in the German war cemetery at Vladslo in Belgium. These powerful and moving sculptures have, rightly, received attention, no doubt partly because of Kollwitz's anti-Nazi credentials and because she has a recognized place in the history of twentieth-century art. Along with Jagger's work on the Artillery Memorial and Reyner Hoff's figures on the ANZAC Memorial in Sydney, these surely rank among the very finest works of sculpture to emerge from the catastrophe of the Great War.[10]

It would be good if, in future, the British public, which is taking an increasing interest in war memorials, could be less insular, less exclusively concerned with the British experience, and visit – and honour – the memorials and cemeteries of all the other nations – both allied and enemy – and so begin to understand the Great War as a European calamity, a continental civil war, whose consequences are still with us. Whether such large numbers will continue to visit these shrines in France, Belgium and elsewhere must be a matter for speculation. Interest in the Great War will surely peak with its centenary and then decline after 2018, as, inevitably, its significance and resonance to younger generations will surely diminish as time passes. And here memorials may have a role to play to make sure that the catastrophe of 1914–18 is not forgotten, just as the surviving memorials of earlier conflicts are still able to evoke the past for those interested and able to read them.

The continuing maintenance of war memorials and cemeteries is another matter, however. While civilization as we know it survives, those memorials that are prominent in towns and villages will surely still be valued while those that are of conspicuous artistic or historical importance and thus 'listed' –

placed on the statutory list of buildings of architectural and / or historical importance – are most likely to be preserved. Whether British war cemeteries and memorials abroad will survive is less certain. A few have already perished through war or urban expansion in nations which have no reason to respect others the continuing presence of British dead or the tangible reminders of the British interpretation of history, but the principal threat to them must be financial. The time must surely come when the income required by the Commonwealth War Graves Commission for its exemplary care and maintenance programmes will be questioned by governments but, as this money comes from the several Commonwealth nations whose dead lie in the cemeteries, this will probably not happen until one in particular dares to break rank. However, even if one day the Commission is disbanded as of no continuing relevance, others may step in to look after their creations – as has happened with, say, the eighteenth-century British cemeteries in Calcutta. As long as these monumental structures of stone and brick continue to stand, however weathered and battered, they will surely continue to elicit awe and wonder and to raise questions about the capacity of human beings both to create and to destroy.

Notes

1   C20. The magazine of the Twentieth Century Society, Autumn 2007, p.18.

2   Sir Reginald Blomfield (1932), Memoirs of an Architect. London: Macmillan, p.181.

3   M.D.R. Foot, in the Spectator for 1 July 2006, wrote that my book 'takes its military history from Alan Clark and Joan Littlewood', while in the British Army Review for Autumn 2006 Christopher Jary elegantly avers that my military history is 'cobblers' and 'tosh'. As a matter of fact, my military history came from Keegan, Howard, Terraine, Winter, Macdonald, Fergusson et al., although I may have drawn my own conclusions from what I presumed they presented as facts. It seems sad that, in their desire to be revisionist about the repellent Haig, a new generation of military historians seem as callous and jingoistic as their hero and that they (along with far too many of my compatriots), even over 60 years since the end of the Second World War and 90 after the First, still cannot bear the suggestion that the British were ever anything other than consistently honourable and virtuous – and of course victorious. It is cheering, therefore, to come across a broad-minded and honest investigation like 1914–1918: Understanding the Great War (2002, London: Profile Books) by Stéphane Audoin-Rouzeau and Annette Backer, two historians who were co-founders of the Historial de la Grande Guerre at Péronne.

4   David Cannadine, 'War and Death, Grief and Mourning in Modern Britain' in Joachim Whaley (ed.) (1981), Mirrors of Mortality: Studies in the Social History of Death. London: Europa Publications, p.189.

5   A fuller bibliography on war memorials is given in my Memorial to the Missing of the Somme (2007, London: Profile Books).

6   Nicola Gordon Bowe and Elizabeth Cumming (1998), *The Arts and Crafts Movement in Dublin & Edinburgh 1885–1925*. Dublin: Irish Academic Press.

7   See the forthcoming special issue of the *Journal of the Society for the Study of Architecture in Canada* volume 33, no.1, 2008, on the Canadian War Memorial at Vimy Ridge.

8   American historians have, however, studied the disturbing implications of the German obsession with monuments and commemorating her war dead in the twentieth century, notably (German-born) George L. Mosse in *Fallen Soldiers: Reshaping the Memory of the World Wars* (1990, Oxford: OUP) and Rudy J. Koshar in *From Monuments to Traces: Artefacts of German Memory 1870–1990* (2000, Berkeley: University of California Press).

9   I recall noticing that a paper on Tischler was delivered at a conference in the United States organized by the Society of Architectural Historians, but I have failed to trace this.

10 For Hoff and the memorial, see Deborah Edwards (ed.) (1999), *'This Vital Flesh': The Sculpture of Rayner Hoff and his School*. Sydney: Art Gallery of New South Wales.

Chapter 18

Kleenex at the Ready? Britten's War Requiem: Which War, Whose Requiem?

Ian Bostridge

'Kleenex at the ready ... one goes from the critics to the music, knowing that if one should dare to disagree with "practically everyone", one will be made to feel as if one had failed to stand up for "God Save the Queen".'

Igor Stravinsky's crotchety response to the overwhelming success of Benjamin Britten's 1962 *War Requiem* is easy to dismiss as envy, the master's fear of losing his powers in the face of the younger generation. Stravinsky had written the musical work, the *Rite of Spring*, which, more than any other, seems to express the savagery of twentieth-century conflict, an unbridled musical depiction of primitive blood sacrifice. This iconic masterpiece (originally entitled the 'Great Sacrifice') was premiered little over a year *before* the outbreak of the First World War. It has come to be seen, like Holst's 'Mars, Bringer of War', from *The Planets* suite (completed before August 1914), as a portent.

As if he was scared by what he had summoned into being, Stravinsky's style and musical philosophy underwent radical change after 1914. The war was not to be addressed directly; and Stravinsky's *Soldier's Tale*, written in its last year, is not an emotionally engaged contemporary manifesto but rather a quirky and detached modernist fairy tale. The poised classicism of Stravinsky's later work, his adoption of a sort of formalism, and dogged insistence that music could not express anything but itself, were symptomatic of the retreat from romanticism of any sort that the war had induced, a highbrow incarnation of Noel Coward, the Jazz Age and Bright Young Things. Goodbye to All That, in Robert Graves's words. In that sense, Britten's *War*

Requiem, and all the brouhaha surrounding it, the 'Battle of Britten' as Stravinsky called it, must have seemed distastefully direct and, in its engagement with savagery, a return to the aesthetic of the *Rite of Spring*. In a diary entry in 1931, a student Britten wrote of a performance of the latter work – 'Sacre – bewildering and terrifying. I didn't really enjoy it, but I think it's incredibly marvellous & arresting.'

The Great War did not really touch Britten, except in a more general sense. He was too young (born in November 1913) to remember its course or its rigours, and his close family did not suffer the losses that afflicted so many others. He grew up as an artist, of course, in an atmosphere of post-war disillusionment, of irony and detachment, but three things served to mitigate this: first, and essentially, his self-confessed romanticism as a com- poser; secondly, and despite his progressive interests, his upbringing in a musical culture which was insulated from con- tinental modernism; and thirdly, his view of the artist's social responsibility, forged in the Auden circle in which he moved in the 1930s and allied to his long-standing and apparently visceral pacifism.

All of these currents feed into the *War Requiem* which is a culmination in Britten's work and, rather like the *Rite of Spring* for Stravinsky, a stylistic turning point. It quite consciously works with register and style to achieve a synthesis between public statement and private questioning which is, formally, masterly. The sound and fury of the settings of the Latin mass text itself, with that Stravinskian rhythmic drive and Verdian theatricality, are set against chamber settings of war poetry by Wilfred Owen which combine the instrumental and gestural economy of modernism with the interiority and sheer melody of the romantic. The piece somehow symbolizes reconciliation through the seamless interweaving of Germanic and non- Germanic conceptions of aesthetics, the metaphysical in concert with the human and contingent. For this was how the cultural aspect of the European civil war had manifested itself, a struggle, as the Germans had it, between *Kultur* and *Zivilisation*. The *War Requiem* seems to transcend all this, a hymn of healing as much as a manifesto of pacifism.

If Stravinsky was latching onto something about the *War Requiem* which he distrusted – that an occasional work decrying the European wars of the first half of the twentieth century was bound to be, in his terms if not ours, sentimental – his scoffing at the popular acclaim it attracted was perceptive. For Britten himself was arguably unsettled by the scale of public success – his last opera, *Death in Venice*, is in part a study of an artist hollowed out by celebrity – and after the *War Requiem* forged a more austere and less crowd-pleasing style.

But the *War Requiem* remains, justly, a much-performed and appreciated work, one of the few classical compositions written after 1945 to have had a continuous place in audience affections, and a growing place in the repertoire. I first performed it in 1994 in commemoration of the bombing of Freiburg 50 years before, and while some of the performances in which I have taken part have had similar occasional, commemorative significance, most have not. By the time this piece appears I will have performed it 50 times, probably more than any other piece in my repertoire. It moved audiences and performers in 1962 and, 63 years after the end of the Second World War, 46 years after its composition for the reconsecration of Coventry Cathedral, it continues to speak.

Stravinsky's attack is occasionally resurrected – most trenchantly in recent times perhaps by the critic and novelist Philip Hensher (librettist of Thomas Ades's *Powder her Face*), who described the the *War Requiem* as 'a terrible, literary sort of din'. 'We all know,' he wrote in *The Guardian*, 'what we think of the First World War: it's very sad. We all know what we think of Wilfred Owen's early death: it's very sad. And since the *War Requiem* is about these two deeply moving things, it must, therefore, be deeply moving itself, mustn't it?'

The *War Requiem* uses Owen's poetry for its own purposes, aesthetic and ideological (the poet-soldier Owen was no pacifist), but the piece is not in any sense *about* Owen. We are told nothing about him, although words from a projected preface to his poems do stand on the front page of the score as epigraph: 'My subject is War and the pity of War. The Poetry is in the pity . . . All a poet can do today is warn'. Warning through pity – this is at odds with the Stravinskian aesthetic, dangerously personal, dangerously engaged. 'Some of my right-wing friends loathed it,' Britten is reported to have said, '"though the music is superb, of course," they'd say. But that's neither here nor there to me. The message is what counts.'

The *War Requiem* is, overtly, and perhaps surprisingly, about the First World War. 'The idea of the W.R. *did* come off I think,' Britten wrote to his sister, '. . . & how one thinks of that bloody 1914–18 war especially – I hope it'll make people think a bit.'

This is unexpected in a piece whose commission originated in the destruction of Coventry in 1940. Indeed Britten seems to veer away from addressing many of the experiences of the Second World War in his *Requiem*. He chose an English, a German and a Russian soloist, in his own words, as 'representatives of the three nations that had suffered most during the war'. This was a brilliant aesthetic gambit – the reconciliation of old enemies, English and German presided over by the searing Russian soprano, embodying at times a cruel and somehow alien God, at times an unbearable weight of lamentation – but an odd sentiment to express in view of the Holocaust, Hiroshima and Nagasaki, or the invasion of Poland. Britten had responded darkly and savagely to his one direct experience of the horrors of war – his visit to Belsen with Yehudi Menuhin in 1945 – with a work, *The Holy Sonnets of John Donne* for voice and piano, much of which pulsates with guilt, sin and self-loathing. Britten's return to 1914–18 reflects both the immense significance of that war as the beginning of all the horrors of the twentieth century, and a catastrophe which musicians of the time had been able adequately or directly to address; but also, I think, the awkwardness and wariness of a pacifist who had experienced the second war, seen its horrors but had been present only as a bystander.

In the end, as I have experienced it in performance, and despite Britten's apparent commitment to its pacifist 'message', the *War Requiem* is about far more than twentieth-century war and its horrors. It looks death in the face and presents a terrifying vision of implacable holiness in, for example, the Sanctus. The religion of humanity and the religion of the saints confront each other and achieve an ambiguous resolution.

Chapter 19

Courage, Mon Amie

Terry Castle

'You speak like a green girl, Unsifted in such perilous circumstance.'

Hamlet, 1.3, 101–2

A year ago this past autumn – a year before the old life so shockingly blew away – I made a long-contemplated trip to France and Belgium to see the cemeteries of the First World War. My quest, though transatlantic, was a modest, conventional and somewhat anorakish one: I hoped to locate the grave of my great-uncle, Rifleman Lewis Newton Braddock, 1st/17th (County of London) Battalion (Poplar and Stepney Rifles), the London Regiment, who had died in the war and was buried near Amiens. Facts about him are scarce. My grandmother, whose only brother he was, has been dead now for 20 years. No one else who knew him is still alive. By stringing together odd comments from family members I've learned that he worked as a greengrocer's boy in Derby before joining up in 1915; that he served first in the Sherwood Foresters; that he managed to survive three years before getting killed during the final German retreat in June 1918. My mother, born eight years after his death, claims to have heard as a child that he was shot accidentally – 'by his own guns'. But my uncle Neil, *her* only brother, can't believe 'they would have told the family that'.

Newton was said to be artistic: two dusty little green-grey daubs – both of them Derbyshire landscapes – are among his surviving effects. There are two photographs of him in uniform – one from the beginning of the war, the other from the end. In the first he looks pale, spindly and rather stupid: a poorly fed, late Victorian adolescent overfond of self-abuse. In the second, the one with the moustache, he is stouter, tougher, dreamier, and looks distressingly like both my mother and my cousin Toby. My companion Blakey says he looks like me. I don't see it. I've been fascinated by him – and the Great War – since I first heard of him, at the age of six or so. I'm now 48.

Somebody should write about women obsessed with the First World War. Everybody knows Pat Barker, of course, but there's also Lyn Macdonald – a former BBC producer whose dense, addictive, exhaustively researched oral histories of the war (*1914: The Days of Hope, 1915: The Death of Innocence, Somme, They Called It Passchendaele, The Roses of No Man's Land, To the Last Man: Spring 1918*) are a fairly devastating moral education for the reader. And once you begin to delve, as I have done, into the netherworld of popular military history – battlefield guides, memorial volumes, regimental histories, military-souvenir web-sites – it is peculiar how many lady archivists you encounter. Some of these, it's true, are part of husband-and-wife teams: the prolific Valmai Holt, for example, author, with her husband, of *My Boy Jack? The Search for Kipling's Only Son* (1998). (John Kipling died in his first half-hour in action – at the age of 18 – at Loos in 1915. Though his stricken father carried on a 20-year search for his grave, his remains were not found until 1992.) When not writing, the Holts run a sprightly operation known as Holts History and Battlefield Tours. 'Their *Battlefield Guide to the Somme* and *Battlefield Guide to Ypres*,' reads one cheery promotional blurb, 'have brought these areas to life for tens of thousands of people.'

Other female obsessives work in austere isolation. The late Rose E. B. Coombs MBE, former Special Collections Officer at the Imperial War Museum, is the author of *Before Endeavours Fade: A Guide to the Battlefields of the First World War* (1976 and 1994). Miss Coombs's bleak volume, illustrated with her own amateur snaps, is a necrophile's delight: photograph after photograph, in tiny, eye-straining black and white, of crosses, graves, plaques, inscriptions, bombed-out block-houses converted into monuments, decaying trench relics, dank rows of cypresses, grassed-over mine and shell craters, obscene-looking barrows, and yet more crosses and graves. Some of the photos show boxy 1970s cars parked in the background – a peculiarly depressing sight – and anonymous male tourists with period comb-overs and long sideburns. I bought my second-hand copy through the mail from a military book dealer in Dorset and its once-glossy pages reek of must and damp.

My own war fixation is equally grim and spinsterish, its roots primal and puzzling. My first awareness of the Great War came, quite literally, with the crack-up of my parents' marriage. They had emigrated from England to California in the early 1950s and divorced ten years later, in 1961. (I was born in San Diego in 1953.) It was a bit of a mess – my mother had been having an affair with a lieutenant in the navy – and in the convoluted aftermath my irascible grandfather, a former buyer for the Co-op in St Albans, prevailed on her, the Extremely Guilty Party, to come back to England and rehabilitate herself in some respectable, out of the way spot. My baby sister and I were bundled onto a plane at 4 a.m., me sobbing dolefully at the break-up of my little world. Gone into transatlantic blackness – for ever, it seemed – my cowboy hat and Mickey Mouse books, the pixie-cutted members of my Brownie troop, our blue and white Rambler, and the sunny back patio where my father had, in happier days, filmed me in vivid Kodachrome disporting in a plastic blow-up pool.

Our first few months in England were spent in my grandparents' little brick bungalow, at the foot of Caesar's Camp, near Folkestone. (Their house and lane have since disappeared – razed to make way for the stark, moonscaped run-up to the Channel Tunnel.) It was in those lonely, quiet days – the clock ticking on the mantelpiece, the adults discoursing in another room – that I first examined my great-uncle's bronze memorial disc, which stood on a bookshelf next to my grandmother's Crown Derby. It was six inches across, heavyish, and the same greeny-gold colour as a threepenny bit, a piece of coinage with which I had recently become acquainted. I was immediately charmed by its glint, its inscriptions, its palpable seriousness. It seemed to have survived – like a dense, tooth-breaking wafer – from some unknown time and place. I asked my mother, only slightly babyishly, to ask my grandmother if I could have it – for my new collection of oddments, begun when our plane had stopped in Iceland for refuelling and my mother bought me a ceramic puffin from the tiny airport giftshop. This request – received with embarrassed laughter – was not granted.

The following three years in England, a stagnant time characterized mainly by my mother's depression and sexual loneliness, deepened my war curiosity without clarifying it. We moved to our own little bungalow in nearby Sandgate, at the top of a rise just below the Shorncliffe Army Camp. There were several new things here. I saw my first person without a leg, an old man with a horrible stump, in Sandgate High Street, and though I never mentioned him to anyone, I was terrified for months we would run into him again. The village had its own little grime-blackened war memorial – standard vintage and style – and an air of lugubrious decay unlike anything I had encountered before. The grey waves of the Channel flopped endlessly and drearily on the shingle beach that ran alongside the High Street. This blighted strand, impossible to walk on in bare feet, bore no resemblance to the palm-studded sands of infancy and toddlerhood. I fixated on orange-flavoured Aero bars as a means of survival.

My primary school, Sir John Moore's, was part of the Shorn-cliffe Camp. I have no recollection of the sun shining during my sojourn there. Each day I walked to school and back past deserted, dusky parade-grounds, the occasional ghostly soldier in puttees looming up out of the mist. Except for a few barracks and the red-brick officer quarters, all dating from Napoleonic days, the place seemed largely uninhabited. Once in a while an army lorry lumbered up Artillery Road: my first suicidal fantasy had to do with flinging myself under one in the presence of my horrified parents, now strangely reunited, as if by magic carpet, to witness the act. This, I know, makes it all sound bad: but Sir John Moore's wasn't really so awful – our teacher once took us out to make bark rubbings – and I soon developed a powerful aesthetic attraction to the various uniforms I saw, the officers' peaked caps and regimental insignia especially.

But when I dream of the place – and sometimes I still do – my brain usually fixes on the baleful rituals of Armistice Day. Nothing was explained. Who, or what, was an 'armastiss'? It was never made very clear. Nonetheless, schoolmates and I were duly instructed to bring cut flowers from home – the bottoms of the stems to be moistened with a wrapper of wet tissues in aluminium foil. My mother obliged – I'm not sure how, given that nothing very posy-like grew in the leftover building rubble around our house. And intriguing, too, the break in schoolday routine. At half-past ten we mustered in the playground by the toilets – no talking, straight lines, wipe your noses please – then set off through the camp. We passed by Sir John Moore's pokey little museum, the Folkestone bus stop and the abandoned cinema. We trundled across playing fields, skirted stinging nettles, rounded unknown corners, then ascended a rolling procession of new-old Kentish hills: hills that must have been quite close by, but, uncannily, never seemed to exist except on that particular day. At the top of these, the sky suddenly lifting, an astonishing vista broke out before us: greensward and chalk and *Lear*-like white cliffs, the cold massy sea and lofting gulls, the distant line of France, and everywhere, like some vibrant, disturbing retinal trick, hundreds of identical graves, sweeping down in rows to the cliff edge, as far as the eye could see.

We stayed near the top, of course, our teacher deploying us in little ranks till each of us ended up with our own white marker to stand in front of. The grave at one's feet at once prompted animistic dread. Were you supposed to stand right *on the spot* under which the dead person lay? Could he feel your presence through the grass? If so, it was creepy, possibly even foolhardy, to be there. Might he not, late at night, get up from his grave, glide down Artillery Road, and seek you out? Southern California, a place entirely lacking in cemeteries, offered no precedents. The scariest thing back there had been a Time-Life book of my father's with a picture of a grim, tiny-eyed shark, jaws open wide in prehistoric eagerness. This was far worse: *a ghastly corpse-face at the bedroom window*! The tattered rendition of the Last Post, by a pair of insect-buglers on the hill opposite, didn't help. A prayer was said; the bouquets deposited; the tremors persisted. I had yet to see any *Night of the Living Dead* movies at this point, but when I did, back in San Diego a few years later, alone in the cheerless TV 'den' of the house my father now shared with his new wife and stepdaughters (the same place I was sitting when I saw Oswald get shot), I realized I already knew all about them.

All very sad and picturesque (*poor little female-Terence!*); but enough to explain a 40-year craving for more? For just such a craving – acquisitive, pedantic and obscurely guilt-inducing – is what I ended up with. Not all at once, of course: like most obsessions, this one took a while to get going. In my 20s, as a literature student, I read and acquired the obvious classics: Graves, Owen, Sassoon, Remarque, Barbusse, Brittain, Fussell. But I had lots of other fads and hobbies going too: opera, Baroque painting, Kurosawa films, the *Titanic*, the Romanovs, trashy lesbian novels. Sometimes my preoccupations overlapped: I became fascinated, for example, with the long World War One sequence in Radclyffe Hall's *The Well of Loneliness*. I read up on butch lady ambulance-drivers at the Western Front. But the world had not yet retracted to a grey, dugout-sized, lobe-gripping monomania.

Then, starting in my 30s, things seemed to intensify. I was in England teaching in my university's overseas programme in 1989, as it happened, on the 75th anniversary of the start of the war. (An item on the news one evening, showing tottery, ber-ibboned veterans saluting at the Menin Gate, reduced me to sudden tears.) I began absorbing ever more specialized fare: Macdonald's books, Taylor and Tuchman on the political background, battle histories of Gallipoli, Verdun and Passchen-daele, books about Haig and Kitchener, VAD nurses, brave dead subalterns and monocled mutineers. I read Michael Hurd's desolating biography – *The Ordeal of Ivor Gurney* – on the train to Edinburgh, the city where the nerve-wracked composer, on his way to insanity and death, was hospitalized after being gassed in 1917. I stared at the few surviving pictures of him: the one in a private's tunic (2nd/5th Gloucesters); the one where he's standing, in ill-fitting civvies, alone and blank and looking down at the grass, in the grounds of his asylum in 1922.

And more and more I began investigating the filthy minutiae of 1914–18 trench warfare. John Keegan, the *Face of Battle* man, was my trench guru. I read all his books. I became an armchair expert on Lewis guns and enfilade fire, shrapnel and mortars, wiring parties, trench raids and listening-posts, the tricky timing of the creeping barrage. I pondered the layout of dugouts and communication trenches, the proper distance between parapet and parados, the placement of machine-gun nests (they're always called 'nests'). It seemed at the time, I realized, an odd obsession for a girl. But it seemed to go along with various other ungirlish things about me: my vast bebop collection and dislike of skirts, my aversion (polite) to sleeping with men.

I remember a conversation with a famous feminist poet in the late 1980s in which I grandly pronounced it a 'disgrace' that so few women knew anything about military history. In an apo-theosis of pomposity – and also to see if it would get her goat – I boasted about my great-uncle and proudly asserted that I could *never* have been a pacifist in August 1914.

Over the past ten years the *folie* has only become more involved. A couple of years ago I started collecting first editions of World War One books. (Latest Internet bandersnatch: a battered copy of Reginald Berkeley's *Dawn*, a patriotic tear-jerker, complete with garish pictorial dust jacket, about the martyrdom of Nurse Cavell.)

I've got several faded trench-maps and a tiny, pocket-sized

'Active Service Issue' book of Psalms and Proverbs, issued by the Scripture Gift Mission and Naval and Military Bible Society in 1918. Every year, when I go to London, I load up on greasy wartime postcards in one of the memorabilia shops in Cecil Court. ('Helping an Ambulance through the Mud'; 'Armée Anglaise en Observation'; 'The Destruction at Louvain, Belgium'; 'Tommy at Home in German Dugouts!') I've got a whole shelf on war artists: C. R. W. Nevinson, Paul Nash, William Roberts, Wyndham Lewis, and the skullishly named Muirhead Bone. I've got books about Fabian Ware and the founding of the Commonwealth War Graves Commission. I've a 1920 Blue Guide to *Belgium and the Western Front* and a Michelin Somme guide from 1922 – both published for the so-called 'pilgrims', the aged, widowed and dead-brothered, who flooded France and Flanders after the war seeking the graves of the lost. I have scratchy recordings of 'Pack Up Your Troubles' and 'The Roses of Picardy'; a tape of a (supposed) German bombardment; and yet another of a Cockney BEF veteran describing, rather self-consciously, the retreat from Mons. I have videos and documentaries: Renoir's *Grande Illusion*, Wellman's *Wings*, Bertrand Tavernier's *Life and Nothing But*, and a haunting excerpt from Abel Gance's famous anti-war film *J'Accuse*. And then, too, there are all my mood-setting 'high-brow' CDs – the songs of Gerald Finzi, Vaughan Williams, George Butterworth, Gurney, Ernest Farrar. (The baritone Stephen Varcoe is unsurpassed in this repertoire.) I have but to hear the dark opening bars of Finzi's 'Only a Man Harrowing Clods' to dissolve in sticky war nostalgia and an engorged, unseemly longing for things unseen.

Yet something about my fixation has always bewildered me, as it indubitably has those friends and bedmates forced to enthuse over grimy mementos and The Latest Facts. (Thanks to a troll around at www.fallenheroes.co.uk I recently discovered, for example, that Shorncliffe Camp was a major Great War jumping-off point – notably for the Canadian units who went on to fight, with appalling losses, at Vimy Ridge in 1917. The soldiers in the cemetery were mostly men who had died of wounds or sickness in nearby military hospitals after returning from the front. But a few graves hold other kinds of casualties: a small group of Belgian refugees; a single Portuguese soldier; several members of the Chinese Labour Corps; some civilian victims of a daylight air raid on Folkestone on 25 May 1917, in which 95 people were killed and 195 injured.)[1] I guess an obsession is defined, crudely enough, by the fact that one doesn't understand it. Even as it besets, its determinants remain opaque. (The word 'obsession', interestingly, is originally a military term: in Latin, it signified a siege action, the tactical forerunner of trench warfare.) The obsessions of others embarrass and repel because they seem to dehumanize: to make the obsessed one robotic and alien and unavailable. It's like watching an autistic child humming or scratching or banging on a plate for hours on end.

I suppose it was some desire to get free of a certain robot-feeling – in myself – that prompted my trip to France and Belgium. Not that I was planning on renouncing my books or my collections (nor have I). It was more a matter of, OK, *you've been talking about it for ever – go find him.* Blakey was teaching and couldn't go: but Bridget could, and wanted to, even though she is not from the Braddock side of the family. She turned out to be the ideal companion. She's my first cousin, a south Londoner by way of Ipswich. Our estranged fathers are brothers. We knew each other as children – for a brief time, before my mother took us back to San Diego – but then I didn't see her for two decades, until I looked her up one day in the London telephone book. (After my parents' divorce I'd let all the Castle relatives go to hell.) Bridget, it turned out, had been in the army for 11 years – in Germany and Belfast – and was now running the transport department for a London borough. She is slangy and brusque and ultra-competent – knows all about plumbing and engines and dogs – and regards me, the Prodigal Bluestocking, as a bit feckless. A couple of years ago we went down to Dungeness to see Derek Jarman's garden and ran into a man with his wife and mother-in-law whose car had got stuck in the wet shingle. Bridget had it hitched up in a trice and dragged it free, while the man stood by looking utterly flummoxed and outdone. ('Ex-military,' she said, by way of explanation.) Anyway, Bridget set it all up: our Chunnel car ticket, the package-deal hotel in Ghent, our route map. Needless to say, she drove all the way, from Herne Hill to the outskirts of Ypres, with me a slightly cranked-up presence in the passenger seat.

I'd been hoping, obviously, that the trip might bring some new understanding, might clarify both my relationship with my dead great-uncle and my war-fixation. But no such *éclaircissement* took place, at least not immediately. On the contrary: though a 'success' from a practical standpoint – we found Newton's neat little grave and red geraniums on the second day – the journey seemed only to provoke more disorientation. As Bridget gamely motored us from one memorial to the next, the freezing rain walloping down on the windscreen ('Hooge Crater is just up here'), I found myself less and less able to grasp what I was doing there. I felt misty, numb, a bit ghoulish. I was the Big Girl-Expert – an Unusual and Fascinating Person Now at Last Visiting the Western Front. (*She's slept with more women than her father has!*) But I felt increasingly disgusted with myself. I started thinking that probably a lot of people I knew didn't really like me, were only pretending to.

The nadir came on the second day. We'd spent the first day in and around Ypres – visiting Tyne Cot and neighbouring cemeteries, moping around the In Flanders Fields museum. Ypres itself is a huge bummer, fake and nasty and foul, with machine-cut cobblestones and dead-eyed people everywhere. Numerous renovations were going on, presumably to make the spot more of a 'target' destination for EC tourists (though it's already been flattened and rebuilt more times than anyone can count). We found a Great War souvenir shop, run by a surly Falklands veteran, but I couldn't bring myself to buy anything: not even one of the dull gold cap-badges or orphaned tunic buttons. That night we retreated in a downpour to our Ibis in Ghent Zentrum – the only good news being the charred steak and frites we gobbled down in a place near the cathedral. The hotel was filled with paunchy Benelux businessmen who took one look and didn't bother giving us the eye; the bedroom was cramped and small, with two narrow beds about a foot apart. I got horribly self-conscious at having to undress in front of Bridget, and started blushing. The Incest Taboo, in one of its weirder manifestations, seemed to descend thickly, like a cloud of odourless gas.

The next day we zipped south on a motorway, Moby on the CD player, huge container trucks from Holland and Germany careening by in the rain. Coffee in Albert, a quick gander in the drizzle at the French war memorial in the town square, then on to the giant Lutyens monument to the Missing of the Somme at Thiepval. It was mid-morning, and we were the only people there apart from a sullen group of French *lycée* students playing around on the steps of the thing. (They all had the same annoyed-teenager look: *We're too old to be standing about here!*) The memorial itself is a massively ugly parody-arch in the middle of nowhere. You see it coming up on the horizon from miles away. ('The majestic Memorial to the Missing,' says Miss Coombs, 'stands amid fields still scarred with the trench lines of the Leipzig Redoubt.') Blakey would call it fugly. Loads of Castles among the 73,000-or-so incised names, though nobody known to us. One of them had been in the Bicycle Corps, which made us laugh because it was all so Edwardian and English and pathetic. 'He died heroically – his bicycle shot out from under him.' Housman could have written a poem about it.

Uncle Newton, it turned out, was not far off, halfway between Amiens and Albert, in a pretty little walled 'extension' cemetery at Franvillers filled mainly with Australians. The cemetery was on a small rise, presumably close to the place where he had died, and impeccably maintained. It had three or four farmhouses around it, probably built in the 1960s. I figured I was the fifth person to visit him in the 80 years since his death: the other four being my grandmother, her sister Dolly, her sister's daughter Sue, and my uncle Neil (on his way back from the Italian front in 1945). As Bridget and I unlatched the gate and went in, the sun came out – just like in a Jane Austen novel when the heroine is about to get proposed to. We walked around; we scrutinized the inscription on the Blomfield Cross of Sacrifice. We read the homely greeting-card messages in the memorial book ('Sleep well, lads!'; 'We'll never forget you!'; 'Thinking of you always with love and gratitude', 'Always with us'). Bridget took a photograph of me by the grave – glum and fat and respectful – and that was that.

But even as we began winding back north towards Calais and home in the late afternoon, I suppose we were getting close to having had enough. I started to feel broody and compulsive and Urne-Buriall-ish; the sky got dark and pent again. I asked Bridget, as we drove, if she thought soldiers buried in tidy little battlefield cemeteries like my great-uncle's occupied separate plots. True, they had their individual headstones; but might they not, in the hurry and chaos of war, have simply been piled willy-nilly into a single burial pit somewhere in the vicinity of the present markers? A mass grave, if you like. Bridget said, 'Yes, I'm afraid so,' and kept her handsome grey-blue eyes on the road. We both hunkered down. Then back toward Ypres we decided on one last stop: a little old-fashioned war museum which, according to the guidebook, incorporated some vestiges of front-line trench – something, for all of our perambulations, we hadn't yet seen. We followed an ancient Roman track a mile or two across sodden beetroot fields, made several bumpy turns up a hill and into a copse, then rolled up, even as the rain started again, in the little dirt parking lot.

Dank thoughts in a dank shade. In the front of the 'museum' – a little cluster of dilapidated houses and sheds – was a café, deserted inside except for a couple of bloated Flemish men with wet black moustaches and empty beer glasses. The drill here was: buy your ticket in the café; walk through the two side rooms where the 'exhibits' were; then out into the back garden where the bit of old trench was; then back again. The bleary-eyed proprietor, likewise with moustache, looked like that Belgian serial killer who got caught by Interpol a year or two ago. He contemplated us briefly with deep alcoholic hatred. *How yoo zhay in Inghlissh? Who arrhh zeeez two fhucking dykes?* The place was damp and cold and dirty – old spiked Uhlan helmets and things lined up on a shelf behind him – and smelled like hell.

The place, I learned afterward, is famously horrible. Stephen O'Shea, the wonderful Canadian writer, has a stark riff on it in *Back to the Front*, his extraordinary 1996 account of hitchhiking the entire length of the Western Front. (O'Shea is another catastrophe junkie: his latest book is on the Cathars.) But Bridget and I needed no guidebook to alert us to the vibe. Down one side of the display room we proceeded, dutifully examining the fly-blown war photos on the wall. They got worse as you went along. Battlefield shots first – mudslides, craters, collapsing limbers and dead horses – then a switch to British and German wounded laid out in hospital beds. The photographer, 'Ferdinand of Ypres', had signed each picture in a flowery chemical script (an early example of diversification no doubt: the Ypres *carte de visite* business must have fallen off dramatically when the place got pulverized in November 1914). The last two were clearly Ferdinand's masterpieces: tight, nauseous close-ups of men with ghastly facial injuries: jaws and mouths gone, rubbery slots for noses; an eye or an ear the only human thing left. The one other person in the room with us was a pale young man in a windbreaker, one of the Four Horsemen on his day off. He was busy taking photos of the photos and smiling delightedly.

We passed next through a kind of garage with rusty stuff piled all around – shell casings, barbed wire, rotting Sam Browne belts, a pair of ludicrous French shop-dummies, gaily attired in mismatched officers' uniforms – then on out to the display trenches, snaking off into the woods behind the building. These had a neat, generic, recently packed-down aspect, the corrugated iron supports looking as if they'd just come from the Lille DIY store. Not much to see really, once you'd peered down into them or clambered in – as Bridget briefly did – so we went back in the house and down the other side of the exhibit room. Here was further war debris: ammunition boxes, ancient bully-beef tins and, jarringly, some bits of Nazi regalia and Hitler-junk (a blotted letter to him at the front from his grandmother). I knew Hitler had fought – valiantly – in a Bavarian infantry regiment near the Messines Ridge, but this part of the show seemed nonetheless a mite too enthusiastic. A big dusty swastika banner – sorely in need of dry-cleaning – was draped in a corner, like a prop from the Hall of the Grail scene in Syberberg's postmodern *Parsifal*.

But they saved the best till last. *Zhose ughly girls get snooquered Beeg Time!* Along the far wall by the exit was a long wooden work desk with five or six seats attached – rather like a junior school science class set-up. Mounted at each seat was a beautiful old-fashioned viewing machine – a kind of antique stereopticon – made of brass and polished wood, with a double eyepiece and hand crank. It was all too exquisite and Proustian to resist. Like silent-film cameramen, Bridget and I took our seats and eagerly began to crank.

Yet hellish indeed what assailed us. Trench-pix again – in lots of 20 – but now eternally fixed in a lurid, refulgent, Miltonic 3-D. Sickening and brain-twisting: a clicking, clacking kaleidoscope of atrocities. Don't forget the vertigo. Even as I sat and stared I felt myself lurching forward – into the bright intolerable sunshine of some ruinous as usual summer day in 1917. The light itself was a somatic wedge tilting one into the past. The cerebellum went walkabout.

Granted, the light preserved in old photographs can be unnerving at the best of times. I have a picture in one of my books of Mahler and Richard Strauss stepping out into bright sunlight after a matinée of *Salomé* in Graz in 1906. The Old World sun glinting off the side of Mahler's polished shoe, the sharp edge of Strauss's boater, the geometric shadows thrown onto the wall behind them: these teleport one instantly into the scene. You start remembering what the day was like. But here the illusion of reality was fearsomely, even fiendishly intensified. The febrile glare, conjoined with the stereoscopic depth of field, equalled My God They're Right There: a corpse with flies; a headless body upside down in the sand; two skulls on a battle-field midden; an obscure something or other in *feldgrau*. I got up in disgust after seeing yet another moribund horse, its intestines spilled out and glistening.

In the weeks and months that followed, nothing made very much sense. (After a surreal shopping spree at the vast Eurostar mall outside Calais, Bridget and I got back to Herne Hill without incident.) I confess I was moody. I was on sabbatical; I should have been happy. But I maundered and malingered. On the flight home to San Francisco I stopped for the weekend in Chicago to see Blakey. She politely admired the absurd keychain I'd brought her from Flanders – a laminated reproduction of a 1914 recruiting poster: a cadre of shrewish females exhorting their unfortunate men: 'Women of Britain Say – Go!' (I myself had a plastic, finger-pointing Kitchener – the brave homo-warlord bristling like a 1980s Castro Street clone.) We took my photos of Tyne Cot and Franvillers to be developed at the Walgreens on Michigan Avenue. But then we had a big blow-up fight that evening and she rushed out of her apartment building in a rage. I had to ask the Polish doorman which way she'd gone and ran after her, gesticulating like a Keystone cop, up Lake Shore Drive.

When I got back to California, friends asked about the trip. I gave brief, potted, cousin-rich recountings – sometimes I even described the stereopticon. But I felt like a bit of a sociopath, especially when one of my colleagues looked at me with revulsion as I related the itinerary. At the same time I became irrationally indignant when listeners seemed insufficiently captivated by my odyssey of death. In March I gave a lecture at an esteemed university where I hoped to get a job. (The people there knew that Blakey and I wanted to be together; I had been asked to apply.) The talk had to do with the war and writers of the 1920s – Wyndham Lewis, Woolf, the Sitwells. I showed slides of Claud Lovat Fraser's sad little trench-drawings and expressed, all too dotingly, my love for them. I even mentioned (obliquely) Uncle Newton. It was not a success. The department Medusa – a steely Queer Theorist in bovver boots – decided I was 'wedded to the aesthetic' and needed 'nuking' at once. And so I was. Hopes dashed, I fell into a pompous, protracted, maudlin depression – like Mr Toad when he finds the stoats and ferrets have taken over Toad Hall. Friends kept saying: 'But *they* are the ones who look bad!' But I couldn't get over the ghastly cruelty of it all. I felt like a bullet-ridden blob. The cemetery trip had done something to me – induced a kind of temporary insanity? – but I couldn't get a grip on how or why. I was cabin'd, cribb'd, confin'd, and bound in to saucy doubts and fears.

> My resolution's plac'd, and I have nothing
> Of woman in me; now from head to foot
> I am marble-constant, now the fleeting moon
> No planet is of mine.
>
> *Antony and Cleopatra*, 5.2, 237–40

A clue to the nature of my feelings came only this past autumn, haltingly, in the wake of the attacks on the east coast. Even in balmy California there was no escaping what had happened. Televisions – especially the silly little army of them suspended above the treadmills at the gym I belong to – became existential torture devices. No more *Frasier* reruns or baseball: just Peter Jennings and dirty bombs.

The boys with tattoos flexed nervously. Even the female-to-male transsexuals looked shaken (it's a gay gym). I went through my own quiet days feeling gusty, shocked and forlorn. Blakey was still in Chicago. One evening I broke down and called my father for the first time in three years. He was surprised to hear from me. I mumbled that I was 'calling to see how he was', that I was upset by the attacks. Long, baffled pause. He allowed that he was fine. Silence, followed by clotted *hmmms*. He seemed to apprehend that I wanted something. I started raging inwardly. After a further pause, as if goaded by tiny jump leads, he morosely acknowledged that when he and his brother were evacuated to the north of England in 1940, he thought it was 'the end of the world'. Two weeks later, though, he was feeling 'somewhat better'. Glum Larkinesque half-chuckle. Now this was all unprecedented self-revelation but didn't help much. I asked after his wife and the trombone-playing nephew. He sank back into his customary Arctic mode. I hung up, swearing as always never to call again.

I'd got off the World War One thing after the job fiasco – couldn't bear to look at my lecture notes, had tried to put everything out of my mind. But now it came inching back. I was desperate for something to read in those disordered weeks – something to match up with the lost way I was feeling. I galloped through Ann Wroe's book on Pontius Pilate, but it was too weird and dissociated. I ordered Kenneth Tynan's diaries from Amazon but found I was in no mood for high camp and dominatrixes. I wanted something stolid and sad. With a sense of oh-what-the-hell, I finally picked up a book I'd bought on the trench trip and then instantly lost interest in: a new paperback edition of Vera Brittain's Great War diary – the very diary she later transmuted into her celebrated 1933 war memoir, *Testament of Youth*.

Brittain was hardly an unknown quantity. I'd read *Testament of Youth* in my 20s and had never forgotten the intensity with which she related the primal bereavements of her early years. (I had once observed my grandmother surreptitiously dabbing at her eyes while reading it in the 1970s: her own Great War losses – of fiancé and only brother – duplicated Brittain's exactly.) Yet I couldn't say I had ever exactly warmed to Brittain, as either author or woman. For all the pain and horror she had suffered – and for all the integrity of her subsequent personal and political commitments – she struck me as abrasive and conceited. I tended to agree with Woolf, who, after devouring *Testament of Youth*, applied the usual backhanded praise in a comical diary entry from the 1930s:

> I am reading with extreme greed a book by Vera Brittain. Not that I much like her. A stringy metallic mind, with I suppose, the sort of taste I should dislike in real life. But her story, told in detail, without reserve, of the war, and how she lost lover and brother, and dabbled her hands in entrails, and was forever seeing the dead, and eating scraps, and sitting five on one WC, runs rapidly, vividly across my eyes.

And as I started in, it all began coming back to me: the head girl self-righteousness; the smug rivalry with other women; the gruesome fascination with period bores like Mrs Humphry Ward and Olive Schreiner. (In her wartime letters to the doomed Roland Leighton – her 19-year-old fiancé – Brittain is forever comparing their poetical puppy love to that of the unfortunately named 'Lyndall and Waldo' in *Story of an African Farm*.) Nor did I find much at first to obviate my ill-humour. I've got big irritable underlinings, I see, at just that point, early in 1915, when Brittain, still at Somerville, contemplates enlisting as a VAD nurse:

Janet Adie came to tea to help me learn to typewrite. She is feeling very busy because she now has the secretaryship of one of those soup-kitchen affairs on her shoulders. It does not sound very strenuous occupation; these people who never had anything to do before don't know the meaning of work ... I was told I ought to join this & that & the other. Everyone seems to be *so* keen for me to give up one kind of work for another, & that less useful, but more understandable by them. The general idea seems to be that college is a kind of pleasant occupation which leads to nothing – least of all anything that might be useful when the results of war will cause even graver economic problems than the war itself. If only I can get some work at the Hospital in the summer. I wonder what they will say when they see me doing the nursing which seems to exhaust them all so utterly, & my college work as well! I always come out top in the end, & I always shall.

Yet as I continued to read, something else began coming through too – something less rebarbative. I started noticing, amid all the boasts and bitchiness and careening *ressentiment*, a more vulnerable side to Brittain's personality. I hadn't remembered – at all – what a phobic and self-critical woman she was, or indeed how deeply she had had to struggle, throughout the First World War, with what she felt to be her own pusillanimity. Now, among the myriad painful feelings the attacks of 11 September had evoked in me – grief, despair, outrage – perhaps the most shame-making had been a penetrating awareness of my own cowardice. I worried incessantly about crashes, bombs, sarin gas, throat-slitting, eye-gouging, burning, jumping, falling. I brooded over horrific illnesses – anthrax, smallpox, nuclear sickness, plague – and imagined my own blood, teeming with bacteria, oozing thickly from my pores. I became afraid of bridges and tall buildings and the incendiary, blue-gold beauty of the city in which I lived. My childhood fear of flying revivified, I shed tears of self-disgust when I saw the pregnant Mrs Beamer, whose husband had died on United Flight 93, take the same flight a few weeks later, to show her resilience in the face of disaster. While straining to appear normal, I felt a vertiginous dread – of life itself – soar and frolic within me, like an evil biplane on the loose. I was not brave, it seemed, as men were – or even semi-stoical. I struggled with hysterical girlishness. It was an archaic and humiliating problem. I was female – and a wretched poltroon.

Yet signs of similar struggle – against girl-frights of such magnitude that she 'ached', she said, 'for a cold heart & a passionless indifference' – were everywhere in Vera Brittain's journals. And perhaps because I was already alert to the theme, I found myself peculiarly affected by her testimony. I rapidly consumed the remaining diaries, reread *Testament of Youth* (in a single great dollop), then turned to Paul Berry and Mark Bostridge's excellent Brittain biography of 1995. Before I knew it I was up to my ears again in Great War *matériel*, but this time with a difference. I was getting a weensy bit more honest, at some cost to my amour propre. To confess in public that you are afraid of death – and violent death especially – is to break a powerful taboo. Simple people will pity you and say nothing; the sophisticated will accuse you of being insufferably bourgeois. ('Spirited men and women' – or so maintains the title character in Bellow's *Ravelstein* – 'were devoted to the pursuit of love. By contrast the bourgeois was dominated by fears of violent death.') Yet precisely in Brittain's unsentimental revelation of her fear and candid hankering after the kind of physical bravery she saw in the men she knew at the front, I found not only a partial clue to the meaning of my war obsession but a necessary insight into my own less admissible hopes and fears.

Brittain's own anxieties, to be sure, were to some degree part of a difficult family inheritance. As Berry and Bostridge point out, she was a delicate woman: small and gamine in appearance, even in her starched VAD uniform. (Her brother Edward, who won a Military Cross on the first day of the Somme and died in June 1918, a few days after my Uncle Newton, towers over her by at least a foot in family photographs.) And in many ways she was delicate in spirit too. Insanity ran in the family – she worried greatly as an adult about a 'bad, bad nervous inheritance' in the Brittain line – and she was prone all her life to irrational frights and fancies. In an unfinished autobiographical novel from the 1920s she recalls the panic produced in her as a child by the sight of a 'leering' full moon:

The little girl in the big armchair had gazed at it, tense with fear, till at last it grew into a face with two wicked eyes & an evilly grinning mouth. Unable to bear it any longer, she hid her face in the cushions, but only for a few moments; the moon had a dreadful fascination which impelled her, quite against her will, to look up at it again. This time the grin was wider than ever & one great eye, leering obscenely at her, suddenly closed in a tremendous & unmistakable wink. Four-year-old Virginia was not at any time remarkable in her courage ... Flinging herself back into the chair, she burst into prolonged & piercing screams.

Similar hallucinations plagued her later in life. In one of the stranger asides in *Testament of Youth*, she describes a 'horrible delusion' she suffered after being demobilized in 1918. Returning to her studies at Somerville, traumatized and embittered by her war losses, she seemed to perceive – each time she looked at herself in the mirror – a 'dark shadow' on her face, suggestive of a beard. For 18 months she was tormented by this 'sinister fungus' and feared she was becoming a witch. In the memoir she attributes the fantasy to the strain she was under and passes over it relatively quickly. ('I have since been told that hallucinations and dreams and insomnia are normal symptoms of over-fatigue and excessive strain, and that, had I consulted an intelligent doctor immediately after the war, I might have been spared the exhausting battle against nervous breakdown which I waged for 18 months.') Yet one has a sense, here and elsewhere, of a woman painfully susceptible to mental distress. Despite her subsequent achievements as journalist, public speaker and political activist – or so say Berry and Bostridge – Brittain had always 'to fight hard for what little confidence she achieved, and even in old age the predominant impression she created among those meeting her for the first time was of a woman who seemed to be in a state of almost perpetual worry'.

But cowardice, as Brittain herself knew well, was also something more or less imprinted on women. By coddling and patronizing its female members, society enforced in them a kind of physical timidity; then, with infuriating circularity, defined such timidity as effeminate and despicable. Both practically and philosophically Brittain rebelled against the linkage. In *Testament of Youth* she recalls, broodingly enough, the violent 'inferiority complex' she felt in the early days of the war with regard to her lover Roland. He had enlisted in the Norfolks and would soon have his courage 'tested' in the most literal way possible. Yet while fearing for his safety Brittain envied him the trial. When he admitted in a letter how proud he was to be going to the front –

174

it relieved him of the appearance of a 'cowardly shirking of my obvious duty' – she declared, with palpable chagrin, that 'women get all the dreariness of war, and none of its exhilaration'. By 'exhilaration' she meant, among other things, a certain exemption from self-contempt. Women got to hand out white feathers – notoriously – but the gesture took on its odium precisely because women themselves epitomized 'cowardly shirking' so perfectly. They were the skulkers and moochers and tremulous babies of modern life: emasculated beings in need of protection, forbearance and forgiveness.

Everyone knows what Brittain did: made herself as manly as possible by becoming a nurse on the Western Front. (Her subsequent beard-in-the-mirror fantasy suggests the psychic intensity of her rejection of conventional femininity.) It was as if by getting as close to the fighting as she could – within striking distance of long-range German artillery – she sought to subject herself to the same practical test of bravery imposed on Roland and her brother Edward. Her war diaries make unabashedly clear the impinging wish: to *act as a man would* and be emboldened thereby. 'I had no idea she would get so thrilled as she seemed about the nursing,' she writes in 1915 after telling her classics tutor at Somerville that she is signing up for war service; 'she seemed to put it quite on the level of a man's deed by agreeing with me that I ought not to put the speedy starting of my career forward as an excuse, any more than a man should against enlisting'. Joining up was doing something 'on a level' with a man – facing up to fear like a soldier – and 'all part of the hard path I have assigned myself to tread'.

Which is not to say that Brittain entirely mastered her fearfulness. During her two years of nursing she was often afraid, and sometimes abjectly so. On her way by ship to Malta – her first foreign posting – she dreaded being blown up by enemy mines. During an air raid on Etaples during the final German advance in 1918 her teeth 'chattered with sheer terror'. But always there to sustain her was the faith that one might be inspirited – as if by magic – simply by mimicking, as far as possible, the stoic attitudes of men. Men had a certain mana, it seemed: a native supply of aplomb and insouciance that a courage-hungry woman might draw on. Blood transfusion technology, sadly, had yet to be perfected at the time of the First World War; thousands of soldiers who died from blood loss at casualty clearing stations might have been saved in later wars. Yet if haemoglobin could not always be transfused, valour might be. By placing herself in harm's way, or as near to it as she could get, Brittain seems to have hoped to absorb, as if by osmosis, the palpable gallantry of the men she loved and admired.

After Roland's death in 1915 by sniper bullet near Lou-vencourt, Brittain immediately elevated him, talismanically, to the role of chief exemplar and courage-infuser. Since his death was less than glorious – he seems merely to have lifted his head up inopportunely while slithering on his stomach through No Man's Land on a routine night-time patrol – Brittain's post-humous exaltation of him depended on some ambitious mental manoeuvres. In the weeks after his death she repeatedly sought to assure herself that despite the humiliating manner of his demise he was as brave an English warrior as any Arthurian knight. As she wrote in February 1916:

> I had another letter tonight from Roland's servant, giving a few more illuminating details of His death. It proves Him conclusively not to have thrown His life away recklessly or needlessly. He was hit because he was the *last* man to leave the dangerous area for the comparative safety of the trench, and so was at the post where the Roland we worship would always have wished to be when he met Death face to face.

'Worship' is the operative word. In *Testament of Youth* Brittain presents herself as godless and disillusioned, but it is clear from the ardent tributes to Roland in the diaries that she viewed him, for a time at least, as a sort of new Jesus Christ, whose martial self-sacrifice had made possible the 'salvation' of others – including her own. Almost as soon as Roland was killed, she began referring to him with a god-like 'He': 'Whether it was absolutely necessary for Him to go [on the fatal patrol] is questionable, but He would not have been He if He had not, for not only did He like to do everything Himself to make sure it was done thoroughly, but He would never allow anyone, especially an inferior, to take a risk he would not take Himself.' She herself became 'His' principal devotee and disciple, the mystic practi-tioner of a new sort of *imitatio Christi*, as her entries from 1916 make clear:

> *Sunday, 2 January.* We had more details today – fuller, more personal, more interesting, & so much sadder ... Two

sentences – one in the Colonel's letter & one in the Chaplain's hurt me more than anything. The Colonel says, 'The Boy was wonderfully brave,' and the Chaplain 'He died at 11 p.m. after a very gallant fight.' Yes, he would have been wonderfully brave; he would have made a gallant fight, even though unconsciously, with that marvellous vitality of his. None ever had more to live for; none could ever have wanted to live more ... I can wish to do nothing better than to act as He has acted, right up to the end.

Monday, 31 January. There was very much of a Zeppelin scare tonight. The Hospital was in utter darkness, passages black, lamps out, blinds down. I stood at the window of my ward, feeling strangely indifferent to anything that might happen. Since He had given up all safety, I was glad to be in London, which is not safe.

Sunday, 22 October. We had a simple sermon comparing harvest with the Resurrection of the Dead, & sang the hymn 'On the Resurrection Morning' to end with. I don't believe half the theology implied in these things, of course, & yet it is all a reminder. 'I could not if I would forget' – Roland. But I never would, since in all this hard life He is my great & sole inspiration, & if it were not for Him I should not be here.

In 1917, when Roland's old schoolfriend Victor, blinded by a bullet at Arras, lies dying in a London hospital, she admits that one reason she can't bear to lose him is because in his 'accurate, clear & reverent memory of Him, Roland seems to live still'. 'All that I ask,' she concludes, 'is that I may fulfil my own small weary part in this War in such a way as to be worthy of Them, who die & suffer pain.'

In the nervy state that gripped me after 11 September, such reflections struck me with new and incriminating force. Had I resisted Brittain for so long – cast her off as an important Not-Me – precisely because, deep down, I felt so much like her? I found out now, with a sudden embarrassed pang, precisely how much I sympathized – both with her anxiety and with the florid hope that the men she knew might infect her, so to speak, with physical courage. Not very butch of me, I know – *not very feminist*. But I had to confess it: I admired and coveted – quite desperately at times – the insane, uncomplaining relentless bravery of men.

I hear the shrieks. I write this knowing full well that some readers will find such veneration wholly charmless, part of an objectionable idealization of war or some absurd reversion to worn-out sex roles. So let me try to be a bit more precise. It seems to have something to do, first of all, with *walking*. Walking, paradoxically, is one of the great leitmotifs of the First World War. (I say 'paradoxically' because we are so used to imagining the nightmarish stasis of the trench world – a stasis more notional, perhaps, than actual. Even in times of relative quiet the typical front-line trench was an anthill of comings and goings.) Under normal conditions British soldiers travelled to the battle sector by troop train; contemporary accounts of 'going up the line' are full of descriptions of men crammed into creaking box-cars, and the slow, juddering rides towards Abbeville or Béthune. (How often the physical imagery of the First War anticipates, diabolically, that of the Second.) But on disembarking, soldiers usually had to march – sometimes for ten or twenty miles – toward billets, reserve trenches and other staging-areas behind the lines. 'This in fact,' Malcolm Brown writes in *Tommy Goes to War*, 'was the classic progress "up the line": train to the railhead, after which the Tommy had to fall back on the standard means of troop-transportation in the First World War – his own feet.' All the famous soldier-songs of the time – 'Here We Are', 'Tipperary', 'Mademoiselle from Armentières' – were first and foremost marching songs.

The route was long, exhausting and often indelibly frightening – especially for the tyro soldier seeing warfare up close for the first time. One subaltern, quoted by Brown, wrote:

> Yesterday as we were jingling over the cobbles past the danger zone, sure enough, away to the right came *Ponk! Ze-e-e-e-e-ee-E-Bang!* right over our heads. Again: *Ponk: Ze-e-e-e-ee-E-Bang!* A little nearer. The road just there is bare of cover, but a little way along on the right was a large barn, shell-holed. I would have given quids and quids just to run to that barn: but I am in front of my column, so I merely glance up in a casual way (what an effort) as if I'd been reared on shrapnel, whereas it's my baptism!

Another described his company being scattered by a German shell on their first march up the line near Bailleul: 'My back and pack were struck by a shower of debris and flying dirt while quite a number of men fell and bled for their country. Jack Duncan was in front of me and he received a severe wound from this, our first shell. He was carried onto the pavement and left for the attention of the doctor.'

Getting into the front-line trench itself meant further dreadful walking: a crabbed, head-down slog along battered communication trenches or over rotting duckboards, sometimes under heavy shelling or machine-gun fire. The journey to the front lines around Ypres – invariably made at night, through pools of mud and the reamy stench of dead animals and men – was notoriously ghastly. Leon Wolff writes in *In Flanders Fields*:

> The boards were covered with slime, or submerged, or shattered every few yards. The heavy laden troopers (60 lb of clothing, equipment and weapons were carried per man) kept slipping and colliding. Many toppled into shell-craters and had to be hauled out by comrades extending rifle-butts. And falling into even a shallow hole was often revolting, for the water was foul with decaying equipment, excrement, and perhaps something dead; or its surface might be covered with old, sour mustard gas. It was not uncommon for a man to vomit when being extricated from something like this.

And many fell, never to be dragged out. At Passchendaele, in the satanic months of October and November 1917, soldiers going up the line would often see the heads or hands of hapless predecessors protruding from the muck.

Animals, it seems, knew better – that such walking was intolerable. 'In one official history,' Wolff notes, 'there is a picture ... captioned "Bogged", of a mule in a shell-hole. His hindquarters are deep in the mud; only his head and shoulders protrude. In utter despair his head rests in the mud, eyes half-closed. Many mules had panicked, had fought merely to stand on visible portions of the planking, and could be made to move only with much coaxing and punishment.' The collapsing pack-mule is a vignette out of Sterne's *A Sentimental Journey* – but here gone awry and nightmarish.

The most celebrated walking of all was that of soldiers going 'over the top'. In order to stay in sync with the barrage and each other, attacking troops were strictly enjoined not to run. Once up over the parapet and into No Man's Land, they were required to proceed in a stylized, almost courtly, fashion – one man every two yards, rifles at the port, bayonets fixed, everyone moving forward in slow and regular waves. And thus unfurled what one writer calls 'the classic drama of the Western Front', the solemn, pavane-like motion of men towards machine-gun fire and death:

> In the flame and clamour and greasy smoke the British slogged forward deliberately, almost unhurriedly. They moved from crater to crater, but even in the craters they were not safe, for the German gunners streamed bullets against the edges of the holes and wounded many men lying near the rims. As the British walked, some seemed to pause and bow their heads; they sank carefully to their knees; they rolled over without haste and then lay quietly in the soft, almost caressing mud.

There is something beyond uncanny in such scenes. On the first day of the Somme, defending German gunners watched in amazement as row upon row of British soldiers plodded calmly towards them, only to be cut down in swathes. For the oncoming troops, it took every ounce of courage not to break formation – even as hellfire raged, crumps exploded and ground churned up around them. For the few who survived, the dream-like walk towards enemy trenches remained ever after, in the words of Leon Wolff, 'an intensely personal journey etched in [the] memory like the Stations of the Cross'.

As Paul Fussell long ago pointed out, the passage over No Man's Land was indeed a Christ-like transit, a hideous stroll into the Valley of Death. Like the assault on the Somme, the Passion begins – kinaesthetically and archetypally – in heroic pedestrianism: the tedious trudge 'up the line' to the boneyard known as Golgotha. Jesus is the first man in history to walk unwaveringly towards his own death. And ultimate masculine fortitude – at least in the modern West – has never lost its association with this Christ-like, goal-oriented walking. It is striking how many accounts of the destruction of the World Trade Center obsessively replay the image of doomed firemen and police walking into the towers and up the fatal stairwells – with exactly the same steady, flowing motion of attacking soldiers in the Great War. In a recent *Newsweek* report on the last minutes of Bill Feehan, a deputy commissioner of the New York City Fire Department killed in the collapse of the North Tower, he is seen exhorting his subordinates to walk just so:

> Feehan's men – Guidetti, Goldbach and two other deputy commissioners, Tom McDonald and Tom Fitzpatrick – began rushing to the elevator. 'Now, hold it, guys,' said Feehan, wearing a wry smile, holding his arms to the side and waving his palms down, like a teacher calming rambunctious school-children. 'Do we really want to run to this? Or should we walk to it?' Feehan was following an old dictum: 'Firemen should never run.' It was important to stay calm, to size up the job before rushing in.

Panic-stricken civilians making their way down were staggered – or so one reads again and again – by the sight of 'firefighters loaded with gear, trudging their way up the stairs. Everyone stepped aside to let them pass, watching them in awe.' Onward, Christian soldiers.

Cynics will no doubt want to debunk this heroic image of World War One walking: they will call attention to the fact that men who balked at the whistle – the signal for the start of the assault – faced being shot on the spot by their commanding officers. True enough. It's also true that other frightened soldiers simply faded from the scene, only to be caught and punished later. (The Ypres museum has a sad little pamphlet for sale commemorating the 306 British troops officially tried and 'shot at dawn' for cowardice or desertion.) Kipling – Kipling! – has the following wrenching couplet in his *Epitaphs* (1919):

> I could not look on Death, which being known,
> Men led me to him, blindfold and alone.
>
> ('The Coward')

Yet, relatively speaking, very few men seem to have failed thus in their duty. Those who did so were usually blatantly shell-shocked or otherwise unfit. However amazing in retrospect, the vast majority of ordinary soldiers accepted the martial tasks assigned them, even when such tasks were plainly suicidal. The most moving British novel to come out of the war, Frederic

Manning's *Her Privates We* (1930), may be taken as a fitful, yet forceful, demonstration of this fact. The hero, a laconic private soldier named Bourne, commits himself to a night-time trench raid, though he knows it is doomed to fail. When asked by his foolish commanding officer if he has any objection to going, Bourne feels 'something in him dilate enormously, and then contract to nothing again', but says only that he is 'quite ready' to go. He goes; he dies; and the book ends.

If you're a woman – and a woman haunted by feelings of cowardice – it's hard to know where to stand with all of this. You regret the appalling, absurd waste of life. You excoriate the madness of the system. You rail against war. You see the savage toll the cult of heroism takes – has always taken – on men and boys. But painful too – at times exorbitantly so, once you become sensitized to it – the near-total exclusion of your own sex from such primal dramas of unflinching physical courage. You feel at a moral deficit. You wonder, perhaps dubiously, if you would be capable of such nobility under the circumstances – of moving forward calmly. You fear the worst. For Brittain was right: women have seldom been asked to exert their valour in this direct, theatrical, entirely wasteful and (yet) sublime fashion. Certainly I never have.

From early childhood I have searched with little success for a woman who might show me – in some comparable and quite literal way – how to walk towards death. Few have offered themselves as models. A psychoanalyst I know says this is because women are pre-eminently concerned with 'life': children and the raising of children. They have no interest in walking towards death. Given half a chance they walk away from death. It's 'pure and simple biology', the shrink says. But whence my own odd questing? Some retardation of normal development? Some sad hormonal jousting with the male of the species? Some dissatisfaction with simply staying put and waiting for things to happen? Last week I went to see the film version of *Lord of the Rings* – not having thought about Tolkien since I was 12. The trilogy's a death-trip of course – a long weary trudge through mud, mines, ravaged woods and orc-infested caves. As I pondered the dire, cacophonous, corpse-laden wastelands through which Frodo and his friends are forced to travel – now digitalized and Dolbyized and fiercely estranging (like video games and cyberterrorism) – I found myself wondering whether Tolkien had been a soldier on the Western Front. I couldn't remember. I got home and looked him up: he fought on the Somme with the Lancashire Fusiliers.

True, a woman on her way to public execution in some degree resembles a soldier going over the top. As a child, I uncovered a few such women, and studied them as best I could. But a certain intimacy, kinship – even friendliness – was almost always lacking. They never felt like companions. There was Joan of Arc, but I found her celebrated visions freakish and her personality aloof. I was not raised a Catholic, so stories of female saints and martyrs made little or no impression. I was too young for the terrible dramas of the Holocaust and Resistance. There was the afore-mentioned Edith Cavell – her fate, I find, is luridly described in a children's *Pageant of History* book I still have on my shelves – but it would take a while before I understood her actions in context. (Calling me, not long ago, from the grotty pay-phone near the latter's memorial at the foot of Charing Cross Road, Blakey had to endure me squeaking away, at 8,000 miles' distance, 'But of course she was a spy! The Germans had every right to shoot her! She knew it!' and so on.) Only now do I begin to find the high starched collar, iron-grey hair and sweeping black cape oddly alluring. *No, sir, I do not require a blindfold.*

The French Revolution, to be sure, offers instances of almost picturesque feminine gallantry – though it's hardly fashionable to say so. Madame Roland was famously poised on the scaffold: she let Lamarche, a feeble old man being executed with her, go first so he would not have the sight of her own headless corpse before him as he approached the guillotine. Marie Antoinette, former cocotte, was even more so. Hounded, half-starved, white-haired and decrepit at the age of 34 – from chronic menstrual flux and the gross abuse of her jailers – the no-good *Autrichienne* became quite staggeringly noble in her final moments. David's harrowing sketch of her, set down from life as she rolled by in the death-cart on her way to execution, is the unexpected emblem of a stupendous and electrifying heroism.

The French Revolution is also the setting for the only major work of art – the only one that I can think of at least – devoted profoundly and exclusively to the topic of feminine courage: Francis Poulenc's 1957 opera *Dialogues of the Carmelites*. Based on a play by Bernanos and a novel by Gertrud von Le Fort, *Die letzte am Schafott* (*The Last to the Scaffold*), the opera turns on the struggle of Soeur Blanche de l'Agonie du Christ, a novice in the Carmelite order at Compiègne, to master the dread that assails her when the sisters of the convent are arrested during the Terror. The plot has its origin in fact: Marie de l'Incarnation, a Carmelite nun who survived the Revolution, tells a similar story in her memoirs. (And how odd, the World War One freak notes, that it should all have taken place at Compiègne: British GHQ during the retreat from Mons and site of the signing of the Armistice in 1918.)[2] When the other sisters take a vow of martyrdom, Blanche runs away and hides for several weeks at her father's house. Mortified by her own cowardice, however, she secretly follows her fellow nuns when they are taken to Paris for execution. In the opera's final moments, as the condemned women march to the guillotine singing the *Salve Regina* – a voice falling out with each ferocious slice on the cymbals – Blanche suddenly materializes from the crowd and joins in the procession. Hers is the only voice left, soaring up in triumph, when the last blade-stroke comes down and the curtain drops.

But Blanche is a bit of a pill too – a sexless high soprano and one of those blonde, seraphic goody-goodies one could never stand in primary school. Charlotte Brontë would have loathed her. And for every Blanche, it seems, there are always women like the unhappy Lange Vaubernier – better known as Madame du Barry, the one-time mistress of Louis XV. On *her* way to execution, according to Lamartine's *Histoire des Girondins* (1847), the aging harlot flung back her veil, 'in order that her countenance might move the people' and 'did not cease to invoke pity, in the most humiliating terms'. The poet, spokesman of the People, is extravagantly contemptuous:

> Tears flowed incessantly from her eyes upon her bosom. Her piercing cries prevailed over the noise of the wheels and the clamour of the multitude. It seemed as if the knife struck this woman beforehand, and deprived her a thousand times of life.
>
> 'Life! Life!' she cried; 'life for my repentance! – life for all my devotion to the Republic! – life for all my riches to the nation!'
>
> The people laughed and shrugged their shoulders. They showed her, by signs, the pillow of the guillotine, upon which her charming head was about to sleep. The passage of the courtesan to the scaffold was but one lamentation. Under the knife she still wept. The Court had enervated her soul. She alone, among all the women executed, died a

coward, because she died neither for opinion, for virtue, nor for love, but for vice. She dishonoured the scaffold as she had dishonoured the throne.

Poor old Lange. *See yah. Wouldn't wanna be yah.*

At a certain point one just gives up and decides to go with the men. They're so much closer to home, after all. Unless one is insane or a sex fanatic, it's impossible to identify much with Joan of Arc or Marie Antoinette; whereas one's estimable Uncle Newton, soft moustache and all, seems just a few decades and a Chunnel trip away. I sometimes feel I could call him up on the phone. He lives in the same world as I do – the familiar vale of sorrows, fuck-ups and relentless, chain-reaction human disasters. (How acutely one feels the 11 September atrocity to be, like so much else in our time, simply one of the hundreds of geopolitical aftershocks of the First World War. Palestine, after all, began its long, sad modern history in 1917, when Allenby's army drove off the Turks at Gaza and occupied Jerusalem.)[3] And compelling indeed is the knowledge that I myself can now walk exactly where he walked. The worst signs of battle have long disappeared from the Western Front but the war-tourism industry battens still on the morbid hankering of visitors to stroll freely about those very places (Loos, Menin, Hooge, Stuff Trench, Polygon Wood, Vimy, Festubert, Beaumont Hamel, Gheluvelt, Neuve-Chapelle) where walking – of any sort – was once so foul and frightening. One can now wander unimpeded over spots formerly blasted by gun and shell fire, where lifting one's head above the parapet, even by an inch, meant getting it blown off. One feels floaty and tall and invulnerable, like a ghost. You imagine getting hit all over – positively laced with bullets – but it doesn't hurt at all.

And then, too, there's the mana effect: the hope that by treading just so, on the very spot, some ancient family backbone will be magically imparted. (After I came back from my trip I found it oddly difficult to brush the Somme mud off my hiking shoes.) Travelling through Picardy and Flanders, it's hard to forget that the soil itself is full of once-sentient matter, now dissolved but still in situ. We are inclined to make fun of Rupert Brooke-style animism these days, perhaps because his creepy brand of dirt-magic is still so weirdly potent:

There shall be
In that rich earth a richer dust concealed;
A dust whom England bore, shaped, made aware,
Gave, once, her flowers to love, her ways to roam,
A body of England's, breathing English air,
Washed by the rivers, blest by suns of home.

Yet it's only a short step from Brooke's patriotic composting to fantasies of an even more atavistic sort. Almost as soon as the first Great War cemeteries were opened to the public, senti-mental grave-visitors sought to absorb the magical rigour of the dead. In *The Unending Vigil* (1967), his history of the Com-monwealth War Graves Commission, Philip Longworth relates a saccharine tale of a French child at Versailles – a 'heroic little thing ... doomed by a disease of the spine' – who insisted on tending the graves of her 'chers soldats anglais' until her sickness defeated her. The punning import of the story is so obvious as to be risible: how else to ward off 'spinelessness' in the face of mortality? I've got *her* number, and she, undoubtedly, has mine.

So I want my great-uncle to make me brave – is that what it boils down to? To place his hand in the small of my back and give me that first shove up onto the fire-step? To start me off on my wind-up-toy-like way into No Man's Land? That's an answer for the moment, I suppose – but no more than that. It would be nice to be sturdier and less addled – not such a twit on wheels. It would be gratifying to impress everyone with my handsome, jut-jawed selflessness. ('I now perceive one immense omission in my *Psychology*,' William James once wrote: 'the deepest principle of Human Nature is *the craving to be appreciated*.') Somewhere, it seems, there *must* be a lost baby picture of me – at my father's perhaps? – in which I look just like Mel Gibson in *Gallipoli*. Glug, glug, glug!

At the same time I see how kooky and notional it all is. How can I be sure, for example, that my great-uncle even died bravely? His service record seems to have disappeared: according to the Public Record Office website, it looks to have been one of the hundreds of thousands of such records destroyed during the Blitz. Perhaps he was a puny little time-serving fellow who just happened to be in the wrong place at the wrong time. My mother's vague recollection of him being shot by 'his own guns' is worrying: perhaps he was sitting in a dugout drinking a cup of tea, or nibbling on a piece of chocolate (the family vice), and simply got blown up by accident. Perhaps he was picked off by an errant bullet while using the company latrine. Perhaps he started jabbering in terror one day and his sergeant major just had to brain him in homicidal exasperation. Such things were all part of the 'normal wastage' of the war. I have a great deal invested, I realize, in the image of him not being wasted. I prefer to view him stalking forward coolly, his fellow Poplar and Stepney Rifles at his side, across the muddy, blood-drenched plains of the Ancre.

But even if my fantasy about him is accurate, do I really need him to show me the way? I've got this far, after all, on my own two feet. Might it not be the case, terrors notwithstanding, that most people end up 'walking towards death' in a fairly resolute fashion whether they plan to or not? One of the few times, paradoxically, I've found myself in apparent physical danger, when a bomb warning went off deep in one of the Tube tunnels at Charing Cross and everyone had to evacuate in a hurry, I not only remained calm but felt peculiarly philosophical. The long-legged platform guard skedaddled at once – I can still see him bounding up the escalator steps two or three at a time – leaving a little group of tourists and children and old-age pensioners to scramble along after him. I ran about a third of the way up the escalator, panting horribly – it was one of those extra-long ones and for some reason wasn't moving – then thought, *Oh fuck this, I'm too tired to run any more! I don't care if I get blown up!* It was like the old French and Saunders skit: *my leg-bones have gone away.* So I walked the rest of the way, more or less sedately, ultimately surfacing in Trafalgar Square. The crowds and the pigeons were bustling about as usual. No bomb went off, that week or later.

Silliest of all perhaps: whom do I hope to impress with my virile equipoise? My mother? My father? Siegfried Sassoon?[3] Vera Brittain? Miss Coombs? None, I confess, has ever asked for such a proof of character. Blakey couldn't care less. She's staying with me till next September, working away in the downstairs room, where she's just figured out a way to type on a laptop while lying down. The dog loves it because he gets to spend the whole day snoozing on the bed with her while she muses. She's stuck with me all this dreary past year, though I'm not sure what she really thinks – either about my war-obsession or the 'walking towards death' stuff. She is interested in evolutionary psychology and selfish genes. Given such an intellectual framework, the First

World War, like all genocidal conflicts, poses certain conceptual difficulties. How could it have been possible for millions of men to squander their DNA in such a reckless fashion? It's a stumper, I agree.

The other day we looked at an old photo in one of my books of a parade of volunteers, still dressed in their civilian clothes, marching down a London street in August 1914. War has just been declared. The men look tough and expectant; a military band is playing and women gaze down from balconies and windows. I had just realized to my great excitement that the narrow roadway in the picture (at first generic-looking Edwardian) was actually Villiers Street, the busy pedestrian thoroughfare that runs down from the Strand to Embankment. There on one side of the picture, clearly visible once you get your bearings, is the dark, somewhat dusty façade of Gordon's Wine Bar. It looks almost exactly as it does now.

I went there the first time, I recall, with Bridget, one late autumn night in 1987, during the honeymoon phase of our cousinhood. (It was the same night – we discovered later – as the terrible fire at King's Cross.) Down steep wooden steps into a smoky medieval crypt where they served up our burgundy and plonk. Strange, as always, the curving back of time. One of the worst things about the First World War – from the vantage point of 2002 – is that you think you've got to the end of thinking about it, then something makes you start all over again. This picture, for instance. I would prefer to move on and out – from gloomy 1918 especially – but I keep getting sent back to the beginning, as if stuck in some kind of Möbius loop. It's totally unlikely, as I said to Blakey, that my great-uncle could be one of the men in the parade, coming from the Midlands as he did. (The new Sherwood Forester battalions of 1914 and 1915 formed up in Derby and Newark.) But that didn't keep me – as soon as Blakey went back to work – from screwing in my monocle and inspecting the men like a staff general. It was a tough job: I had first to remove all the cloth caps and boaters, add rifles and packs and khaki, then connect the fatal dots. And even then, all I could really see – staring crazily upward, as if already dazed by the fumes from the dugout brazier – was my own once-boyish face.

Notes

1 John Keegan on the unhappy exploits of the Portuguese Army in World War One: 'Portugal, historically Britain's oldest ally, declared war on Germany and Austria in March 1916. It eventually sent two divisions to the Western Front, armed and equipped by the British. Put into the line at Neuve-Chapelle, in the British sector south of Ypres, they were attacked during the second great German offensive of 9 April 1918, broke and ran. Large numbers of prisoners were taken. The Portuguese, an unsophisticated and rural people, were unsuited to the strains of industrial warfare and it was unwise of the Portuguese Government to have taken sides. It would have been better advised to imitate Spain in standing apart.' *An Illustrated History of the First World War* (2001, New York: Knopf).

2 Like Sarajevo, Belfast and Dallas, Compiègne would seem to be one of the strangely doom-laden minor cities in history: my 1920 *Guide to Belgium and the Western Front* notes that Joan of Arc was captured and turned over to the English there in 1430; Marie Antoinette, aged 15, met her future husband the Dauphin there in 1770; and Tsar Nicholas and the Tsarina were received by President Loubet at the famous nearby château in 1901.

3 Siegfried Sassoon, in *Memoirs of an Infantry Officer* (1930, London: Faber and Faber): 'Markington had gloomily informed me that our [War] Aims were essentially acquisitive, what we were fighting for was the Mesopotamian Oil Wells. A jolly fine swindle it would have been for me, if I'd been killed in April for an Oil Well!'

Quotations from Vera Brittain are used by permission of her literary executors.

Chapter 20

A *Biplane* in *Gnomeregan: Popular Culture* and the *First World War*

Esther MacCallum-Stewart

Popular culture is still a hugely diverse field, with many sub-categories still emerging and struggling to define themselves. The First World War hangs in an unusual position within this construction, as it is at once something rigorously constructed through a series of ideological forms and also at large in culture as icon, symbol and actuality. It has also been extensively studied elsewhere, most famously through literary and historical fields.

For popular culture, however, the First World War is important because of its symbolic value. This conception has undergone significant change over the last century, and has been greatly influenced by other factors, including those of political and social belief. Here, the perception of what the war is seen to stand for as a cultural artefact often overrides the actual detail. World War One is seen as a key moment in the formation of British national identity, as a war gone terribly wrong, and one of idealism and disillusion, of change, and of class outweighing common sense. It is a war, like most others, that is frequently denoted by slogans: 'lions led by donkeys', 'mud, blood and endless poetry', and of course Wilfred Owen's 'old Lie: Dulce et decorum est pro patria mori'. None of these signifiers is particularly clear or well-formed; in fact most rest upon emotive ideals or concepts, rather than actual details, but at the same time they are perceived to be a solid construction. The war has formed into what I have described as a cultural 'parable', a mythic retelling of the war with a specifically moral purpose. This parable informs much of popular culture as it provides a wonderfully strident version of what happened which is heavy with irony, sympathy and a justification for the rather ghoulish (but very human) obsession with an event that caused such carnage. While none of the events that this parable presents are false, they are extremely exclusive, focusing on certain aspects of the war, such as the horrors of the Western Front, the poets and writers, the dogged but forthright private and the uncaring civilian and the mulish general. They are also riven with more recent beliefs about World War One – beliefs which have changed gradually throughout the last century, but largely now portray the war itself as 'futile' (a word which many historians will dispute), and the people who took part as unwitting victims or cruel overlords. These ideals can be seen in practice through Stephen Fry's portrayal of General Hogmanay Melchett in *Blackadder Goes Forth* (1989), perhaps one of the best examples of how fictional archetypes have often been adopted as representing truisms about the war.

Popular culture is a moveable feast of ideas and contradictions, thus it is also true that it is able to express very different viewpoints as well as sustaining an internal hegemony. The following section examines how diverse popular culture can be in its ideas about the war, but also how it can provide more positive depictions – challenging its readers to consider their own beliefs and often escaping the critique of more academic eyes. This section also looks at the ways in which new media – specifically the development of Web 2.0 – has changed the ways that information about the war is disseminated and offers a way forward for popular representations of the war.

The Remembrance Day service every November is a typical example of how popular culture diverges in expression. Surrounding the (largely unattended) parades and ceremonies, the media usually stirs up a moment of political turmoil, questioning the ways that 'respect' is duly accorded to the dead. In 2006, this revolved around newsreader Jon Snow's refusal to wear a poppy during his appearances on the Channel Four news. While even the British Legion stated that wearing a poppy was a voluntary action, Snow was criticized heavily for this decision, with *The Guardian* interviewing a veteran of the Gulf War who stated, 'Any questioning of the poppy can only cause anguish to the people that have worn it with pride over the years, the families of those who gave their lives and those people who are still doing so' (Plumbridge in Bell: 2006). This argument is symptomatic of the hysteria that surrounds any deviation from the normative response to the war – in this case 'all' poppy wearers, not simply veterans, are deemed to be targets of Snow's decision.

In this case, popular beliefs about the war mean that any changes from presumed normative responses are immediately targeted as disrespectful. Snow argued that his decision not to wear a poppy was that any affiliation through wearing ribbons or badges aligned him with a political movement of some description. While his argument was both reasoned and specifically not the expression of a pro- or anti-war stance, this was overruled since the status quo suggests that all newsreaders should wear a poppy, and the caveat attached to this was also that it was done as a mark of respect.

A nebulous line exists in the public mind between what is 'correct' and 'respectful' and what is not, perhaps because the First World War has been so consistently expressed through secondary sources such as poetry, literature and drama. All of these portrayals carry a specific agenda, but because it is often apparently cohesive, the war is overshadowed by an unhealthy dose of ideological bias. The BBC television programme *The Trench* (Colthurst: 2002) suffered similar condemnation in the media, often through articles written prior to the development of the show. The three-part programme aimed to demonstrate daily life in the trenches by using 24 volunteers from Hull. These men lived for two weeks in a recreated trench in France, where they experienced as much as was possible of trench life. This included going on sorties, drill, poor weather conditions, inspections, and the more mundane difficulties of living in cramped, unpredictable conditions with other people. Although *The Trench* was broadcast in the early evening, the programme was primarily targeted at schools, with an extensive campaign promoting the series through posters, a website and an exhibition at the Imperial War Museum that proved so successful that it was extended.

Before the series was even broadcast, however, criticism was rained upon it. How could recreating such a sensitive event ever be practical or realistic? Surely this was the worst kind of schlock reality television, designed to titillate rather than inform? What would the *real* survivors of the war think? In fact, many of the surviving veterans were interviewed for the programme, one of whom visited the site. The programme itself aimed to show the minutiae of daily trench life, getting away from the incorrect preconception that men were constantly going 'over the top' and showing instead the ways in which the army coped with trench occupation. This sensitivity and attention to detail was overlooked in the lambasting of the series as tasteless and disrespectful, with some critics going as far as comparing the programme to recreating the Holocaust. Needless to say, most of the criticism appeared before the show aired, and it is interesting that during the broadcast, reviewers described *The Trench* as surprisingly 'dragging' (Moran: 2002), clearly surprised at the degree to which soldiers had to endure waiting for something to happen.

While perceived ideas of respect and disrespect permeate many representations of the war, it is also true that many other artefacts slip beneath the radar. Some, like the continually bastardized version of Alfred Leete's recruitment poster, have become so commonplace that they no longer attract comment at all, and happily advertise everything from demands for allotment tenants to T-shirts which distort the image to Darth Vader's helmet in place of Kitchener, recruiting stormtroopers for the *Star Wars* Empire. The rise of Web 2.0 and the growth of digital gaming as a pastime that moves far beyond teenagers bashing buttons both epitomize the ways that depictions of the war have changed elsewhere, often to produce highly creative, intelligent new ways of looking at the conflict.

One of the most interesting ways that First World War studies have diversified is through their presence on the web. Historical debate is a popular subject for forums, weblogs, online journals and informative sites. The majority of these sites appreciate the nuances of historical representation, but they also leave interpretation open to the reader by including various opinions, ideas, links or debate as a standardized part of their narratives. Weblogging culture in particular shows an awareness of the politicized nature of historical inquiry, as well as prompting cross-pollination and alternative ways of approaching war studies. A study done by Brett Holman of Airminded in March 2007 estimated that 26 per cent of all military bloggers focus on the two world wars (Holman: 2007).

Overall, weblogs and their authors are well aware of the revisionism that has taken place in First World War studies, and often engage this directly as their subject matter. The information-sharing nature of forums and encyclopaedic sites such as Spartacus.net can prompt debates as lively as those in more formal academic structures such as the Society for First World

War Studies. Overall, the development of web-based technology to advance both the ideas and the information available about the First World War is regarded positively by its numerous authors.

Blogging has also been seen as a way of democratizing research. Anyone with a computer can access and comment on blogs, and a plethora of free hosting sites exist for people to create their own blogs. As a medium for sharing thought and research, blogging presents a fast way to circulate ideas, news and thoughts about the war. The academic playing field is far more level in online communication, with journals and informative sites such as the St Mihiel Trip-Wire (2002–present) deliberately mixing contributions between enthusiasts and people employed in the field, blurring these distinctions in a positive manner and allowing the sharing of ideas rather than one-upmanship. The fear of sharing academic information which can restrict universities in their uses of the web is now largely seen as redundant by users, with both groups presenting diverse responses to the war, and a great deal of valid debate taking place as a result, often on public sites where divergent opinions can be shared.

Elsewhere in the digital world, the development of games that use the war as a motif, or directly engage with its historical detail, are also marked in the ways that they display either unusually neutral views of the world or develop on pre-existing themes in order to provide their own commentary. There seems to be a popular misconception that there are few videogames dealing with the First World War. In fact, the war provides a popular subtext to many games, and is the subject of several others. In this, the use of the First World War is symptomatic of its wider use in popular cultural production – it becomes a stage rather than the whole event, or an ideological example rather than the central subject. In this respect, games also demonstrate the ways that popular culture often accepts the motifs of the war parable as a given, but then uses it in subversive ways.

In videogames, depictions of warfare have become increasingly more detailed over time. This includes extensive reference to military details through graphics, and, with games such as the Medal of Honor (1999–present) series, giving players more historical detail in the form of rewards (files, photographs, videos and additional information) for good play. A misconception of wargames in particular is that they reside solely in the First Person Shooter (FPS) genre, rather than appearing in more diverse contexts. Thus, although World War One is a frequent topic for historical resource games such as Victoria (2003), in which the player manages a country through political, social and military change, scenarios from the First World War are also included as special challenges in many versions of the Civilisation games, for example (1990–2007). The player must manage her resources in order to fight the battles, or simply survive throughout the time period. Notably, players are also able to pick from a variety of different countries in these games, thus allowing them to experience the relative challenges of each country. This mode of play allows a counterfactual experience in which, although a different outcome is almost inevitable to the historical one, players are able to manipulate events, troops and resources, all of which are often accompanied by a very high level of explanatory detail as to how they performed in the past. Increasingly, this type of management, or 'God' game, has bled over into education, and Firaxis, the designers of Civilisation III (2001) attribute its continuing sales to its popularity as a learning tool (Squire and Steinkuehler: 2005).

Similarly, aerial dogfighting games have also seen popularity, Knights of the Sky (1990) and Red Baron (1990) being early versions of these. The war has recently seen an upsurge in interest again through the successful Half-Life mod,[*] The Trenches (2006) and the forthcoming To End All Wars (2007).

The ethos of the First World War is also surprisingly apparent in many games with large-scale narratives. The Massively Multiplayer Online Roleplaying Game World of Warcraft (2004–present) epitomizes this pattern, utilizing recognizable signifiers from the war to connote specific ideas. So, for example, technological development in this fantasy world ends with artefacts from World War One, most notably in the form of ruined biplanes placed around the world and zeppelins which help players move from place to place. These icons are supported by narratives (through quests and comments made by Non Player Characters in the world) that suggest technology beyond this

[*] Mods, or 'modifications' are patches which players create themselves which give the game additional content which overlays the existing game. This content provides extra features, scenarios, levels and animations. Many game companies allow their source code to be freely available to coders, since mods often become more popular than the original version of the game and can therefore comprise a significant part of sales. The most successful mod ever is the Counter-Strike (1999–2007) mod for the Half-Life engine, which is still played more than the original game itself and was given a commercial release of its own. In 2007, Counter-Strike still had 32,479 servers, hosting 92,312 active players at the time of recording (Gamespy: 2007).

point in history is dangerous or inappropriate, having led to disaster. Similarly, certain days set aside to respect fallen heroes, and shrines to fallen warriors embedded in the landscape of the world, also draw the player's attention to the consequences of warfare by directly linking them to memorialization.

Conclusion

Overall, the attention paid to the war in popular culture is still developing. As revisionist ideas begin to filter down, popular culture is often more free to investigate new ways of understanding the war through different experiences, since the way it uses these ideas is not only diverse but also accepts that a wide variety of ideas are already in existence. In this sense, popular culture moves ideas forwards, using parable tropes in unexpected ways, often to highlight their fixed nature and suggest alternatives. Although *The Trench* was unsuccessful, pioneering history projects in virtual worlds such as Second Life (2004–present) suggest that in general, a new era of experimentation is beginning, certainly in the way that history in general is perceived. The recreation of trenches in this world is in line with the way that it demonstrates history already – through recreation and simulation. Thus the perceived offence of the act is displaced, and the people who use Second Life are accustomed to learning through manipulation of their surroundings, thus approaching the subject in a different manner. Thus, popular culture is often free to move onwards from more traditional perspectives, taking a historical event and moulding it as a form of bricolage, as well as developing ideas in new directions.

In terms of development, popular culture is always a reflection of what continues above it in academic research, yet the patterns and distortions that these reflections throw out can often occur in different, sometimes genuinely challenging, ways. As the First World War assimilates itself into our culture, so it becomes familiar through its usage in popular representations. And in this case, it is the familiarity with the war from the multitude of other disciplines that investigate it that allows expansion.

Further Reading

Bell, Dan (2006), 'Snow accuses Remembrance Day critics of "poppy fascism'". *The Guardian*: Friday, 10 November 2006.

Colthurst, David. (Dir.) (2002), *The Trench*. BBC: 15–29 March 2002.

Curtis, Richard, and Ben Elton (Dir) (1989), *Blackadder Goes Forth*. BBC: 28 September–2 November 1989.

Hanlon, Mike, et al., St Mihiel Trip-Wire (2002–present). Available at *http://www.worldwar1.com/tripwire/smtw.htm* [cited 25/07/07].

Holman, Brett (2007), 'State of the military historioblogosphere, March 2007'. Available at *Airminded, http://airminded.org/2007/03/18/state-of-the-military-historioblogosphere-march-2007/* [cited 25/07/07].

International Society for First World War Studies (2004–present). Available at *http://doc-iep.univ-lyon2.fr/wwi/* [cited 25/07/07].

Moran, Caitlin (2002), 'Smile if you're hard enough'. *The Times*: Features, 22 March 2002.

Squire, Kurt and Constance Steinkuehler (2005), 'Meet the Gamers'. *Library Journal*: 15 April 2005. Available at *http://www.libraryjournal.com/article/CA516033.html* [cited 25/07/07].

Chapter 21

A View from the Trenches: An Introduction to the Archaeology of the Western Front

Tony Pollard

There has recently been an upsurge of interest in the archaeology of the recent past, not least within the field of conflict archaeology, which is itself a nascent sub-discipline within the wider sphere of historical archaeology. Particularly noticeable within this general trend has been a growing interest in the archaeology of the First World War, with much of that attention devoted to the Western Front.

Up until now the field has been led by a small group of archaeologists and historians, both professional and amateur. Playing a central role here has been 'No Mans Land', a group of British archaeologists who over the last five years or so have carried out a number of projects on the Western Front in both France and Belgium, many of them taking leave from their own jobs in academic institutions or archaeological field units to take part in projects. See Fraser and Brown in further reading section for a good example of their work.

Over recent years, excavations have been carried out on trench systems, grave sites and dugouts. In looking for a motive for this increased archaeological interest, we perhaps need to look to a more general increase in interest in the First World War among members of the general public, certainly in the UK, where virtually no village or town is lacking a memorial to local men lost in the conflict. A personal connection to the battlefields of Flanders and elsewhere on the Western Front is also reflected in the dramatic growth of interest in family history, a pursuit which has ironically resulted in people today knowing more about what their great-uncles or great-grandfathers did in the First World War than their immediate families ever did.

What has become almost a national obsession with the war is also reflected in television documentaries, books and newspaper articles. (There is barely a week goes by when papers such as the *Daily Mail* don't print a story with some reference to World War One.)

Nor is this upsurge limited to the British side: Jon Price has described British First World War remains on the Western Front as 'Orphan Heritage' but this is a concept which in reality is losing some of its validity as French and Belgian archaeologists become increasingly involved. There can be little doubt that this hunger to learn more about what used to be called the Great War is closely related to the realization that almost all of those who fought in it are now dead and that very few of these extraordinary people left will not be with us for long, a fact reinforced by a recent spate of momentous anniversaries.

While 2006 marked the 90th anniversary of the battle of the Somme, 2007 saw a similar round of commemoration of events centred on the series of engagements collectively remembered as Passchendaele (Third Battle of Ypres), while 2008 marks the end of the war. The Passchendaele anniversary meant more to one man then most. Harry Patch was born in 1898 and in 2007 was the last man living to have fought in the Battle of Passchendaele. In late July 2007, Harry revisited the scene of some of the bloodiest fighting of the Great War, including Passchendaele, where he served as a Lewis gunner in the Duke of Cornwall's Light Infantry. Harry, who was eventually invalided out of the fighting due to a shrapnel wound, is among the last of a dying breed, and very soon veterans of the Great War will be an extinct species. (The week before Harry's visit saw the death of the last Scottish veteran – 107-year-old Bill Young who served in the Royal Flying Corps; his death left just five known British veterans, including Harry, and this figure may well have been reduced further still by the time this volume is published.) The passing of the last of these remarkable men will see an event currently encapsulated within living memory, however tenuously, passing entirely into history.

With this passing, our understanding of the First World War will also rely more than ever on archaeology; it has after all been analysed by historians for the almost 90 years since the Armistice. What is it, though, that currently motivates the archaeological investigation of First World War remains?

Chance has played a role here, as some of the most evocative sites have been discovered while excavating for the types of remains more normally associated with the archaeologist. In 2001, for example, the excavation of an incredibly rich Romano-Celtic settlement and ritual complex in advance of warehouse construction near Arras unexpectedly uncovered a mass grave containing the remains of 20 British soldiers, identified as men from the 10th Battalion of the Lincolnshire Regiment and killed in the Battle of Arras in 1917. In keeping with any site containing human remains, the grave was carefully excavated by municipal archaeologist Alain Jacques and his team and the release of photographs of the skeletons lying side by side excited a good degree of media attention, especially as they seemed to have their arms interlinked – good companions in death just as they had been in life. The reality, however, was a little more prosaic: the bodies had been laid in the grave with their hands resting across their laps, but as decay and the pressure of earth forced the arms outwards they crossed with those of their neighbours and thus on first exposure appeared to be interlinked.

One of the few programmes of investigation explicitly directed toward First World War remains, as opposed to being incidental to the investigation of earlier sites, took place prior to the construction of the A19 road in the Ieper (Ypres) region of Belgian Flanders. In 2002, in response to a campaign orchestrated by various groups, including historians, archaeologists, veterans' organizations and heritage conservation bodies, the Institute for the Archaeological Heritage of the Flemish Community (IAP) was instructed by the Ministry of Culture to examine a 4.5-mile-long stretch of the proposed route known to coincide with First World War remains. A programme of fieldwalking backed up by documentary research resulted in the excavation of nine areas, including trench systems at Turco Farm and Crossroads Farm. Importantly for the long-term growth of the discipline, the project also set the stage for the inauguration of the Department of First World War Archaeology, under the umbrella of IAP, in November 2003.

Modern aerial photographs include soil or crop marks indicating the presence of ancient sites, be they Neolithic long houses or Roman villas, but many of them also portray the characteristic zigzagged or castellated shape of wartime trenches, perhaps cutting through or passing close by these older archaeological sites. Not so long ago, these legacies of war would have been ignored or even caused consternation as they demonstrated how much damage had been caused to ancient sites by wartime activity. However, discoveries such as the mass grave near Arras and the A19 project have helped to bring about a change in this attitude. (Thanks to media coverage many people now have some awareness of the phalanx of skeletons at the former, but how many know anything of the astounding ancient site into which their grave had been cut?)

The media, and most particularly television, has certainly played an important role in bringing about this shift in awareness and has done much to promote work that a few years ago, and to a degree even today, traditional archaeological funding agencies would not consider worthy of support. Television series such as the BBC funded *Two Men in a Trench* have not only bankrolled field projects but also brought battlefields to the attention of an international audience, many of whom had no idea that archaeology had much to tell us about conflict and warfare. This trend has continued with the First World War, and a number of projects have taken place over the last two or three years thanks to funding from British and overseas (mainly Canadian) production companies. The field has also benefited from the proliferation of non-terrestrial channels commissioning history-based programmes – for example, the History Channel, Discovery, National Geographic. Documentaries with titles like *Finding the Fallen, Battlefield Detectives* and *Digging up the Trenches* have all shown archaeologists at work in the fields of Flanders as they re-excavated trenches and exhumed the remains of fallen soldiers. Alongside these overtly archaeological programmes, television's interest in the conflict has also given rise to programmes such as *The Trench* (BBC), which packaged history as what is generally known as 'reality TV' by throwing together a group of young men and trying to recreate the living conditions of the Western Front in a muddy trench. It was a controversial approach (which television people usually like to refer to as an 'experiment') and some criticized it, perhaps not unfairly, for claiming to portray anything like the true experience of those who suffered so terribly on the Western Front.

There are those who might suggest that approaches to the archaeology of the First World War have been slow to advance beyond the type of relic hunting espoused in John Laffin's 1987 book *Battlefield Archaeology* and to a degree practised by everyone who brings home a spent bullet or shrapnel ball as a souvenir from the battlefields. Not that these sites don't have them to spare – in Flanders there are places where the amount of iron in the soil has created a geological ferrous layer upwards of a metre thick, a kind of man-made iron pan created by the 'rain of steel' that fell on these fields between 1914 and 1918. With this in mind, it is perhaps reassuring that despite recent criticisms of the lack of adequate history teaching in schools, what appear to be increasing numbers of British school children are making visits to the Western Front.

There is, however, a world of difference between picking up a bullet or a shrapnel ball from the edge of a ploughed field and the activities of unprincipled collectors who seek out burials specifically for the personal possessions that may have been buried alongside the dead soldier. These are then sold on to collectors, while the human remains may be handed on to the authorities, though with any means of identifying the individual having been removed. Metal detecting is illegal in France and Belgium but this does not mean to say that it is not practised by trophy hunters.

As far as research is concerned, though, things have certainly moved on since Laffin's time. Work by anthropologist Nick Saunders, whose latest study of 'trench art' reflects a renewed interest in materiality among anthropologists and archaeologists, has given some idea of how social theory can be applied to this material. Work like this provides a potential stepping stone to the development of a viable research agenda, which encompasses landscapes, archaeological sites, material culture and the other physical manifestations of the conflict. In so doing, it will place First World War archaeology on an equal footing with other fields of interest.

It is essential that this theoretical framework grows with the methodological advances which are currently being made on First World War sites. For there can be little doubt that the quality of evidence is increasing as more sites are investigated; knowing what to do with this evidence is perhaps not so apparent.

One example of how methodologies are developing, and also a demonstration that not all projects are financed by television or result from development control, was recently undertaken in northern France. The investigation at Fromelles was financed by the Australian government and involved the search for the mass graves of Australian and British soldiers buried by the Germans in 1916. The main aims of the project were to establish whether

Allied troops killed in the Battle of Fromelles (19–20 July 1916) were buried in a series of pits alluded to in a set of German orders and visible on a number of wartime aerial photographs, and secondly, to establish the likelihood of the bodies still being present on the site – as they may have been exhumed and reburied elsewhere after the war. Large numbers of battlefield graves were exhumed by the various armies after the war and the remains reinterred with full military honours in the many cemeteries maintained by the Commonwealth War Graves Commission; these have become places of pilgrimage for so many, even 90 years after the war.

The battle itself was the type of military debacle so often associated with the Western Front, and the decisions made by the British High Command were much in keeping with the image of heartless ineptitude that has long inhabited the popular imagination. The plan was to prevent the enemy from sending troops out of the line to reinforce the Somme, further to the south, which since 1 July had been the location of a massive Allied assault. Australian and British troops were sent over the top to take German front- and second-line trenches, with few if any tactical objectives beyond that. The softening-up bombardment by Allied heavy guns had little impact on the heavily fortified defences, which included a series of buried concrete bunkers, and despite some units reaching their goals, thousands of men where cut down by German machine guns. Following the failure of the first wave, elements of which were either mown down in No Man's Land or became trapped in the enemy trenches and the indefensible ground behind them, a second wave was ordered forward. This order was rescinded at the eleventh hour but word never reached the Australians, who went forth into another murderous hail of bullets. The Australians were from the 5th Division of the Australian Imperial Force, which had arrived in France just days before, and the British troops were drawn from the 61st Division. After the fighting was over, around 5,500 Australian troops had been killed, wounded or captured (1,917 of these killed and 400 captured), while around 1,500 British troops were either killed or wounded.

In the days following the battle the bodies of the Allied dead, many of which lay in the German trenches, were collected up by the Germans and carried well behind the lines on a light trench railway to a place called Pheasant Wood. There, up to 400 of them were buried by a party drawn from the 16th Bavarian

Reserve Regiment, which fought in the battle and just happened to have a 27-year-old corporal called Adolf Hitler among its ranks (perhaps inevitably this coincidence has not been lost in the media coverage which followed the fieldwork). The graves were backfilled and largely forgotten, until an Australian called Lambis Englezos began a campaign for the recovery and reburial of the missing of Fromelles (the names of the missing are marked on nearby memorials). The result has been a non-invasive archaeological evaluation of the site commissioned by the Australian government.

Aerial reconnaissance photographs taken just days after the battle show eight freshly dug linear pits behind Pheasant Wood, adjacent to the light railway which runs from the front line almost two kilometres to the north. By the end of July 1916 five of the pits had been backfilled, presumably with the bodies of Australian and possibly British dead in them. Other than references to the digging of the pits, 'for 400', and the movement of the dead in the Bavarian regiment's war diary, there had never been any confirmation that the bodies were buried at Pheasant Wood, and there was no local tradition of any unmarked burials within the nearby village of Fromelles – though the civilian population was almost entirely removed during the war when the place was turned into something akin to an entrenched fortress (the impact of the conflict on civilian populations and settlements is also an issue which is open to study by archaeologists). To add to the uncertainty, it was believed by some that if bodies had been present they must surely have been recovered by reburial parties after the war, though again the documentary evidence for this appeared to be lacking.

Given that the project was to be non-invasive in character an integrated research methodology, which combined topographic, geophysical and metal-detector surveys supported by a programme of archive research, was applied to the site, with fieldwork carried out over two weeks in May 2007. Each element provided its own contribution to obtaining an overall picture of the site and the activities which had taken place on it. The topographic survey revealed subtle depressions and ridges not only related to the backfilled pits but also the former railway and a communication trench which at one point passed beneath it (stone ballast from the railway was observed as a ploughed out scatter next to the grass-covered area under survey). Metal-detector survey, which although it included the extraction of artefacts from the ploughed soil was still classified as non-invasive as only shallow signals were investigated, quickly confirmed that Australian soldiers were buried in the pits as two medallions with ANZAC (Australian and New Zealand Army Corps) and AIF (Australian Imperial Force) insignia were recovered from positions adjacent to two of the former pits. One of these insignia also bears a place name which from initial archive research appears to be associated with only one of the upwards of 2,000 men listed as having no known grave on the memorial wall in the cemetery at VC Corner on the Fromelles battlefield.

Having provided compelling evidence that Australians were buried on the site, the metal-detector survey then went on to indicate that they had not been disinterred after the war – British shells (expended shrapnel of various calibres), probably related to the final push on Fromelles and the Aubers ridge in Autumn 1918, were recovered in situ at a depth of around half a metre in the area around the pits, while geophysical spikes suggested their presence in the fills of the pits themselves – these would have been disturbed if the pits had been re-dug to remove bodies. This picture was reinforced by the geophysical surveys that identified only weak anomalies corresponding to the pits – one would expect the disturbance caused by the later recovery of bodies to have heightened these anomalies.

Although it has proven itself an essential, if not indeed the key, component of the archaeological investigation of pre-twentieth-century battlefields, researchers have generally shied away from using the metal detector as a survey tool on First World War sites – though this does not hold true of relic hunters. On the face of it, the reasons for this reluctance seem entirely understandable. One of the most daunting aspects of the war is undoubtedly its scale. Whereas battlefields from earlier periods tend to occupy a limited portion of any given landscape and represent short-term events, during which armies of limited size deployed weapons on a non-industrial scale, the Western Front is characterized by a vast territory and battles fought over weeks if not months by huge armies using mass-produced weapons delivering projectiles on an unprecedented scale.

Fromelles provided an ideal opportunity to test the potential for metal-detecting survey on sites associated with industrial-scale warfare, and not just those from the First World War. It paid dividends. The survey recovered evidence for Australian dead on the site and further indicated that the grave pits had not been later disturbed.

Certainly, evaluation will be required to verify these findings but with minimal intervention the programme appears to have provided a valuable insight into the nature, extent and potential condition of the archaeological deposits, which may include the survival of soft tissue in the damp clay, and will serve to inform any future programme of invasive investigation on the site. Decisions on what happens next rest with the Australian, British and French governments, but whatever action is decided upon it is likely to serve as an important precedent for the treatment of previously unmarked military mass graves from the First World War and indeed from later conflicts – particularly those sites under no direct threat from development.

Fromelles has not only demonstrated the practical benefits of metal-detector survey but also the role of geophysical survey (albeit in difficult clay soil which provides less than perfect resolution), which like detector survey has up until recently not been a common feature of First World War archaeology. The availability of trench maps and aerial photographs does not make geophysics redundant; far from it: comparison of aerial photographs and trench maps has demonstrated inaccuracies in the latter and some features may survive in the absence of carto-graphic representations.

Geophysical survey is also key to the success of a forthcoming collaborative project which will also involve a group of Belgian archaeologists (and which incidentally will be filmed by a Canadian production company). The site to be investigated, which goes under the rather gothic moniker of 'Vampir', is a deep dugout constructed by a British Royal Engineer's tunnelling company during the first three months of 1918, only to be abandoned days after its completion in the face of the last German offensive of the war. Radar survey and trial trenching succeeded in locating the lost site of the shaft head which will provide access to the system, which, it is hoped, will be well preserved in the water-logged clay.

Although the project, which will involve various types of remote survey and recording, will be financed by the production company, it is motivated by the immediate threat posed by a nearby clay pit, which may ultimately breach the underground chambers. The lack of central or local authority funding for this project is obviously disappointing and is part of a more general malaise, which is not unrelated to unwillingness in some quarters to recognize the real threat that underground complexes pose to buildings and other structures in rural and urban areas.

There are hundreds of miles of tunnels, shafts, chambers and galleries running beneath France and Belgium; many of them do not require unexploded mines to turn them into time bombs. In places such as Nieupoort, on the Belgian coast, the ground is opening up and buildings threaten to fall into the voids created by tunnel collapses. Recent developments, however, look to change this situation. In July 2007, one of these voids, or crown holes, appeared in the military cemetery at Hooge, but it is not just the dead who are at risk here as a hole has also opened up beside the Menin road. A survey requested by the Commonwealth War Graves Commission will hopefully provide vital information that can be used to develop methodologies for the detection, survey and consolidation of these underground sites, which in too many cases are now making their presence felt on the surface.

Thanks to the work of a small number of archaeologists in recent years we now have the tools to do the archaeology of the First World War justice. What lies ahead is the difficult task of ensuring that they are applied as part of a meaningful research framework and not just for the delectation of television audiences or as a means of removing problematic barriers to development. Accomplishing this is perhaps one of the most exciting challenges facing conflict archaeology today.

Further Reading

Doyle, P., P. Barton and J. Vandewalle (2005), 'Archaeology of a Great War dugout: Beecham Farm, Passchendaele, Belgium', *Journal of Conflict Archaeology* 1, 45–66.

Fraser, A. and M. Brown (2007), 'Mud, Blood and Missing Men: Excavations at Serre, Somme, France', in Pollard, T. and I. Banks (eds) (2007), *Scorched Earth: Studies in the Archaeology of Conflict.* Brill.

Jacobs, K. (2007), *Nieupoort Sector 1917.* Dorpsstraat (Belgium): De Krijger,.

Laffin, J. (1987), *Battlefield Archaeology.* London: Ian Allan.

McLaughlin, C. (2006), 'Touchstone and tinderbox: documenting memories inside the North of Ireland's Long Kesh and Maze prison' in Schofield, J., A. Klausmeler and L. Purbrick (eds)

(2006), *Re-mapping the Field: New Approaches in Conflict Archaeology*. Berlin: Werlag, pp. 72–81.

Pollard, T., P. Barton and I. Banks (2007), *The Investigation of Possible Mass Graves at Pheasant Wood, Fromelles*. GUARD report 12005.

Price, J. (2005), 'Orphan heritage: issues in managing the heritage of the Great War in Northern France and Belgium', *Journal of Conflict Archaeology* 1, 181–96.

Purbrick, L. (2007), *Contested Spaces: Sites, Representations and Histories of Conflict*. Basingstoke: Palgrave Macmillan.

Saunders, N. J. (2003), *Trench Art: Materialities and Memories of War*. Oxford: Berg.

Silberman, N. A. (2004), 'In Flanders Fields', *Archaeology* 57, 3.

Schofield, J. (2005), *Combat Archaeology: Material Conflict and Modern Conflict*. London: Duckworth.

Schofield, J. and W. Cocroft (2007), *A Fearsome Heritage: Diverse Legacies of the Cold War*. Oxford: Berg.

Schofield, J., A. Klausmeler and L. Purbrick (eds) (2006), *Re-mapping the Field: New Approaches in Conflict Archaeology*. Berlin: Werlag.

Stichelbaut, B. (2005), 'The application of Great War aerial photography in battlefield archaeology: the example of Flanders', *Journal of Conflict Archaeology* 1, 235–43.

Chapter 22

Remembrance

Dan Todman

The guns fell silent on 11 November 1918, but the minds and voices of those who had lived through the Great War did not. The scale of the war, and the damage it caused, demanded that it should be remembered. So too did the imagined voices of the dead, who, it seemed vital, must be rescued from the anonymity of total war by an effort of memory. Remembrance was therefore an issue for all post-war societies. Ninety years later, there are few left who can remember the war, and even fewer who experienced it as adults. Yet remembrance persists in at least some of the former belligerent nations, with anniversaries marked by elaborate ceremonies and extensive media coverage. In the last 20 years, moreover, the study of remembrance has been one of the most dynamic areas of academic research into the war. Remembrance is, therefore, 'a part of history' in several ways.

What are some of the key themes that have emerged from these histories of remembrance? It is apparent that remembrance is complex, and that any study must consider more than the particular ceremonies or symbols attached to, for example, 11 November or 1 July. Even those who were there and could remember the war at first hand had their frames of interpretation shaped by pre-war popular culture as well as battlefield experiences. The way in which subsequent generations have thought about the war – and even whether they have thought about it at all – can only be understood by examining the many influences that shaped their 'war in the head', in the American historian Samuel Hynes' useful phrase. Those who study remembrance have to consider such diverse material as veterans' reunions, disability pensions, comics, school curricula, souvenirs and the package tourist trade.

Although it is seen by societies and by individuals as a significant event, war poses problems of recollection and remembrance. Those researchers who have combined the latest psychological and neurological findings with historical work have suggested that the intense emotions of combat mean that memory traces are laid down more deeply than at other times, but are less easily accessible. Veterans can find it difficult to control their memories – either to compose them into a story that can be told, or to prevent their recall at seemingly inappropriate stimuli. The historian Marc Bloch, serving as an infantryman in the French Army, knew that he should try to remember his first day of battle, but found in retrospect that he could not compose the disjointed images in his head into a coherent narrative. He compared his memories to a film strip in which some frames had been removed and others placed out of order. In contrast, the British career soldier Gerald Templer was still dreaming a week before his death in 1979 of the sounds and sights of a transport park of horses hit by a salvo of shells.

Experience at the sharp end caused problems of memory, therefore, but the size, scope and destructive power of the First World War also caused particular difficulties of representation. The artist John Singer Sargent and the film director D. W. Griffith (not a man afraid of the on-screen epic) both felt, when they travelled to the Western Front, that to depict it in its entirety was more than paint, canvas or celluloid could achieve. Total war, moreover, required a set of military roles that did not fit with conventional stereotypes of soldiering. Clerks, railwaymen and meteorologists were all crucial to the performance of armies on the Western Front, but men fulfilling these roles were not well equipped to boast about their martial exploits.

Most traumatically, the nature of death in modern war transgressed traditions of mourning. Soldiers died out of sight of their comrades, were blown to pieces, or their graves were swallowed by the maw of battle. Many of those left behind had no body to mourn over, nor even a location in a foreign field where they knew that their son, husband or brother was buried. Remembrance in the post-war period in particular must be seen as an effort to come to terms with these challenges. For many of the bereaved, remembrance was about rescuing their loved one from the anonymity of death. Ironically, however, the effect of the enduring remembrance of the war has been reductive. The ambiguities and contradictions of wartime experience, which were reflected in the range of remembrance activity just after 1918, have been homogenized by repetition so that now an even more limited, partial version remains. We might see this, in fact, as a requirement of remembrance: only because they are reduced to a few, easily transmittable and widely understood myths are historical events preserved in culture. Where remembrance remains too problematic, ideas about the past are more likely to be obscured than discussed.

One of the reasons that remembrance is complex but reductive is that it is collective. It is characterized by the sharing of ideas about the past and the dead. It includes, but is not limited to, the memories of those who experienced events at first hand. The form and content of these memories is affected by the social context in which they are rehearsed, so that recollections that fit with wider cultural expectations are strengthened and those that run counter to prevailing attitudes are left unspoken and may be forgotten. It makes little sense, however, to talk about those who commemorated the Somme in France in 2006 'remembering' the battle. They could do no such thing, although they might be able to remember others telling them about it. Unlike battlefield relics or photographs, memories cannot be inherited, and to assume that the collective process of remembrance functions in the same way as the individual process of remembrance may be profoundly misleading. Remembrance also, therefore, includes the beliefs and behaviour of those born long after the war ended. It is this that makes it such a useful category, for in its generality it is a more effective term than 'memory'.

The collective nature of remembrance means that it revolves around compromise. For example, Adrian Gregory's work on the commemoration of Armistice Day between the wars (*The Silence of Memory*, 1994, Oxford: Berg) has shown how the desire of some British veterans raucously to celebrate the anniversary of their survival had to adapt to meet the circumstances of the 1920s. Elaborate festivities by the well-off were deemed tactless when many other veterans were out of work. Even worse, celebrations of survival were seen to cause pain to the bereaved. Veterans therefore came under considerable social pressure, which transformed drunken parties into nostalgic celebrations of supposed social unity, embodied in the communal singing of the Festival of Remembrance at the Albert Hall.

The remembrance of the First World War was also influenced by widely different emotional, social and political needs. While there were clear incentives for political leaders to control remembrance, it was seldom if ever imposed entirely 'from above'. Particularly in those countries that remained democratic, remembrance was also shaped by pressure from below. The clearest example of this, from the British case, is examined in work by Gregory, Alex King and David Lloyd on the construction of the Cenotaph and the burial of the Unknown Warrior. Originally erected as a temporary monument to represent the dead at the parade to celebrate the signing of peace in 1919, Sir Edward Lutyens' masterful design attracted such an outpouring of public emotion that the government had to adapt its plans and rebuild the wood, plaster and canvas version in more permanent stone. The unveiling of this new memorial in 1920, at the same time as the burial of a symbolic unidentifiable body from the Western Front in Westminster Abbey, was again the subject of intense interest and saw official plans modified to meet public demand. For example, politicians were forced to give up their seats for the ceremony in the Abbey when it was revealed that bereaved mothers and veterans could not otherwise be accommodated. The bereaved were not always so successful in getting the government to agree to their demands. Despite the pleas of families who desperately wanted either to be able to repatriate the bodies of their dead soldiers, or to mark their graves with tombstones of their own design, the authorities insisted that all servicemen should be buried close to where they fell, in the cemeteries of the Imperial (later Commonwealth) War Graves Commission. This was not merely a matter of economy and aesthetics, although both played their part. Emphasizing the social unity achieved in death by British soldiers of all ranks and classes made a powerful political statement in the turbulent 1920s.

The design of those cemeteries – the echoing of country churchyards, and the use of crusading Christian iconography – indicates the tendency of remembrance towards tradition and conservatism rather than radicalism. This is perhaps the greatest shift in the consensus of academic discussion of remembrance over the last 20 years. Two influential early texts, Paul Fussell's *The Great War and Modern Memory* (1975, New York: OUP) and Modris Eksteins' *The Rites of Spring* (1989, Boston, MA: Houghton Mifflin), argued that the war ushered in a new, modernist approach in the arts and that it changed forever the way in which war was written about and represented. Most historians would now suggest that these works drew on too narrow a set of sources and judged inadequately the range of responses to the trauma of war. Rather than rejecting tradition, religion, visions of martial glory and the heightened rhetoric of patriotism, many communities seem to have turned precisely to these continuities to find reassurance and explanation. Stefan Goebel's recent comparative work on medievalism in Britain and Germany during and after the First World War makes it clear just how strong this tendency was. Faced with the confusion and meaninglessness of death in modern war, Britons and Germans were more likely to depict the dead as chivalric knights than as dehumanized automata, ironically engaged in a futile struggle. Despite its inaccuracies, its polemic tone and clear status as a work of literary criticism, rather than historical analysis, Fussell's work is still far too frequently cited as a core text in popular studies of remembrance and even of the First World War as a whole.

How wars are thought of after they end is, of course, deeply dependent on what happens next. For Britain in particular, in which the recent surge in popular remembrance of the war is perhaps most obvious, context is all. Viewed through the distorting lenses of insularity, subsequent economic depression and the advent of another global conflagration, after 1945 the Great War became established in British culture as a symbol of tragedy, unparalleled loss of life, sorrow and futility. This fits only partially with the means of remembrance established between the wars, when the need to justify the loss of life and to console the bereaved was so much stronger. Few Britons would now be able to see the war as a 'Great Deliverance', the term George V used when he congratulated his nation in 1918. In neither case, however, have the British placed the country's war effort in relation to that of other combatants, or asked whether the apparent fascination with the war is unique or peculiar. Viewed relatively, the history of remembrance confirms just how fortunate Britain was throughout the twentieth century. Terrible though Britain and the Empire's losses were in the First World War, they paled in comparison to those of her allies and enemies. Britain mobilized about 125 servicemen from every 1,000 citizens, about 16 of whom were killed. Germany mobilized about 154 and lost 30, and the equivalent figures for France were 168 and 34. Britain not only emerged amongst the victors in 1918 but also escaped relatively lightly from the Second World War.

The expulsion from mainland Europe in 1940 ensured that there was no repeat of a great attritional campaign involving a con-scripted mass army fighting the main force of continental power. Britain also avoided the terrible moral and ethical questions for remembrance posed by occupation, genocide or defeat. It was therefore unsurprising that the First World War should continue to signify what was worst about war.

The maintenance of a more or less democratic political system also shaped the form and tone of remembrance. As Catherine Merridale's study of death and memory in modern Russia, *Night of Stone* (2001, New York: Viking), makes clear, for example, remembrance under a totalitarian regime was a very different matter. In Britain, those who challenged the norms of remem-brance, or whose recollections differed from the mainstream, risked social censure. In Communist Russia – as under many other totalitarian regimes – they ran a high risk of death.

It seems likely that research in the immediate future will concentrate on specific longitudinal case studies, comparative analyses and demography. There is probably less work now to do on national remembrance and individual memory than on the intermediate levels of small communities bound together by location or experience. Borrowing from social anthropology, Jay Winter, whose scholarship has been a driving force in the study of remembrance, has emphasized the role of the 'fictive kinships' formed by bereavement and war experience. The field would still benefit from further analysis of these kinships – be they war memorial committees, veterans clubs or later family history associations – from their inception until the present day. While Winter has recently suggested that comparative histories are likely to emphasize only national distinctiveness in remem-brance, it is clear that any studies in this field need to be informed by an awareness of what happened in other countries. Recent work has examined the way in which occupation was experienced and remembered in Belgium and north-eastern Italy, as well as war remembrance within imperial as well as metropolitan Britain and France. Here, comparative work can serve as a useful reminder of the global nature of a war seen all too often in parochial terms. At a broader level, there may be room for informative comparisons based on population statistics. It is at least arguable that the change in popular remembrance of the war in post-1945 Britain depended on the disappearance of a generation of bereaved parents whose grief acted as a taboo in the 1920s and 1930s. This suggests the importance of demographic change in altering the boundaries of what can acceptably be said. The effect of population change – by aging or migration – on shared beliefs about the war would reward further study, perhaps particularly in Britain where remembrance remains relatively strong, and the government has become increasingly interested in the use of past wars to foster national identity.

Notwithstanding its current popularity, the future of the remembrance of the First World War outside the ivory tower is less certain. There can be no doubt that the 100th anniversary of the war and the deaths of the final participants will be events of major significance. If nothing else, the First World War is a useful site for national and supra-national bodies to form identities and emphasize their importance. Whether a centenary commemoration organized by the EU, the UN or the British government will accurately reflect academic historians' views on the war is another matter.

The real question, however, is whether those currently involved in remembrance will be able to pass their interest in the First World War on to their children. The grandchildren of those who fought the war absorbed at least some of their fascination at their grandparents' knees in the 1960s, or through conversations with their parents. That experiential link will disappear, and it may be that it is the process of discovery, rather than an attachment to the First World War in particular, that has made it so attractive to later generations. It has been suggested that the current boom in family history and commemoration is the result of a mix of the need to find meaning and location in a dislocated modern world, and of specific trends in demography and leisure fashion. The first need will not disappear – the future will not become any more certain, and the pace of technological and social change will if anything accelerate – but the latter two may leave the remembrance of the First World War more vulnerable. If subsequent generations undertake family history for reassurance, it seems likely that they will look to 'rediscover' the Second World War – which will then lie similarly just beyond the boundary of lived memory – rather than its predecessor.

Further Reading

Audoin-Rouzeau, Stephane and Annette Becker (2002), *14–18: Understanding the Great War*. London: Profile.

Bourne, John, Peter Liddle and Ian Whitehead (eds) (2000), *The Great World War 1914–1945*, Vol I: *Lightning Strikes Twice*, Vol II: *Who Won? Who Lost?* London: HarperCollins.

Gregory, Adrian (1994), *The Silence of Memory: Armistice Day 1918–1946*. Oxford: Berg.

Merridale, Catherine (2001), *Night of Stone: Death and Memory in Twentieth Century Russia*. London: Granta.

Piehler, G. Kurt (1995), *Remembering War the American Way*. Washington and London: Smithsonian Institution Press.

Sherman, Daniel (2000), *The Construction of Memory in Inter-War France*. London: University of Chicago Press.

Thomson, Alistair (1994), *Anzac Memories: Living with the Legend*. Oxford: OUP.

Winter, Jay (2006), *Remembering War: The Great War Between Memory and History in the Twentieth Century*. New Haven, CT: Yale UP.

——(1995), *Sites of Memory, Sites of Mourning: The Great War in European Cultural History*. Cambridge: CUP.

Index